The Last
German Victory

The Last German Victory

Operation Market Garden, 1944

Aaron Bates

Pen & Sword
MILITARY

First published in Great Britain in 2021 by
Pen & Sword Military
An imprint of
Pen & Sword Books Ltd
Yorkshire – Philadelphia

Copyright © Aaron Bates 2021

ISBN 978 1 39900 076 5

The right of Aaron Bates to be identified as Author of this work has been asserted by him in accordance with the Copyright, Designs and Patents Act 1988.

A CIP catalogue record for this book is
available from the British Library.

All rights reserved. No part of this book may be reproduced or transmitted in any form or by any means, electronic or mechanical including photocopying, recording or by any information storage and retrieval system, without permission from the Publisher in writing.

Typeset by Mac Style
Printed and bound in the UK by CPI Group (UK) Ltd,
Croydon, CR0 4YY.

Pen & Sword Books Limited incorporates the imprints of Atlas, Archaeology, Aviation, Discovery, Family History, Fiction, History, Maritime, Military, Military Classics, Politics, Select, Transport, True Crime, Air World, Frontline Publishing, Leo Cooper, Remember When, Seaforth Publishing, The Praetorian Press, Wharncliffe Local History, Wharncliffe Transport, Wharncliffe True Crime and White Owl.

For a complete list of Pen & Sword titles please contact

PEN & SWORD BOOKS LIMITED
47 Church Street, Barnsley, South Yorkshire, S70 2AS, England
E-mail: enquiries@pen-and-sword.co.uk
Website: www.pen-and-sword.co.uk

Or

PEN AND SWORD BOOKS
1950 Lawrence Rd, Havertown, PA 19083, USA
E-mail: Uspen-and-sword@casematepublishers.com
Website: www.penandswordbooks.com

Contents

Foreword		vi
Acknowledgements		viii
Chapter 1	Introduction: 'A Difficult Operation, Attended by Considerable Risks'	1
Chapter 2	Point of Departure – A Brief Historiography of the Market Garden Campaign	10
Chapter 3	Thriving Amidst Chaos: The Origins and Nature of German Tactical and Command Doctrine	26
Chapter 4	'Leaping into a Hornet's Nest': The Role of German Tactical and Command Doctrine in Operation Market Garden	39
Chapter 5	Fencing with a Sledgehammer: The Origins and Nature of British Tactical and Command Doctrine and its Role in Operation Garden	72
Chapter 6	No Mere Matter of Marching: The Role of British Tactical and Command Doctrine in Operation Market	93
Chapter 7	Little More than Guts and Bayonets: British Doctrine and the Role of Firepower in Operation Market Garden	109
Chapter 8	The Thin Grey Line: German Doctrine and the Role of Firepower in Operation Market Garden	138
Chapter 9	Conclusions	161
Notes		170
Bibliography		197
Index		202

Foreword

In the publishing world history dustjackets typically promise new narratives, which are forever recasting, reinterpreting and reconceiving. That certainly does happen, but it is much less common than the sometimes overblown claims suggest, especially in high turn-out fields like the Second World War. When I read *The Last German Victory*, it was clear to me that the contribution to the field warranted a re-evaluation of everything I thought I knew about the campaign. Bates is plausibly recasting how we understand the events that led to the failure of Operation Market Garden. While operational accounts tend to follow the action and provide the blow-by-blow reconstructions so loved by readers, this method, as Bates shows, can miss the essential point. Individual commanders and their particular decisions almost always arise from an institutional culture, which is reinforced by doctrine and relentless training. It is not to suggest that officers don't have individual agency, but that this exists on a spectrum strictly defined by their service environment and military experience. Moreover, military culture among the major powers of the Second World War differed hugely and has all too infrequently formed the subject of comparative study in accounting for operational success. While Montgomery's claim that he enjoyed 90 per cent success in Operation Market Garden has certainly been challenged before, no one has reconstructed the campaign in light of culture, doctrine and training to shift the emphasis away from the day-to-day affairs and cast the events in broader institutional terms. Not only does Bates show the virtue of a broader engagement, the implications support his assertion that many of the key outcomes were pre-ordained. As the title suggests, the conception of Market Garden played to German strengths, which by September 1944 reflects how little Allied commanders actually understood about the *Wehrmacht*. In fact, one can also say it reflects an inability to understand the serious limitations of their own forces. In many respects Market Garden is a cautionary tale of the dangers of institutionalization, which only underwrites the virtue of actively and consciously seeking new perspectives. It is a first-rate study that gives us not just a new perspective on Operation Market Garden, but provides a model for why military culture matters.

David Stahel
The University of New South Wales, July 2021

Acknowledgements

I would like to express my appreciation for the efforts of some of the people who made this work possible. Most notably, I would like to thank Dr Alexander Hill, who advised me through the writing of the graduate thesis that would become this book and who continued to provide useful advice and feedback throughout the writing process. I would also like to thank Dr David Stahel for taking time out of a busy schedule to look at and critique various drafts of the work, and Dr Timothy Stapleton, who (alongside Dr Hill) made the initial suggestion to develop my thesis into a book. I also appreciate the efforts of the editorial staff at Pen & Sword, who provided invaluable advice and support for – and patience with – a first-time author throughout the publication process. Finally, I would like to thank the library and archive staffs at the University of Calgary, the British National Archives at Kew, and the German *Bundesarchiv/Militärarchiv* in Freiburg for providing the materials and assistance that made my research possible. I would particularly like to express my deepest gratitude to Ms Barbara Kiesow at the Freiburg archives, who provided invaluable guidance and assistance to a first-time archival researcher (with a sometimes spotty grasp of spoken German!) and always made me feel welcome at her facility.

Chapter 1

Introduction: 'A Difficult Operation, Attended by Considerable Risks'[1]

Early in the afternoon of 17 September 1944, just after the fifth anniversary of the beginning of the Second World War, the skies over German-occupied Holland were filled with a massive armada of over 4,300 aircraft belonging to both Great Britain's Royal Air Force (RAF) and the United States Army Air Force (USAAF). At the heart of this air fleet, protected and supported by 1,240 fighters and 1,113 bombers, were 1,534 transport aircraft and 491 cargo gliders carrying approximately 16,500 men of the 1st Allied Airborne Army. This was the largest single force of airborne soldiers ever to be deployed in combat – a force that would be dropped and landed shortly after 1300 that day near the Dutch towns of Eindhoven, Nijmegen, and Arnhem, in pursuit of the Western Allies' latest offensive effort against the forces of Nazi Germany, Operation Market Garden.[2] The operation was sent off with high hopes and expectations from the Allied leadership, particularly the operation's chief architect, the newly promoted Field Marshal Bernard Law Montgomery, commander of the British 21st Army Group, to which the 1st Allied Airborne Army was attached.

The primary purpose behind Montgomery's plan was to breach the barrier of the Rhine River, the last major geographical obstacle between the Allied forces and an invasion of Germany itself in the wake of their victory over the German *Westheer* (Western Army) in France the previous month. The forces of the airborne army were to capture and secure key bridges and other crossing points over all the water obstacles along the main road leading north from the town of Neerpelt on the southern Dutch border to the city of Arnhem on the far side of the Lower Rhine (the northernmost tributary of the Rhine proper). This landing was to provide a secure 'carpet' of occupied territory that would allow the forces of the British 2nd Army, led by the XXX Corps, to quickly rush through

2 The Last German Victory

to the banks of the Zuider Zee (or Ijsselmeer) in northern Holland and establish a bridgehead behind both the Rhine and the line of the *Westwall* fortifications along the German border.[3] From this bridgehead, Montgomery hoped to launch a final, decisive, advance into the North German Plain and Germany's primary industrial region, the Ruhr, the

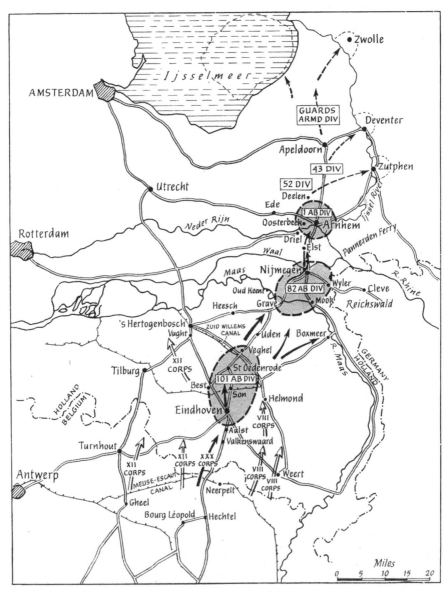

The Market Garden plan. (*Courtesy of John Waddy*, A Tour of the Arnhem Battlefields)

loss of which would cripple German war production and bring about a swift end to the prolonged conflict in Europe.[4]

Operation Market Garden developed out of the promising, but also difficult, situation that the Allies found themselves in during the early autumn of 1944. Operation Overlord, the Allied invasion of France via Normandy, had, after months of hard fighting against a skilled and determined foe, finally overcome the forces of the German 7. *Armee* and 5. *Panzerarmee* by the middle of August, with Allied forces breaking out of their beachhead south of Saint-Lô on 25 July, sweeping into the German rear and eventually achieving a partial encirclement of the remaining German forces around the town of Falaise. Although the trap closed too slowly, allowing large numbers of German troops to escape, the Allied victory still effectively reduced the great bulk of German forces in Western Europe to a tattered and panicked mass of fugitives fleeing back towards the German border in a near complete rout.[5] The Allies quickly followed up the German retreat, liberating virtually the whole of France and pushing through Belgium to the borders of Holland and Germany itself.[6] However, they soon found themselves victims of their own success. With most of the French ports along the Atlantic Coast either demolished by the retreating Germans or still occupied by garrisons determined to hold out as long as possible, the Normandy beaches and the Norman port of Cherbourg remained the Allies' only available facilities on the continent for unloading supplies shipped over from Great Britain. Thus, with their main supply points over 300 miles behind the front lines by the beginning of September, and with the French rail networks still largely out of action from the Allies' pre-landing air interdiction campaign, Allied forces all along the line began to grind to a halt in the face of severe shortages of the fuel, ammunition, and other supplies needed to continue their offensive.[7]

As the Allied advance began to lose momentum after the victory in Normandy and rapid progress through Belgium, a major dispute over strategy developed among the senior Allied commanders. The Allied Supreme Commander, American General Dwight Eisenhower, favoured continuing the original Allied strategy of advancing slowly and steadily along a broad front, keeping as much as possible of the remaining German forces engaged all across the line, preventing them from massing reserves for an effective counterattack and ensuring that no single Allied force got too far ahead of the others and became unduly exposed.[8] Field

Marshal Montgomery, however, preferred an alternative strategy in light of the unexpected rout of German forces from France. Montgomery believed that the Allies should take advantage of the complete disarray that the *Westheer* was in after its retreat and thrust rapidly forward at a single point, concentrating their efforts to quickly breach the remaining German defences before their forces could recover enough to muster effective opposition.[9] As Montgomery himself put it: 'My own view, which I presented to the Supreme Commander, was that one powerful full-blooded thrust across the Rhine and into the heart of Germany, backed by the whole of the resources of the Allied Armies, would be likely to achieve decisive results.'[10]

Naturally, Montgomery intended that his own 21st Army Group would conduct the decisive thrust, ensuring that the often arrogant and vain general, whose ego was still smarting from having lost the command of the whole of the Allied ground forces when Eisenhower had assumed the active field command at the beginning of September, would be able to claim the bulk of the credit and glory for the Allied victory.[11] The reasoning behind his offensive, however, was a product of considerations beyond mere self-interest; the Field Marshal, as well as the British government, was naturally eager to spare the war-weary citizens of Great Britain, whose cities were at that very moment suffering under attack from Germany's V-1 (*Vergeltungswaffe* – 'vengeance weapon') flying bombs, another winter of wartime hardship.[12] Montgomery's plan, whatever its assumptions, risks, and flaws, was a manifestation of a wider British hope – increasingly a virtual necessity by late 1944 – to bring a rapid resolution to a conflict that was straining their national resources and public resolve to the very limit.

Eisenhower was, however, largely unmoved by Montgomery's repeated and increasingly vociferous entreaties to alter his strategy. For one, the supreme commander was unconvinced that Montgomery's forces – or any others the Allies had available – would be able to achieve such a decisive victory so quickly given the strained Allied logistical situation, and feared that attempting to do so would simply result in them rapidly grinding to a halt in a dangerously overextended position.[13] Furthermore, from a political perspective, Eisenhower was unwilling to halt and divert supplies from the American forces advancing further south – particularly those of the highly successful and popular Lieutenant General George

Patton – to enable the efforts of Montgomery's British troops, knowing that such a decision would face an intense backlash from the American government and public.[14] As such, he ordered Montgomery to instead focus on clearing the still-occupied approaches to the Belgian port of Antwerp, which had fallen to the Allied advance on 8 September, allowing its extensive harbour facilities to be opened to Allied traffic and thus addressing the growing logistical crisis.[15]

To placate the bitterly disappointed Field Marshal, Eisenhower did agree to give his 21st Army Group a degree of priority for supplies and also – critically – authorized him to make use of the Allied forces' last remaining strategic reserve, the newly formed 1st Allied Airborne Army, to aid in his future operations.[16] Montgomery quickly began formulating plans to make use of this potentially highly useful asset and, on 10 September 1944, he met with Eisenhower to again push for his 'narrow thrust' strategy, this time offering a concrete plan to achieve his objectives in the form of Operation Market Garden. Though Eisenhower remained dubious of the practicality of Montgomery's wider intentions to push on into the Ruhr once the operation was successful (and thus forbade him from planning such operations in advance), he was quite impressed with the boldness of the plan that the normally cautious Montgomery had proposed and hoped that it could at least secure a useable bridgehead over the Rhine before winter set in, giving the Allies a useful point of departure when offensive operations resumed in earnest in the spring. As such, he enthusiastically approved Operation Market Garden, with its D-Day being set for 17 September.[17]

Despite the hopes of Montgomery and Eisenhower, the scale of the operation, and its innovative combination of airborne and deep mechanized operations, Market Garden was to end in defeat, disappointment, and the deferment of the end of the war in Europe for another seven months. Though crossings across the Maas and Waal Rivers, as well as several major canals, were captured through the efforts of the American 82nd and 101st Airborne Divisions and XXX Corps, extending the Allied front line all the way up to the Lower Rhine, the Germans managed to hold the Allied forces there, just short of their final goal. Though the British 1st Airborne Division, dropped at Arnhem to secure the final bridges over the Lower Rhine, managed to temporarily secure the northern end of the main road bridge, it soon came under intense counterattack and was eventually overwhelmed by the Germans, with less than a quarter of the approximately 10,000 men with which the division had landed escaping back across the Lower Rhine on the night of 25/26 September.[18] Though the Germans also suffered fairly heavy casualties in the course of the battle, their efforts managed to achieve what was arguably their last true operational level success in the war in the West, defeating a significant Allied thrust that might have unhinged their entire defensive effort. At the same time, German forces inflicted significant losses upon the Allied forces involved, achieved a notable propaganda coup to boost the morale of their exhausted forces and civil population, and bought vital time for the preparation of their large-scale counteroffensive plan, Operation *Wacht am Rhein* (Watch on the Rhine), which was launched in the Ardennes in December, resulting in the famous 'Battle of the Bulge'.

Operation Market Garden, and particularly the critical Battle of Arnhem, has been the subject of an extensive body of both popular and scholarly literature in the decades since the end of the war. A matter of central concern in most works has almost invariably been the reasons for the operation's failure – often seen, in light of Montgomery's lofty ultimate ambitions for it, as a lost opportunity for the Allies to bring the war to an end months earlier than was actually the case, and thus to avoid the bloody fighting on both the Western and Eastern fronts in the war's final months and even to possibly pre-empt the prolonged Soviet occupation of large swathes of Eastern Europe. Most criticism has generally been focused on the specific decisions made by Montgomery and his subordinate commanders both in formulating the plan and in putting it into action, particularly with regards to the plans for the airlift that delivered the airborne troops to the battlefield. Matters such as the decision to divide the drops of the three airborne divisions into multiple waves across three days, or the selection of landing zones for the Arnhem mission that were an average of 8 miles away from the 1st Airborne Division's objective bridges have been cited as critical factors in the defeat at Arnhem, effectively wasting the initial surprise the landings achieved and forcing the 1st Airborne to have to fight its way through to its objectives with only a limited portion of its total strength. However, the recent and ground-breaking work done by historian Sebastian Ritchie on the Market Garden campaign draws into question the notion that it was flawed detail in an otherwise sound plan that led to Allied defeat. Ritchie, focusing on a detailed examination of the air plans for the operation, effectively argues that the flaws in those plans were less a matter of mistakes in planning as they were the result of unavoidable limitations inherent in conducting an airborne operation of such depth and scale, given the resources available to the Allied air forces. Ritchie points out, for example, that the Allies simply lacked the number of aircraft necessary to drop the whole of the 1st Allied Airborne Army in a single effort, and that limits of turn-around time between missions and the lack of proper night-flying training among many of the Allied transport pilots effectively ruled out multiple drops within a single day. As such, Ritchie draws into question the prevailing idea that Market Garden was a good plan that was foiled only by specific decisions made in executing it and instead suggests that it was a badly flawed, impractical, and generally unreasonable idea from its very inception. For Ritchie, the Market Garden plan was put into action by commanders that either failed or refused to recognize and accept the limitations of the forces under their command in a single-minded and myopic pursuit of what they saw as a fleeting opportunity to win the war at a stroke.[19]

This work draws upon the approach employed by Ritchie to question the basic feasibility of Operation Market Garden from another perspective, that is by examining the degree to which the two competing forces involved were actually suited, in terms of their combat doctrine, for the unique circumstances and demands that the battle thrust upon them. For the purposes of this work, 'doctrine' is taken to mean the formal and informal rules and common practices that governed how military forces were prepared to fight, including their training, organization, and equipment. On one side this book looks at the doctrine and capabilities of 1st Allied Airborne Army, executing the 'Market' (airborne) element of the plan, and those of the British 2nd Army that executed Operation 'Garden' (the ground advance), and on the other, the forces of the German *Wehrmacht* (Armed Forces) operating under the command of *Heeresgruppe* (Army Group) *B*. With regards to the Allied forces, in order to keep this 'compare/contrast' approach as focused as possible, the author has concentrated primarily on the case of the British forces involved in the fighting; though the actions of the two American airborne divisions will be discussed where appropriate, a full evaluation of the role that American combat doctrine played in the campaign will have to await a future work.

This should by no means be seen as a dismissal of the important role that American forces played in the Market Garden fighting, but merely as a literary choice by the author to focus on the particularly stark contrast that the campaign shows between British and German doctrine.

Upon examination, it is clear that the doctrine in use by both sides during the fighting in Holland in September 1944 played a central role in bringing about both the Allied defeat and the German victory. German doctrine, which emphasized principles of highly aggressive leadership based around independent action taken by commanders through the exercise of their own initiative at all levels of command, as well as small-unit firepower and tactical proficiency, ensured that the relatively weak forces available to *Heeresgruppe B* were able to react extremely quickly and effectively to the sudden Allied landings. In doing so they were able to virtually negate the surprise that was so critical to the success of the Allied plan and then outmatch the Allied forces in the scattered and confused fighting that followed, where small-unit initiative and effectiveness was at a premium. Conversely, the Market Garden plan proved to be extremely poorly matched to the capabilities of the Allied, and particularly the British, forces involved. With British successes in the Second World War to date having been achieved largely through the use of carefully laid and cautiously executed plans under strong centralized control, as well as through an overwhelming level of fire support provided by artillery and air power, Operation Market Garden effectively saw the 21st Army Group willingly place their forces at a severe disadvantage in not playing to those strengths. The Allied operational plans depended upon their forces acting with a degree of speed, independent initiative, and small-unit tactical proficiency that they had rarely displayed before – nor been prepared to by their doctrine and training – and with only a fraction of the centrally controlled firepower upon which their offensive efforts had come to rely. Ordered to do what was largely beyond the capabilities that had been factored into their doctrine, the Allied forces were understandably unsuccessful, in spite of a determined effort that very nearly snatched an unlikely victory from the jaws of defeat. Essentially, Operation Market Garden saw Field Marshal Montgomery abandon the methods and carefully controlled and maintained conditions that had just won him and his troops a decisive victory in Normandy, in favour of trying to challenge the Germans on their own terms, in the very circumstances in which they most excelled. Under these conditions, it can hardly be surprising that the Germans were able to achieve a degree of localized combat superiority at key points in the battle, gain the upper hand, and eventually defeat the Allied thrust.

As such, the outcome of the fighting during Operation Market Garden, though far from predetermined, owed at least as much, and possibly more, to deeply ingrained systemic factors within the two opposing militaries as it did to the specific decisions made by the various commanders involved at the time. It is a truism that armies fight the way that their doctrine and training has prepared them to; as such, it is an absolutely essential factor for commanders to make their plans with careful consideration of such basic factors as what their forces are actually capable of. Unfortunately, as the case of Operation Market Garden shows, all too often in history ambition trumps reality in the plans that political and military leaders make, and, as at Arnhem, it is all too often the ordinary soldier that pays the price of such derelictions of judgement.

Chapter 2

Point of Departure – A Brief Historiography of the Market Garden Campaign

In the seventy-six years since the campaign took place, Operation Market Garden has become the subject of a voluminous body of writing. Beyond the numerous eyewitness accounts of the fighting written by participants ranging from senior commanders to ordinary soldiers, the Market Garden campaign has been a popular subject for historical writing, with an extensive secondary literature that includes both scholarly and more popular works. Among these works are narrative histories of the campaign as a whole, as well as more focused accounts of the various battles that comprised the wider campaign, and of the various military units that waged them. The challenge for any would-be researcher is thus not in finding material, but in sifting through that material to find those works that most usefully contribute to the debates about, and understanding of, the Market Garden campaign.

Perhaps the most prominent sub-set within this literature is the numerous narrative accounts that seek to describe, and occasionally to analyse, the events of the campaign. An in many ways obvious starting point for discussing this literature is Cornelius Ryan's 1974 monograph *A Bridge Too Far*, undoubtedly the most well-known book on the Market Garden campaign and one which, along with the 1977 film based upon it, has had an immense influence in shaping both public perceptions of the campaign and the scholarly literature and debates surrounding it.[1] This author has not seen a single work on the topic that has not used or engaged with the evidence and arguments presented in Ryan's book to some degree. *A Bridge Too Far* is largely a straightforward, if detailed and in-depth, narrative of the events of the Market Garden campaign, written from both official documents and from information gathered by an exhaustive series of interviews conducted by Ryan with various surviving participants in the campaign, including a selection of commanders, officers, and common soldiers from the Allied and German forces involved, as well as Dutch civilians that were caught up in the fighting. This wide variety of sources not only ensures an engaging narrative, but also provides considerable insight into the inner workings of Market Garden from various perspectives, providing much useful material for a researcher to work with in assessing the way in which the battle was planned and fought and the reasons for its eventual outcome.

Beyond its detailed narrative account, Ryan's work was also one of the first serious efforts to critically evaluate the conduct of the campaign. For the most part, the mostly 'official' histories and memoirs that preceded it paid relatively little attention to the campaign, sandwiched as it was between the much larger, more famous, and more successful campaigns in Normandy and the Ardennes. What little coverage there was generally followed the line presented in the memoirs of Field Marshal Montgomery, who described the campaign as 'ninety per cent successful', only barely frustrated by circumstances beyond his control.[2] Ryan, in contrast, was highly critical of the planning and execution of Market Garden, examining both in considerable detail to illustrate how numerous errors and omissions by Allied leadership contributed greatly to the operation's failure and the loss of the 1st Airborne Division. As part of this critical approach, Ryan made effective use of his numerous sources to not only point out where Allied commanders went wrong, but to actually seek the deeper reasons why they made the decisions they did. Though sometimes harsh in his criticisms, Ryan usually made an effort to investigate the context in which decisions were made and the degree to which circumstances and factors outside the control of commanders constrained their available options and thus present a more nuanced critique.

On the downside, however, the nature of Ryan's source base also ensures a degree of bias throughout the work. He shows a distinct tendency to lionize those figures who contributed most extensively to his research effort, such as the commander of the American 82nd Airborne Division, Major General James Gavin, II. *SS-Panzer Korps* commander, *General der Waffen-SS* Wilhelm Bittrich, and his two divisional commanders, *Obersturmbannführer* (Senior Battalion Commander) Walter Harzer and *Brigadeführer* (Brigade Commander) Heinz Harmel, as well as a handful of senior officers from the British 1st Airborne Division. These men are clearly depicted as the 'heroes' of the piece, with their contributions and those of the formations they commanded being emphasized at the expense of others. Although the available evidence does indicate that Ryan's assessments are not entirely incorrect, as the actions of the figures he focuses on were generally prominent – indeed, often decisive – in some events of the campaign, his focus at times distorts and exaggerates their roles in and significance to wider events. Moreover, Ryan generally seems to accept their accounts of events at face value, with very limited effort at concerted criticism, even where their stories seem to diverge from those presented by other sources. Consequently, these personalities clearly seem to exercise a disproportionate influence over the story Ryan tells and the conclusions that he draws.

Conversely, those figures that made little or no contribution to Ryan's interviews – such as 1st Airborne Corps commanding officer (CO) Lieutenant General Frederick Browning or *Generalfeldmarschall* (Field Marshal) Walther Model, commander of the German *Heeresgruppe B*, both of whom died before Ryan began his research – often come off quite poorly. These individuals are seemingly made to shoulder the bulk of the blame for the various mistakes that were made, while naturally lacking the ability to defend themselves or the decisions they made in the way that their above-mentioned contemporaries so energetically did. Though it is perhaps understandable that Ryan chose to focus on those individuals and formations for which he had the most material, this does result in a somewhat distorted picture of the campaign. Ryan's narrative suggests, for example, that the German side of the battle was waged almost exclusively by the forces of the Waffen-SS, with the efforts of other Wehrmacht formations being underplayed or even denigrated by his (mostly ex-SS) German sources. Ryan also is perhaps a bit too credulous in accepting the post-facto critiques of higher level planning by the field officers that compose the bulk of his source base. For example, he extensively cites or quotes the scathing indictments made by Major General Roy Urquhart and Brigadier John Hackett of the 1st Airborne Division of many of the decisions made by their superiors before and during the battle, critiques that often draw heavily upon the benefit of hindsight without accounting for what information those superiors actually had available to them at the time or other factors that may have constrained their choices. This problem also illustrates Ryan's subtle bias towards a 'lions led by donkeys' perspective on the campaign, as he is clearly far more critical of the decisions made by the senior leadership on both sides than he is towards those of front-line 'fighting' commanders or troops.[3] Throughout the book, Ryan proves generally unwilling to attach any real responsibility for the outcome on those actually engaged on the ground, or to make any critique of the way in which they actually fought.

Despite these flaws, Ryan's work still holds up fairly well in spite of its age. Though more useful as a narrative than an analytical work, the sheer amount of material that Ryan includes, particularly in terms of personal testimonies, ensures that *A Bridge Too Far* still has value for any researcher. Moreover, the book remains virtually a required starting point for any investigation of the literature surrounding Market Garden, if only because virtually all subsequent works use or engage with it in some significant fashion, seeking in some way to reinforce, refine, or refute Ryan's conclusions.

Notable among the various works that have followed more or less directly in the path laid by *A Bridge Too Far* are Martin Middlebrook's *Arnhem 1944: The Airborne Battle*, Peter Harclerode's *Arnhem: A Tragedy of Errors*, and A.D. Harvey's *Arnhem*.[4] Middlebrook and Harclerode's works – both published as part of the broad surge of popularly oriented literature on the liberation of North-West Europe that accompanied the fiftieth anniversary of the 1944–5 campaign – are both quite 'conventional' in their narratives and interpretations. Both largely follow Ryan's example quite closely in their overall structure, argumentation, sources consulted, and conclusions. Middlebrook, in particular, openly states that his book is intended merely to provide a detailed description of the Arnhem fighting to a wider audience, and that he is making no major revisions or revelations in interpreting the campaign. Despite this, his work retains a degree of utility for the scholarly reader in its detailed accounts of the numerous small battles fought by the 1st Airborne Division around Arnhem and Oosterbeek. These are accompanied by a useful amount of new material derived from interviews with, or written accounts by, junior officers and enlisted men of the division, providing a more detailed and well-supported 'soldier's eye' view of the actual fighting than has previously been available.

Harclerode's account is largely similar, although with a broader – if less detailed – focus on the events of the wider Market Garden campaign beyond Arnhem and the operating area of the 1st Airborne Division. Harclerode does, however, include one major point of revisionism – a former Guardsman himself, he devotes a considerable portion of his work to a defence of the actions of the British XXX Corps – and in particular the Guards Armoured Division, which led its advance during Market Garden – against the criticisms of most previous writers on the campaign. These critics have often charged that the formation conducted its advance with a degree of excessive caution and a lack of urgency that they argue was a – or even *the* – major factor in ensuring that the 1st Airborne Division could not be relieved in time. Harclerode effectively points out the many external factors that limited the speed of XXX Corps' advance, including a lack of infantry manpower, the extremely narrow frontage in which they had to operate, and the prevailing insufficiency of clear knowledge of enemy strength or positions, and thus argues that their slow pace was not simply a matter of timidity or a lack of drive. Thus, while the work breaks little new ground on the campaign as a whole, Harclerode's effort to explore the wider context behind XXX Corps' difficulties in the campaign leads the reader to reconsider the way in which factors beyond just command decisions can influence combat operations and thus how the degree to which a combat unit is actually capable of carrying out the orders it is given may matter at least as much as the degree to which those orders were themselves right or wrong in a given situation.

In his 2001 work, A.D. Harvey makes an effort to depart from traditional interpretations of the battle, challenging the significance of some of the factors that Ryan and those who followed him have asserted were decisive in the failure of the operation, such as the choice of landing zones for the 1st Airborne Division or the apparent slowness of XXX Corps' advance. Instead, he attributes the defeat of the 1st Division largely to its inability to muster sufficient fighting power quickly enough to match the rapid German response, largely due to the division's airlift insertion being spread across several days. Though this perception of an imbalance in relative fighting power is indeed a useful insight, Harvey fails to more closely examine possible reasons for it beyond a simple lack of numbers for the British Airborne. Given that the Germans were also severely short in manpower in the Arnhem area during the decisive first few days of the battle, there seems to be a critical gap in Harvey's explanation for why the Germans were able to gain the upper hand here – one that this work seeks to address. Furthermore, Harvey's assessment of the overall planning for Market Garden is at times frustratingly inconsistent: though he states early on that he believes that the overall plan was a fairly practical and feasible one, doomed only by a poor operational execution, he suggests at other times that it was excessively ambitious in several respects and all too often failed to match its ends to the available means, particularly in terms of planning for the airlift. This disconnect leaves the reader uncertain as to his actual conclusions on the practicality of the Market Garden plan, which limits the utility of his overall analysis.

One of the most useful of the narrative-style works on Operation Market Garden, however, follows a very different approach from those that have come before or since. Robert J. Kershaw's *It Never Snows in September*, originally published in 1990, is currently the only major scholarly work in English to make a comprehensive study of the fighting in Holland in September 1944 from the German perspective.[5] Kershaw makes use not only of the generally under-employed (if admittedly highly fragmentary) German archival sources for the battle, but also a number of personal interviews and an extensive collection of private correspondence and testimonies. He uses these to provide a detailed account that covers both high-level German planning and command decision making, as well as numerous 'trench-level' accounts from front-line officers and soldiers to provide a broad perspective of the German experience of the battle. Kershaw examines not only how German units actually fought the battle, but also how they assembled the various improvised forces they employed, using several 'case studies' to show the way in which functional combat units were rapidly assembled from assorted groups of stragglers, trainees, and reservists. Though Kershaw's analysis of German combat performance is relatively limited, the very fact that his work delves into largely unexplored scholarly territory ensures that his efforts cannot help but uncover new perspectives and force a reassessment of old conclusions. The most critical of these revisions – the idea that the outcome of Operation Market Garden was as much a matter of what the Germans did right as what the Allies did wrong – was a major driving force behind the current work.

With regards to more analytical works on Operation Market Garden, two recent books have made a major contribution to the scholarship on the campaign by opening new fields of inquiry and debate. The first,

Sebastian Ritchie's *Arnhem: Myth and Reality*, as mentioned in the introduction, is perhaps the most significant challenge to conventional interpretations of the campaign that has been written since *A Bridge Too Far*.[6] At the core of Ritchie's thesis is the challenge he makes to three 'myths' that he sees as having long dominated scholarship on the operation. The first of these is the idea that airborne operations prior to Market Garden had been almost entirely successful (and thus that its failure was an exceptional and unusual result), with the second being the idea that Montgomery's initial plan for Market Garden was a bold and brilliant masterstroke at the strategic and higher operational level, which only failed due to poor execution of those plans at the operational and grand tactical level by less competent subordinates. The third is the idea that the bulk of the failings in the planning for the operation were the fault of the Allied air forces, which have often been accused of ignoring the specific requirements of the ground forces in forming their plans for both the airlift and air support efforts, preferring instead to prioritize their own concerns and preserve their own forces at the expense of their ground-bound comrades.

Regarding the first myth, Ritchie's detailed exploration of both German and Allied airborne operations in the years prior to Market Garden clearly shows that such operations had invariably been difficult and disproportionately costly undertakings and that they almost never achieved the full degree of success that their planners anticipated. For the third myth, Ritchie takes advantage of his expertise in the history of airpower and air forces to examine the plans made by the air forces for Market Garden in greater detail and depth than any previous historian has done, placing them within their proper context, and critiquing them with an appropriate appreciation of the strengths and limitations inherent to military airpower. As such, he concludes that the apparent failings of the air forces in Market Garden, particular in the selection of landing zones, the extended timeline for the airlift, and the relatively limited provision of close air support, were not the result of carelessness or inter-service rivalries. Instead, Ritchie suggests that these failings were primarily a product of the fact that the framework operational plans – developed independently by Montgomery and the 1st Allied Airborne Army HQ and imposed upon the air forces with minimal consultation or opportunity for feedback or criticism – simply failed to account for

A Brief Historiography of the Market Garden Campaign 17

the available resources and technical limitations of the air forces under the circumstances prevailing in September 1944. Thus, Ritchie argues that the air forces' planners simply did the best they could in the face of severe pressures and limitations and that the flaws in those plans were not simple errors, but rather unavoidable consequences of those complicating factors – a fact that he argues previous historians of Market Garden, who have generally focused almost exclusively upon the ground forces, have never fully appreciated.

Finally, the second myth falls apart as a natural consequence of the critiques Ritchie makes of the other two; given the unrealistic reliance that Montgomery's plan for Market Garden placed upon absolute success to achieve its goals – a degree of success never before achieved by airborne operations – and his failure to realistically assess the ability of the air forces to actually execute the plans he made, it is clear that it can hardly be termed a masterwork of planning and that Market Garden's flaws as a military operation started right at the very top. Thus, by examining Market Garden within the broader context of airborne operations in general and with a proper appreciation for the way that airpower works, Ritchie has produced a new history of the operation that forces any future scholars to carefully reconsider the reasons behind its failure.

Perhaps less ground-breaking, but nevertheless useful in light of the varied approaches and ideas it introduces to the discussion is *Operation Market Garden – The Campaign for the Low Countries, Autumn 1944: Seventy Years On*, a collected volume of essays written for the 'Highway to the Reich' conference held at Wolverhampton University in September 2014 in commemoration of the seventieth anniversary of the campaign.[7] The central focus of this volume is an effort to challenge some of the myths and misunderstandings that have surrounded the operation by exploring several specific aspects of it in greater depth and detail. Among the more useful essays for the purposes of the current work are those of John Peaty, who examines the role that the dwindling supply of British infantry manpower in late 1944 had in impeding the combat performance of British units in the campaign; of Russell A. Hart, who investigates the improvised formation and deployment of the 406. *Landesschützen Division* and the significant (but rarely appreciated) contribution it made to the German victory; and that of Peter Preston-Hough, whose re-examination of an apparently disastrous assault made by *SS-Hauptsturmführer* (Senior

Company Commander) Viktor Gräbner's 9. *SS-Panzer-Aufklärungs-Abteilung* (9th SS Armoured Reconnaissance Battalion or Detachment) on the second day of the battle, serves to illustrate the way in which apparently small and insignificant actions could have a considerable effect upon wider operations. Overall, the tightly focused and multi-varied nature of these essays allows the reader to develop an appreciation for various small but significant aspects of the campaign that may be missed in more broadly focused works.

Moving beyond works specifically written about Operation Market Garden and the Battle of Arnhem, the effort in this work to investigate how the British and German armies actually fought the battle, and the degree to which their differing approaches to combat shaped the operation's outcome, has benefited greatly from the numerous works written on the development and practice of combat doctrine in both armies.

Perhaps the most useful works for developing an understanding of the origins and nature of the German Army's tactical doctrine in the Second World War are Robert M. Citino's *The Path to Blitzkrieg: Doctrine and Training in the German Army, 1920–1939* and James S. Corum's *The Roots of Blitzkrieg: Hans von Seeckt and German Military Reform*.[8] These two works take similar approaches to similar subject matter, tracing the tactical doctrine that proved so effective for the German Army in the Second World War back to reforms enacted in the early years following the German defeat in the First World War. Both authors argue that these reforms were spearheaded largely by *Generaloberst* (Colonel General) Hans von Seeckt, the de facto Chief of Staff of the reformed German Army, the *Reichswehr*, from 1919–26, who sought to rebuild the army with a new doctrine that combined the best aspects of the old Imperial Army with the lessons learned in the First World War. They show that Seeckt combined the best aspects of traditional German doctrine, particularly its emphasis upon encouraging aggression, mobility, initiative, and independent thinking among its officers and men, with the most significant developments to come out of the First World War, particularly in the field of small-unit infantry 'stormtroop' tactics and in concepts of motorized and mechanized warfare, to produce a modernized army that relied more upon mobility and the high quality of its forces than raw numbers and mass to achieve victories. Citino and Corum argue that it was this highly flexible and decentralized doctrine, coupled with the high standards of training introduced within the *Reichswehr* to ensure that doctrine could be successfully carried out, that provided the German Army of the Second World War with a general (if very hard to effectively quantify) qualitative advantage over the Allied forces at the tactical level, particularly in confused and rapidly changing situations such as those faced in Market Garden.

Despite their general similarities, Citino and Corum's works also differ usefully in several ways. Most notably, Citino focuses more upon in-depth discussions of the various doctrinal manuals produced by the *Reichswehr* between 1919 and 1935, as well as on annual reports on the army's manoeuvres, and on the discussions that took place within the army's journal literature in the period, to trace the development and promulgation of the new doctrine throughout the army and its effects upon its performance. Corum, on the other hand, focuses instead upon the details of the training programmes established by the *Reichswehr* for officers, non-commissioned officers (NCOs), and enlisted men, showing how the concepts introduced in the new doctrine were effectively put into practice and instilled into the minds of soldiers at all levels. Each book thus provides useful details of the development of German doctrine and training that help to fill in some of the gaps in the other.

These two works are also usefully supplemented by another Citino work, *The German Way of War: From the Thirty Years' War to the Third Reich*, which seeks to trace the origins of the German doctrinal traditions mentioned above back to their points of origin in the wars of the seventeenth century. Citino argues that the 'German way of war,' focused on manoeuvre warfare and achieving quick, decisive battlefield victories through tactical superiority, developed out of the perennial strategic problems faced by Germany (and the states of Brandenburg and Prussia that preceded it) due to its geography – its relatively small size, limited resources, and, critically, the fact that it has generally been surrounded by potential enemies. Citino shows that Germany – lacking the territory, manpower, or resources to sacrifice ground or fight a war of attrition – instead sought to fight wars on its own terms by seizing the initiative and attacking before it could be attacked in turn, forcing their enemies onto the defensive and allowing German forces to dictate the course of events to a large degree. Citino also argues that the disadvantages faced by the German states encouraged both a long-standing focus upon high standards of training, as their armies would generally need a qualitative advantage to overcome enemies that outnumbered them, and a tradition of subordinate commanders being permitted to exercise a considerable degree of independence in carrying out the orders of their superiors. The latter was important because hard-pressed German forces could not afford to waste any fleeting opportunities encountered on the battlefield by waiting for orders to exploit them to come from above.

Overall, these last three works all serve to demonstrate the nature and origins of the doctrine and tactical proficiency that proved so useful to the German Army in the Second World War as a whole, and during the Market Garden fighting in particular. They also show the fact that these German military qualities were the product not simply of short-term changes to manuals of instruction and training methods, but of long-standing traditions instilled into the very heart of German military culture for decades in terms of specific doctrine, and centuries in terms of the broader principles. As such, it is hardly surprising that their opponents had so much difficulty in adapting to and overcoming these German advantages in the short time they had available, and that the process was far from complete in autumn 1944, even after four years of war.

Turning to the British Army, several works have explored the difficulties the British Army of the Second World War faced in developing effective combat doctrine and tactics, particularly with regards to the infantry combat that predominated during Market Garden. Jeremy A. Krang's *The British Army and the People's War 1939–1945*, David French's *Raising Churchill's Army: The British Army and the War Against Germany, 1919–1945*, and Timothy Harrison Place's *Military Training in the British Army 1940–1944: From Dunkirk to D-Day* all make the observation that the combat performance of the 'front line' or 'closing' arms of the British Army in the Second World War – that is, the infantry and armoured forces – was, in general, mediocre.[9] They note that the tactics used by British infantry and tankers were generally outdated and overly simplistic, that the quality of training among both their officers and enlisted men was usually fairly low, and that British forces generally relied heavily upon superior numbers and weight of materiel, particularly an overwhelming amount of artillery and air support, to defeat their German opponents, and often still suffered a disproportionate scale of losses in doing so.

Though they broadly agree on the general flaws of the British Army, these three authors differ to some degree in what they see as the reasons for this tactical weakness. Krang sees it largely as the result of a strong tradition of conservatism within the British Army as a social institution, one in which it was often not elderly and hidebound senior generals that resisted change and innovation, as is frequently charged, but instead a sizeable proportion of the long-serving, middle-ranking officers and NCOs throughout the field forces who all too often steadfastly resisted efforts by the War Office and other central command organs to update and revise the tactics and methods with which they were comfortably familiar, even when their inadequacy had been manifestly demonstrated by failures in the field. Krang argues that this resistance was enabled largely by the army's Regimental System, which made standards and methods of training an almost entirely sovereign responsibility of battalion and (to a lesser extent) divisional commanders; this ensured that whatever efforts the army made to develop its tactics and training could never easily become standardized, as commanding officers could largely adopt or ignore doctrinal directives as they saw fit. This drag upon tactical development ensured that, despite the extensive information accrued from the experiences of the first five years of the war, and the lengthy training period available for most British units before the invasion of Europe, British combat doctrine and training standards still remained well behind those of the Germans in late 1944.

French's book, however, disagrees with some of Krang's conclusions, arguing that the British Army of the interwar period was not as conservative as is often thought and that it did make a considerable effort to modernize itself in line with the lessons of the First World War, developing a new doctrine through the 1920s that embraced modern concepts of combined arms warfare and mechanization. French argues, however, that the army was largely unsuccessful in actually putting this doctrine into practice, being hampered by its retention of a highly rigid centrally controlled command system and a tendency to excessive caution that emphasized preservation of strength and morale over the exploitation of opportunities, both of which were informed by a general disregard among the upper ranks for the intelligence and resilience of the average enlisted man. French argues these flaws ensured that the British Army remained far too inflexible and slow in its reactions on the battlefield to make the best use of the potential of its doctrine. French does agree with Krang on the point of training, however, arguing that the lack of centralized enforcement of standards for training, and a general failure to pay sufficient attention to it, ensured that what advances were made in doctrine and tactics were only intermittently – and often incorrectly or incompletely – promulgated among the troops.

French, however, does not take an entirely negative view of the British Army's fighting efforts, arguing that they did eventually learn how to play to their strengths, particularly in the effective use of massed artillery firepower, and, along with their allies, eventually managed to win the war against the Germans in spite of their advantages. This conclusion that the British Army was able to achieve success as long as it could play to its strengths, however, leads the reader to consider the possible consequences that would likely result when the army exited its 'comfort zone' of superior firepower – as it did in Market Garden.

Timothy Place's book follows an approach largely similar to that of French, arguing that the British Army's greatest failing was its inability to effectively and consistently convey appropriate doctrine to its troops via training. To illustrate this, Place examines the cases of three different divisions to show that the tactical proficiency of units was often just the 'luck of the draw', with successful units generally benefitting from having been fortuitously assigned commanding officers who paid sufficient attention to training efforts, actually took the time to properly learn the doctrine, and had sufficient experience and/or good judgement to determine those methods and standards that were best suited to the demands of modern combat. The fact that one of the divisions he studies, and whose training standards he specifically criticizes – the Guards Armoured Division – was, as mentioned above, prominent in Market Garden makes Place's work particularly useful to this study, providing some explanation for the difficulties the unit experienced in the battle. Overall, these three works help the reader to understand the very serious shortcomings that British forces were operating with, even in late 1944, and to appreciate the fact that what successes they did achieve were based upon fighting according to very specific methods that minimized those flaws – methods that, for the most part, could not be effectively used during Market Garden, leaving the British Army at a notable disadvantage.

A Brief Historiography of the Market Garden Campaign   23

Stephen A. Hart's *Montgomery and 'Colossal Cracks': The 21st Army Group in Northwest Europe*, serves as a highly useful counterpoint to the more critical views of the Second World War British Army expressed in the preceding works.[10] Hart argues that the slow, cautious, firepower-centric approach to combat taken by the British Army in North-West Europe in 1944 was far more effective than many of its critics have suggested. Hart argues that Montgomery, and other like-minded commanders, deliberately chose to adopt this doctrine because of the specific circumstances faced by the British Army and nation in the latter half of the Second World War. With the British Army finding itself well behind its German opponents in the kind of training and leadership needed to effectively employ the type of fast-moving, mobile armoured tactics that had gained the Germans so much success in the early years of the war, and with the British government facing a looming shortage of manpower and considerable concerns about the morale and will of their people to carry on the fight, Montgomery's battle methodology, first deployed in the North African desert at El Alamein and honed to a high level of effectiveness thereafter, played to British strengths and minimized their weaknesses. By relying upon overwhelming firepower delivered by artillery and tactical airpower and by constructing elaborate and cautious plans with relatively limited objectives, Montgomery was able to both preserve his country's precious manpower and potentially fragile morale and avoid 'playing the Germans' game' by trying to engage in the type of fast-moving, free-form warfare for which his own forces were not adequately prepared.

Hart further argues that, far from hampering Allied efforts in Normandy as some have charged, Montgomery's 'Colossal Cracks' doctrine was in fact chiefly responsible for the degree of success that the Allies achieved there, with the firepower allowing the Allies to steadily wear down the Germans, in spite of their often superior tactics and equipment, while the caution and careful planning greatly reduced the opportunities the Germans might have had to inflict a serious reverse upon them. Hart thus demonstrates that the British Army had established an effective and successful method of waging war by autumn 1944, which leads a student of Market Garden to consider the degree to which that operation's failure came due to divergences from the model that had just proven so effective in Normandy.

24 The Last German Victory

Finally, although its specific subject matter does not touch directly on the Market Garden campaign, or even the Second World War, Martin Samuels' *Command or Control? Command, Training and Tactics in the British and German Armies, 1888–1918* provides a very useful comparative study of the differences in the doctrine and combat philosophies of the German and British armies in the late nineteenth and early twentieth centuries – one that remains largely applicable to the Second World War as well.[11] Samuels argues that the very different responses developed by the militaries of each nation to the challenges of modern warfare faced in the period were the result of deep differences in their cultural views on the broader nature of warfare. Samuels argues that the German leadership, in the tradition of famed Prussian military theorist Carl von Clausewitz, saw combat as an inherently and immutably chaotic and unpredictable thing, in which it was impossible to make entirely reliable predictions or rigid plans for how events would develop; this in turn led to them believing that success in combat could only be achieved by learning to operate effectively within these conditions of chaos. Thus, the Germans adopted a system of decentralized command, developing a high level of skill, independence, and initiative as widely as possible among their officers and men to ensure their ability to react to changing situations and exploit fleeting local opportunities without the direction from above that was so subject to delays or interruptions.

In contrast, Samuels argues that British leadership believed that while combat was naturally chaotic, that chaos could be effectively mitigated and made subject to order, given a sufficient degree of strict central control by commanders and rigid discipline and obedience to orders among their troops; effectively, they chose to implement a command system to resist chaos rather than accept it, as the Germans did. Samuels argues that all the differences between the doctrine and tactics of the two nations effectively trace back to these differing views on the nature of combat and that, in the end, the more flexible German system proved much better suited to actually coping with the realities of modern warfare than did that of the British, which was never really able to establish the degree of control it aspired to. Samuels also argues that this deeper philosophical difference between the two armies was a major reason why the British were unable to successfully adopt German-style methods, despite several efforts to do so – the German way of thinking that was so central to the effectiveness of their decentralized command system was simply too alien to the British Army's cultural mindset to be rapidly adopted. In light of the chaotic conditions that generally prevailed on both sides throughout the events of operation Market Garden, Samuels' arguments on how the way that each military perceived and coped with chaos in combat influenced the way they fought are highly instructive.

Chapter 3

Thriving Amidst Chaos: The Origins and Nature of German Tactical and Command Doctrine

The nature of German combat doctrine – the principles and concepts that informed the tactics, training, and organization of their fighting forces – was central to the success of *Heeresgruppe B* against Operation Market Garden in September 1944. It allowed the forces of the army group to react quickly and effectively to the surprise attack, successfully disrupt the Allied battle plan, and contain a potentially decisive Allied breakthrough. The doctrine employed by the German *Wehrmacht* in the Second World War was to some extent a product of their experiences in the First World War, but also drew upon a long tradition of German warfare and particularly the key principles of independent and aggressive battlefield leadership and tactical proficiency. Such a doctrine ensured that the *Wehrmacht* was almost ideally suited to the confused, chaotic, and rapidly changing nature of a combined airborne-mechanized operation such as Market Garden, allowing it to quickly retake the initiative from the Allied forces and seize the upper hand in the ensuing fighting.

Historical Origins of Germany's Doctrinal Principles

One of the most important and long-standing elements of German military doctrine was a general perception of warfare as an unavoidably chaotic and unpredictable activity.[1] This idea was perhaps first articulated by the Prussian staff officer and military theorist Carl von Clausewitz in his famous work *Vom Kriege* (*On War*). In this work, Clausewitz speaks extensively on the concept of 'friction': the wide variety of omnipresent and often unavoidable factors, both major and minor, that could complicate or disrupt the implementation of military plans under real world conditions, ensuring that those plans could virtually never be executed exactly as intended.[2] The concept, however, was already a prominent feature in German military thought well before Clausewitz penned his treatise, dating back to the earliest days of the modern Prussian state. At its core, this philosophy of combat postulated the idea that, as a violent, emotionally charged activity waged between competing human minds, war was simply too complex to be fully understood, predicted, or governed according to set rational principles – that the conduct of war was far more of an art than it was a science.[3]

This philosophy of warfare in turn shaped the way that German doctrine viewed leadership and command. Given that they saw battle as an extremely chaotic and unpredictable affair, the prevailing view among most prominent German military leaders through history, such as the 'Great Elector' Friedrich Wilhelm of Brandenburg, Frederick the Great, and Helmut von Moltke the Elder, as well as their military establishments, was that combat doctrine could not simply be a set of prescriptive rules or formulas for what were the best actions for a commander to take in any given situation in battle, as there were simply too many possible variations and complicating factors to accurately predict in advance. Instead, German doctrine saw the key element of effective leadership as being the ability to quickly and accurately assess a situation and then to draw upon both one's knowledge and creativity in figuring out and applying a solution tailored to the specific circumstances and conditions faced. German doctrine has thus generally been less a set of firm 'commandments' than a set of loose principles to guide a commander in judging the situations they faced and making appropriate decisions.[4] Moreover, because friction would naturally impede the ability of a commander of any sizeable force to both obtain an accurate assessment of the situation on any given portion of the battlefield, and to effectively communicate his orders to the various sub-units under his command, German doctrine placed a high premium on the ability of subordinate commanders to exercise independent initiative and make their own assessments and decisions according to whatever local threats or opportunities presented themselves, without firm direction or specific orders from the centre.[5]

As such, one of the defining principles of modern German military doctrine is a concept that has generally become known as *'Auftragstaktik'*, which translates loosely as 'mission tactics'. The term was first explicitly expressed by *Generalfeldmarschall* Helmut von Moltke the Elder, Chief of Staff of the Prussian (and later Imperial German) Army in the era of the German Wars of Unification. However, like Clausewitz's 'friction', the basic concept was traceable as far back as the reigns of the eighteenth-century Prussian King Friedrich II (better known to posterity as Frederick the Great) and Friedrich Wilhelm, the seventeenth-century *Großer Kürfurst* ('Great Elector') of Brandenburg-Prussia.[6] The essence of *Auftragstaktik* was the idea that a senior commander should not issue detailed orders telling their subordinates precisely what to do and when to do it, but rather should only outline the general tasks or 'missions' they wanted accomplished, while leaving any specific details of conducting the battle for those subordinates to figure out and decide for themselves according to the specific situations they encountered.[7] It is important to note that this did not grant subordinate commanders total freedom to do as they wished; they were still expected to conform to the general intent of a superior's overall plans and were held responsible for any consequences of their actions. However, within that broad framework German commanders were generally granted a wide degree of freedom – and responsibility – to exercise their own initiative, conduct their own battles, interpret and alter orders as they saw fit, and even to disobey orders that they believed were no longer appropriate to a situation.[8] In its earliest form through the seventeenth, eighteenth, and nineteenth centuries, known as '*Weisenführung*' or 'leadership by directive', *Auftragstaktik* only extended this freedom of action down to the most senior subordinates of an army commander, such as corps or division commanders, but, as will be discussed more later, the twentieth century saw the principle extended down to even the smallest units of an army.[9]

Coupled to this emphasis on initiative within German doctrine was an equally strong focus upon rapid and aggressive offensive action. This offensive orientation was largely the result of the general strategic situation that almost invariably confronted Germany and its predecessor states throughout the last several centuries, that of being a relatively small and resource-poor country surrounded by potential enemies that could muster superior human and material resources. This situation made defensive conflicts and prolonged wars of attrition impractical, as the German states generally lacked both the geographic depth and the reserves of fighting men and materiel that such strategies required.[10]

Since the seventeenth century, German military leaders had sought to resolve this problem by seeking to wage short, decisive wars. They sought to seize and hold the strategic and operational initiative in any conflict by taking to the offensive as swiftly and aggressively as possible, throwing their opponents onto the defensive and allowing them to concentrate their own more limited strength at a time and place of their own choosing to defeat the enemy's forces as swiftly as possible, ideally in a single, decisive battle.[11] As such, German doctrine heavily emphasized the importance of boldness and aggression in effective military leadership, asserting that any commander should seek to take the offensive whenever and wherever possible in order to seize the initiative and force their opponent to react, rather than allowing that opponent to carry out their own plans. According to this way of thinking, taking action was in and of itself a virtue, with even mistaken actions being seen as preferable to idly waiting for orders or more information in an uncertain situation, as such inaction would simply allow the enemy greater freedom to act themselves.[12]

This overall concept of bold, aggressive, and independent-minded leadership in combat has been a defining feature of German warfare – what Citino has termed 'the German Way of War' – from the mid-seventeenth century onwards, with numerous famous victories such as those of Frederick the Great in the Seven Years War, or those of Moltke in the Wars of Unification, relying heavily upon aggressive independent action pursued by subordinate commanders operating relatively loosely within the framework of an overall plan.[13] At the Battle of Zorndorf in 1758, for example, Frederick the Great's young, but highly talented cavalry commander, *Generalleutnant* (Lieutenant General) Friedrich Wilhelm, Freiherr von Seydlitz, refused several direct orders from the king to counterattack a Russian force that was driving back the Prussian infantry line, believing it would be better to wait for a more opportune moment and to properly reconnoitre the marshy ground across which his regiments were to charge before acting. Seydlitz thus told Frederick's messenger to, 'Tell the king that after the battle my head is at his disposal, but meantime I hope he will permit me to exercise it in his service!' Shortly thereafter, Seydlitz, having found navigable crossing points through the marshland and seen the Russian force exposing its vulnerable flank as it swept past him in pursuit of the Prussian infantry, launched his six regiments in a decisive charge that shattered the Russian advance and allowed Frederick to eventually eke out a hard-fought victory.[14] Seydlitz' calculated disobedience at Zorndorf thus almost perfectly embodied the principles of *Weisenführung* at the time; in refusing Frederick's commands he emphasized the importance of the king trusting his judgement as the commander on the spot, who presumably would have had a better view and understanding than the more distant Frederick of the specific tactical conditions he faced, and allowing him the freedom to act as he saw fit in pursuit of the overall battle plan, while also explicitly taking personal responsibility should his judgement have proven mistaken. That Frederick accepted this 'insubordination' shows the prevalence of these concepts among the Prussian Army's leadership even at this early point; though Frederick issued his initial orders based upon his own perception of the situation, he accepted and trusted that Seydlitz had good reason for acting contrary to them, and allowed him the freedom to fight his own portion of the battle despite his own clear doubts about the situation.

The Turning Point: *Auftragstaktik* in the First World War and the Interwar Period

However, a major turning point for this German doctrine came in the First World War, particularly with regards to *Auftragstaktik*. In the decades prior to the First World War, in the wake of Moltke the Elder's retirement in 1888, the concept of independent leadership had been deemphasized to some degree within the German Army. At this time the German military leadership, following the example of *Generalfeldmarschall* Count Alfred von Schlieffen, the Chief of the General Staff from 1891 to 1906, came to prefer a strategy based upon rigidly controlled and scheduled mobilization and manoeuvre, seeking to take advantage of the sheer mass of Germany's large conscript army.[15] This rigid, mass-based strategy failed utterly in the opening years of the First World War, however, with Germany's powerful but ponderous opening offensive eventually grinding to a halt in the face of modern firepower on the Marne, leaving Germany confronting the very prolonged attritional war it had long sought to avoid. Unsurprisingly, many among the German military establishment sought a solution to the growing trench deadlock in the successful practices of the past. Given that Germany still had little hope of winning the defensive war of attrition they had found themselves

The Origins and Nature of German Tactical and Command Doctrine 31

in, the German military remained committed to seeking a return to a decisive offensive war. It was also realized, however, that the rigid, mass-based methods of the Schlieffen era were entirely unsuited to the conditions of modern war and that any offensive would require entirely different methods to succeed.[16]

While the French and British armies sought a solution to the stalemate mainly in technology – such as the use of tanks and increasingly elaborate artillery programmes – the Germans sought their answer mainly in a reform of their combat tactics, largely through the application of the principles of *Auftragstaktik* to an unprecedented degree. One of the chief problems encountered in the wielding of military forces in the First World War was that of command and control; the level of dispersion necessary for forces to have any chance of surviving in the face of modern firepower completely overwhelmed traditional methods of central command that relied on vocal, visual, or cable-based communication. Once out of their trenches, any sizeable attacking force quickly became uncontrollable by any central commander, leaving the attack to dissolve into chaos in the face of enemy fire and unexpected developments.[17]

In light of their long-standing views on the ubiquity and inevitability of chaos on the battlefield, the German military sought to solve this problem not by improving central control, but by devolving a large degree of command responsibility down to the smallest units of the army: companies, platoons, and even squads. The German military thus developed what James Corum called 'the greatest German tactical achievement of the war': the famous stormtroop tactics. At the heart of this concept – initially developed through local experimentation by individual units at the front – was the restructuring of the above-mentioned small units into nearly fully independent units capable of employing both firepower and tactical manoeuvre on the battlefield. These units, supplied with their own organic firepower in the form of machine guns, trench mortars, and light infantry guns, were trained to operate and manoeuvre independently and aggressively, matching their tactics to the specific resistance and terrain encountered to maintain offensive momentum in the face of battlefield confusion.[18] The result of this was the effective expansion of the principles of *Auftragstaktik* throughout the entire army, as stormtroop tactics naturally required individual small-unit leaders and even individual soldiers to take an increasing degree of responsibility for their own conduct on the battlefield, as they would have to be able to assess their own situations and make appropriate decisions. Thus, after a prolonged period of retraining while remaining on the defensive throughout 1916 and 1917, the German Army deployed its stormtroop tactics with considerable tactical-level success in the last year of the war, particularly in their successful counteroffensive at Cambrai in November 1917 and in the *'Kaiserschlacht'* (Emperor's Battle) offensives of spring 1918. Though the Germans failed to achieve the decisive victory they sought, the effectiveness of their stormtroop tactics in battle was widely acknowledged.

In the wake of its defeat in the First World War and the signing of the Treaty of Versailles, the Imperial German Army was disbanded in 1919, with a new army, the *Reichswehr*, being formed to replace it. This new army, however, retained most of the traditional doctrinal principles of the old, and also learned well from the experience of the First World War. As head of the *Truppenamt*, or 'Troops Office', the de facto successor to the disbanded General Staff, the leading figure in the formation of the *Reichswehr* was *Generaloberst* Hans von Seeckt. Seeckt had been a highly successful staff officer in the First World War, and is now widely seen as the man perhaps most responsible for the impressive battlefield performance of the German *Wehrmacht* in the early years of the Second World War.[19] Almost immediately after the war, Seeckt commissioned an exhaustive investigation of the experiences of the army in the First World War and the effectiveness of German doctrine, seeking to ascertain both what went wrong and what had proven successful.[20] The results of this comprehensive 'self-evaluation' largely confirmed Seeckt's existing ideas on the basic viability of traditional German doctrine, with its focus upon decisive offensive action, flexibility, and initiative, suggesting that the German defeat was due mainly to a failure to properly apply those principles.[21] Seeckt had spent the bulk of his wartime career on the Eastern Front, where he was prominent in the planning of several successful offensives, such as the Battle of Gorlice-Tarnow and the invasions of Serbia and Rumania. He believed that the stalemate on the Western Front had been primarily the result of the fact that the armies there were simply too big and unwieldly to effectively manoeuvre in the relatively limited available space, forcing them to rely on simple brute force and attrition. Seeckt thus believed that traditional German mobile

The Origins and Nature of German Tactical and Command Doctrine 33

offensive warfare, or *'Bewegungskrieg'*, was still entirely possible for a smaller, but more manoeuvrable and better trained army.

The Wehrmacht's Founding Documents: *FuG* and *Truppenführung*

The primary result of Seeckt's efforts was a new core doctrinal manual for the *Reichswehr*, *Führung und Gefecht der verbundenen Waffen* (*Combat and Command of the Combined Arms*), or '*FuG*', published in two parts in September 1921 and June 1923. This new doctrine effectively updated traditional German doctrine for the demands of modern warfare, incorporating the new tactical developments of the First World War.[22] *FuG* remained the primary source of combat doctrine for the *Reichswehr* throughout most of its short existence, being replaced in 1933 by *Heeresdienstvorschrift 300: Truppenführung* (*Army Service Regulation 300: Troop Leading* or *Unit Command*). *Truppenführung*, however, was largely just a minor revision and update of *FuG*, reproducing virtually all of its main principles and even reprinting some sections almost verbatim; it would remain the central doctrinal manual of the German Army through to the end of the Second World War.[23]

Truppenführung heavily emphasized the principles of independent and aggressive leadership outlined above; though the term *'Auftragstaktik'* is never actually used in the manual, the concept is pervasive throughout the work.[24] Among the key concepts expressed in *Truppenführung* was the idea that strict centralized control was entirely unsuitable to the conditions of modern mobile warfare, and that such conditions instead demanded 'soldiers who can think and act independently, who can make calculated, decisive, and daring use of every situation, and who understand that victory depends on each individual' and 'leaders capable of judgement, with clear vision and foresight, and the ability to make independent and decisive decisions and carry them out unwaveringly and positively'.[25] It thus concluded that, 'The commander must allow his subordinates freedom of action, so long as it does not adversely affect his overall intent', charging that units should be both willing and able to act without orders from above to exploit whatever fleeting opportunities might present themselves at the front, and to modify or discard the specifics of any orders as the situation demanded, as long as they acted in accordance with their commander's overall intentions.[26]

Truppenführung also emphasized the need for commanders to opt for quick decisions and bold, positive action whenever possible, stating that, 'The first criterion in war remains decisive action. Everyone, from the highest commander down to the youngest soldier, must constantly be aware that inaction and neglect incriminate him more severely than any error in the choice of means.'[27] It did qualify this however, stating that 'great successes require boldness and daring, but good judgement must take precedence', emphasizing that, while prompt and aggressive action was generally desirable, commanders still needed to carefully consider their actions, and should not attack carelessly or recklessly in an unsuitable situation. Therefore, *Truppenführung* theoretically sought to instill aggressive leadership, but not a 'berserker' mentality, and while offensive action was emphasized, it was not seen as the sole solution to any given problem.

Expanding upon these concepts, *Truppenführung* also devoted considerable attention to the concept of 'meeting engagements', where two opposing forces met unexpectedly on the march and thus had to engage with minimal advance knowledge or preparation. *Truppenführung* emphasized that such engagements were usually won by the side that was able to assess the situation, make decisions, and act more quickly than the other, which meant that the ability of subordinate commanders in a formation's advance guard to take the initiative and attack while the other side was still confused was critical.[28] It is worth noting that this type of engagement was also heavily emphasized in the *Reichswehr*'s annual exercises, being seen as an ideal way to train officers and troops on how to improvise rapidly in combat.[29]

Moreover, *Truppenführung* also extended its ideas on initiative and aggressive action to defensive warfare. In this, *Truppenführung* drew upon the concept of 'elastic defence' developed in the First World War, in which the defence was based not simply around repulsing the enemy through raw firepower from a single, rigidly held front line, but rather around the employment of local withdrawals and counterattacks from within the depth of a position against any enemy penetrations of the line.[30] Though *Truppenführung* still maintained that firepower was the keystone of any defence, it emphasized that a commander should endeavour to wield this firepower as actively as possible, rather than simply passively awaiting an enemy's attack. *Truppenführung* called upon commanders to aggressively seek out and seize the best possible terrain to maximize the effect of their defensive firepower, to rapidly counterattack any penetration before an enemy could consolidate their position, and to promptly follow up any defeated enemy attack with their own offensive action.[31]

The doctrine expressed in *Truppenführung*, with its calls for quick decision making and action at all levels of command, naturally placed extremely high demands upon the abilities of the officers and men of the German Army; given the considerable freedom it gave soldiers to exercise their own judgement in making critical decisions, the proper development of that judgement would naturally be vital in ensuring the doctrine could be effectively put into action. As such, a key factor in the German doctrinal 'renaissance' of the interwar period was an extensive and intensive programme of training and exercises, introduced by Seeckt alongside *FuG* and carried on by his successors right through the Second World War. Historian James Corum, for example, has argued that the German Army's level of training was the single most significant advantage it had over its opponents in the early years of the Second World War.[32]

Theory into Practice: *Auftragstaktik* and Training in the *Reichswehr* and *Wehrmacht*

Seeckt's training programmes were hardly introducing an entirely new concept to the German military; the idea that the quality of officers and troops was often much more important to combat success than simple numbers had a long-standing basis in German military thought, dating back at least to the days of Frederick the Great, whose musketeers were famously trained to a unmatched level of proficiency in their formation drills and were generally able to fire their muskets significantly faster than their opponents.[33] Seeckt, in turn, strongly believed that the quality of an army's training was far more important to its performance than numerical strength (a factor made even more important in light of the size limitations imposed on the *Reichswehr* by the Treaty of Versailles), and further believed that intensive training would be necessary both to promulgate the *FuG* doctrine throughout the army and to ensure that its officers and men were actually capable of acting as the doctrine directed.[34]

As such, Seeckt instituted a training system that was geared to preparing the army as effectively as possible for the conditions they would face on the battlefield. The primary emphasis of this training was upon developing the skills necessary for effective leadership and decision making, in officers, non-commissioned officers (NCOs), and even enlisted men. At the most basic level, the German Army simply put more time and effort into training its soldiers, and particularly its officers and NCOs, than most other armies. In peacetime a German officer candidate could expect to spend four years in intensive training before they were commissioned – as long as some modern academic doctoral programmes – and though this period was reduced to a still lengthy two years in 1937, in the face of a massive expansion of the army and the looming threat of war, the standards expected in the final examinations remained largely the same.[35] Similarly, German NCOs were selected by performance and examinations on their tactical knowledge, rather than simple seniority as in the British and US armies, and candidates often attended specialized NCO schools to hone their command abilities. This system of selection and training ensured that German NCOs represented a well-trained corps of junior leaders, rather than just 'assistants' to officers, and often performed more important command roles in the field than their counterparts in other armies; it was, for example, quite common for senior NCOs to be assigned to command platoons in the German forces.[36]

Both the *Reichswehr* and *Wehrmacht* also made extensive use of realistic exercises, both using maps and sand-tables and, as frequently as possible, in the field.[37] One of the most important characteristics of these exercises was that commanders and men were expected not simply to carry out a pre-formulated plan (as was generally the case for the exercises of most other armies), but to formulate and execute their own plans based on the specific situations with which they were faced, and to confront and deal with unexpected changes to those situations.[38] Junior officers, NCOs, and even private soldiers would often be able – and even encouraged – to contribute to or critique the formulation of those plans, or even to take turns at playing a command role within their unit, ensuring that virtually every German soldier had at least a basic grasp of the principles of command and tactics.[39] This practical experience in leadership ensured not only that the officers and NCOs of the German Army were given considerable opportunities and resources to develop their sense of tactical judgement and decision-making abilities, but also that the army almost always had a sizeable pool of men willing and able to take the initiative and to assume a higher level of command responsibility when necessary.[40]

Finally, and perhaps most importantly, training in the German Army focused very heavily upon teaching the basics of minor tactics for employment at the 'sharp end' of combat – up to the level of battalion command; by comparison, British and American officer academies generally focused on matters of administration and higher strategy.[41] Given that the German Army saw infantry combat as the most basic and central element of battle, every soldier of every branch of the army was trained in basic infantry tactics before proceeding to any specialist training and the first year of every officer's training was spent learning how to lead and manoeuvre all infantry units from sections up to battalions.[42] This meant that German junior officers and men – even those that were technically not front-line combatants – had a much better grounding in the most basic tasks and demands of front-line infantry combat tactics and leadership than their Allied counterparts.

This high standard of training, standardized across the German Army, ensured not only that the members of the *Wehrmacht* generally possessed the high level of knowledge and skill that the doctrine of *FuG* and *Truppenführung* required, but also that they shared common concepts and ways of thinking about combat, a factor that was crucial to the effective functioning of *Auftragstaktik*. Given the considerable freedom that the various sub-units of the German Army had to operate independently, this common standard of training ensured that they would all generally make decisions and act within a common framework, even without specific direction from above, ensuring that their various independent actions generally maintained a unity of purpose.[43]

Thus, the German Army entered the Second World War with both doctrine and training that produced a high degree of tactical proficiency, initiative, and aggression throughout its ranks, qualities that were reflected by the many notable successes achieved by lower level commanders acting without, or even contrary to, orders, when an opportunity was perceived. Perhaps best known are the examples of Panzer commanders General Heinz Guderian and *Generalmajor* Erwin Rommel in the French campaign of 1940; both of these men, seeing the chaos ahead of them in the Allied rear after having breached Allied lines at the Meuse, chose to disregard orders from the High Command to halt and wait for supporting units to catch up and instead plunged ahead towards the French coast.[44] Their superiors, soon realizing the opportunity their wayward subordinates had uncovered, quickly reinforced these bold thrusts, which eventually resulted in the encirclement of Allied forces at Dunkirk, which all but guaranteed the German victory over France. Beyond famous high-level examples such as the above, the war saw countless instances of small German units, right down to individual companies, platoons, and squads, launching attacks or counterattacks on their own initiative as situations demanded. Though this tendency did not always yield positive results – as such actions and reactions could prove extremely costly if their opponents managed to muster sufficient firepower to meet them – it at the very least ensured that the German forces were often able to seize or at least dispute the initiative from their Allied opponents, forcing them to react and diverting efforts and resources from any offensive efforts of their own.

Chapter 4

'Leaping into a Hornet's Nest': The Role of German Tactical and Command Doctrine in Operation Market Garden

Market Garden: The German Operational Response

Given the nature of German doctrine and training as discussed in the preceding chapter, it should hardly come as any sort of surprise that the German reaction to Market Garden was both rapid and ferocious. Firstly, it is worth noting that the initial Allied airborne landings at Arnhem, Nijmegen, and Eindhoven achieved almost total operational and tactical surprise, with both German after action reports and the fact that *Generalfeldmarshall* Model himself came very close to capture at his *Heeresgruppe B* headquarters in Oosterbeek's Tafelberg Hotel, less than 3 miles from the principal British drop/landing zones, attesting to the fact that the Germans were caught entirely off guard.[1] Moreover, the war diaries of the Allied units involved in the drops almost universally describe facing only the most minimal resistance during and immediately after the landings, with only a few scattered individual German soldiers fleeing or being taken prisoner; the diary of the British 1st Parachute Battalion described the drop as 'perfect, just like an exercise'.[2] An old myth that attributed the presence of the II. *SS-Panzer Korps* just north of Arnhem to the betrayal of the date and location of the landings to the Germans by a Dutch double agent has long since been disproven by both participants and historians.[3] In fact, the corps had been sent to Arnhem specifically because it was seen as a relatively quiet, out of the way place where it could recover and refit from the severe battering it had suffered in Normandy in relative peace.[4] The German command certainly had anticipated an Allied ground offensive in the sector, as the 2nd Army's massive build-up behind the Neerpelt bridgehead was hard to miss.[5] However, though *Generalfeldmarshall* Gerd von Rundstedt (the recently appointed overall commander of German forces on the Western Front) and Model himself were wary of the possibility of Allied airborne operations given the known presence of the 1st Allied Airborne Army in the Allied reserves, they had expected that such an operation would be launched either in support of an assault on the *Westwall* further south in the American sector, or in support of further amphibious landings along the Dutch coast. Although the bridges at Arnhem and Nijmegen were certainly seen as possible targets for Allied airborne operations, landings there were nonetheless not seen as particularly likely.[6]

Despite the shock that the landing of three Allied airborne divisions well behind their lines produced, the German command reacted almost immediately to the new threat. Having fled from the Allied landings, Model's HQ was left temporarily out of action in the early stages of the battle, as he relocated to General Wilhelm Bittrich's II. *SS-Panzer Korps* headquarters at Doetinchem, 16 miles east of Arnhem.[7] This brief 'decapitation' of *Heeresgruppe B*, however, had minimal impact upon the ability of the German forces to respond to the landings. Receiving the first report of the landings at 1330, 15 minutes after the first troops touched down, General Bittrich immediately alerted his two divisions and ordered them to mobilize.[8] As previously mentioned, the 9. '*Hohenstaufen*' and 10. '*Frundsberg*' *SS-Panzer Divisionen* that comprised II. *SS-Panzer Korps* had been badly weakened by their battles in Normandy and were left a mere shadow of their original strength, mustering a total of perhaps 6,000 to 7,000 men out of their combined pre-Normandy strength of nearly 36,000; between 16 and 32 tanks and assault guns out of 382; and about 70 armoured cars and half-tracks out of an original 606.[9] In spite of this much reduced strength, these divisional battlegroups remained a potent force, comprising mostly well-trained, well-equipped, well-led, and highly experienced troops, and they would quickly become the backbone of the German defence against Market Garden.[10]

The rapid reaction of the two SS divisions in the face of the airborne threat benefitted not only from the normal German doctrine and training for rapid and decisive action, but also from the fact that both had undergone an extensive programme of anti-airborne training and exercises in late 1943, while serving as part of General Geyr von Schweppenburg's *Panzergruppe West* in France. This training had taught them that the best way to counter airborne landings was to launch counterattacks against them as quickly as possible, ideally before they could properly organize in the wake of their landings.[11] Moreover, it heavily reemphasized the need for initiative and fast decision making at all levels of command to be able to react and respond quickly enough in the face of such a surprise attack. *Brigadeführer* (Brigade Commander) Heinz Harmel, commanding officer of the 10. *SS-Panzer Division*, later noted: 'At the lower end, NCOs and officers were taught to react quickly and make their own decisions. NCOs were taught not to wait until an order came, but to decide for themselves what to do. This happened during the fighting all the time.'[12]

Thus, in part because of this training, and in part because of Model's ongoing concerns about the looming presence of the Allied airborne force, the remnants of the 9. *SS-Panzer Division*, while awaiting trains to take them back to Germany to refit, had been reorganized into nineteen motorized, company sized *Alarmeinheiten* (alarm units) dispersed at various villages and road junctions throughout the Arnhem area to maximize their ability to detect and rapidly respond to any sudden Allied airborne attack – all of these were within 2 hours march or a ½-hour drive of Arnhem.[13] For similar reasons, the 10. *SS-Panzer Division*, which was to remain in the Arnhem area for its own refit and had been reinforced by elements taken from the withdrawing 9. *Division*, was reorganized into several battalion-sized battle groups, forming a brigade-sized combat group that was redesignated '*Kampfgruppe* (KG) Frundsberg'.[14]

Due to these measures, the two divisional groups were well disposed to respond to Bittrich's call to arms when it came. Most of the various *Kampfgruppen* and alarm units received the alert message within a matter of minutes and were mobilized and ready for action in between 15 minutes and 2 hours, depending upon their individual status and dispositions.[15] This feat of organization was achieved in spite of the fact that both divisions were under the command of the equivalent of mere lieutenant colonels at the time, with *Obersturmbannführer* Walter Harzer having been filling in for a wounded *Brigadeführer* Sylvester Stadlter at the head of the 9. *SS-Panzer Division* since August, and with Frundsberg's Harmel away in Berlin pleading with the High Command for further reinforcements (though he returned the next day after driving through the night from the capital), leaving the Frundsberg *Kampfgruppe* in the hands of an *Obersturmbannführer* Pätsch.[16] Clearly these deputies, and their various subordinates, stepped up admirably to the demands of the situation despite the relative absence of senior officers on the spot.

Despite the extremely fragmented, confusing, and generally limited information regarding the Allied offensive getting back to his HQ at the time, with wildly varying estimates of the strength of the Allied landings and numerous false reports of further landings coming in from across eastern Holland and the German border regions, Bittrich, with his subordinate units already readying themselves for battle, decided to take action based upon on what little information he already had, rather than waste any more time waiting for the situation to clear up, or for instructions from Model.[17] Less than 2 hours after he received the initial word of the landings, Bittrich accurately concluded that, with the bulk of the Allied landings seemingly concentrated around Arnhem and Nijmegen, the bridges in each city were their most likely targets, and had hastily drawn up a battle plan for his corps, directing the 9. *SS-Panzer Division* to advance through and secure Arnhem before attacking the Allied landing zones west of the city, while KG Frundsberg was to proceed to and secure the bridges at Nijmegen.[18]

Upon his arrival at Bittrich's HQ at about 1500, Model took command of the situation, instructing that Bittrich's corps would henceforth be operating directly under *Heeresgruppe B*, but, with regards to the corps' instructions, he simply approved and confirmed the measures that Bittrich had already taken without any changes of note.[19] Instead, he simply incorporated the ongoing efforts of Bittrich's corps into a broader plan for the entire army group, issuing instructions to the three other major formations under his command to counterattack the landings in their respective sectors and secure any local river and canal crossings, much as Bittrich had done with the II. *SS-Panzer Korps*. Before midnight on the 17th, Model had ordered the 1. *Fallschirmarmee* (Parachute Army) to counterattack the American landings (by the 101st Airborne Division) in the Eindhoven area, for the forces of *Wehrkreis Kommando* (Military District Command) VI to join the efforts of the Frundsberg *Kampfgruppe* against the US 82nd Airborne Division around Nijmegen, and for the various rear area security units operating under the *Wehrmachtbefehlshaber Niederlande* (Armed Forces Command Netherlands) Headquarters to support the efforts of the 9. *SS-Panzer Division* by attacking the British landing zones near Arnhem from the west (the 9. *Division* was to attack from the east).[20]

With this series of orders, issued between 2215 and 2315 on the night of 17 September, Model had effectively completed the greater part of his role as the overall operational level commander of the defence against Operation Market Garden, sending his forces into action with a plan that would remain broadly in effect through to the withdrawal of the British 1st Airborne Division on the night of 25/26 September, changing only in matters of detail and emphasis. Less than 12 hours after the initial landings, in spite of the great expectations of the Allied planners that their shock effect would all but paralyse the defenders, German forces throughout Holland and along the German border were already moving in force to oppose them, in spite of the fact that the overall situation was still largely unclear to their senior commanders. Moreover, the most critical elements of that defensive plan had been put into action by relatively junior officers, with a 'mere' corps commander effectively setting the main German defensive reaction into motion on his own initiative and in the face of limited information.

It is also notable that neither Model nor Bittrich included any specific details on how their subordinates were to conduct their operations, merely assigning them specific sectors in which they were responsible for counterattacking any enemy forces present. At this point of the battle the higher HQs had only a bare minimum of incomplete and often contradictory information on the overall situation and, as such, they counted heavily upon the ability of their subordinate commanders to assess their individual local situations and make their own tactical and minor operational decisions within the overall framework of the plan – measures that were, again, entirely consistent with the principles of German doctrine and training discussed above. The fact was that the principles of *Auftragstaktik* that were so prominent in the doctrine and training of the German forces allowed the various component formations of *Heeresgruppe B* to operate effectively with only the most basic guidance from above. This not only greatly simplified Model and Bittrich's command efforts, but also compensated for the rather limited and patchy state of command and communications arrangements that was prevalent throughout German forces in the West in the wake of the defeat in France. General Gustav-Adolf von Zangen, commander of the 15. *Armee* and whose advance units soon joined the battle in the Eindhoven area, later noted that he was never able to establish more than the bare minimum of contact with Model's HQ, ensuring that he was largely left to his own devices in leading his units.[21] Von Zangen further stated that this degree of freedom was vital to his effective waging of the battle, as Model could never be given a clear enough idea of the details of the 15. *Armee*'s situation to effectively direct its efforts from his distant HQ.[22] Given that the battle as a whole was waged largely by a 'crazy-quilt' assemblage of hastily improvised battle groups, many with minimal communications equipment, it would have been almost impossible for Model to command centrally, even had he been inclined to do so.

For the remainder of the battle, Model acted less as a supreme operational commander and more as a coordinator and facilitator, travelling to the various HQs of his subordinates to assess their situations and encourage their efforts, and calling up reinforcements and resources from the Reich and allocating them wherever they were needed.[23] The German practice of *Auftragstaktik* thus allowed Model to conduct the battle with a relatively light hand, trusting his sector and sub-unit commanders to conduct their own battles, while he concentrated the efforts of his own HQ on matters that *could* be effectively managed centrally, such as logistics and the allocation of reserves. Overall, the effectiveness of the response of German higher commanders in the fighting in Holland in September 1944 relied heavily upon the principles of independent and aggressive combat leadership instilled throughout their forces by their long-standing doctrine and training.

Market Garden: The German Tactical Response – Case Study One – *SS-Panzergrenadier Ausbildungs und Ersatz Battalion* 16 at Arnhem, 17 September 1944

At the tactical level, perhaps the most exemplary case of the vital role that the German doctrine of small-unit aggression and initiative played in Market Garden was that of *Sturmbannführer* (Battalion Commander) Josef Krafft and his *SS-Panzergrenadier Ausbildungs und Ersatz Battalion* (motorized infantry training and replacement battalion) *16* in the early hours of the battle on 17 September. Krafft's was an NCO training unit that had been sent to Holland to serve in a garrison role while it carried out its training regime, comprising 12 officers, 65 instructor NCOs, 229 partially trained men, and an eclectic assortment of support weaponry that included mortars, anti-tank and anti-aircraft guns, and heavy rocket launchers.[24] When the British landings began just before 1330 on the 17th, Krafft was exercising elements of his unit in the fields and woods near the western Arnhem suburb of Oosterbeek. Upon sighting the incoming gliders and parachutists, he, like Bittrich, very quickly guessed that the nearby bridges over the Lower Rhine at Arnhem were their most likely target and immediately sent his unit into action. Though he initially set out to counterattack the British airhead with one of his three companies, they were quickly forced to fall back from the drop zones in the face of the overwhelming British numerical superiority. Krafft then turned to establishing a blocking line between the landing zones and Arnhem, covering the two most northerly of the three main routes into the city from the west, the Utrechtseweg and the line of the Ede–Arnhem railway, hoping to at least delay the enemy advance long enough for reinforcements to be mustered to hold the city and its vital bridges.[25] Though Krafft was likely aware that the heavily wooded and built-up terrain of the suburbs on the western approaches to Arnhem would help to conceal the miniscule numbers of his force, and thus maximize the delaying effect their defence might have, it also seems that simply retreating back to Arnhem or beyond in the face of this superior force was something he never seriously considered; given that German doctrine recommended taking the most aggressive course of action that was possible, if Krafft could not attack then he would defend the objective as far forward as he could.

Krafft's small force quickly exerted an effect on the British advance far out of proportion to its numerical strength. The 1st Airborne Division's 1st Airborne Reconnaissance Squadron, which had been ordered to stage a *coup de main* to secure the primary Arnhem road bridge by rushing there from the landing zones up the main Ede–Arnhem road (the Amsterdamseweg) in their machine-gun-armed jeeps, ran into the northern end of Krafft's line soon after they set off. The leading troop was quickly shot up by fire from Krafft's machine guns and mortars, which destroyed the first two jeeps in the column, pinned down the rest of the troop in a 2-hour firefight, and eventually forced the entire squadron to abandon their mission and retreat back to the landing zones.[26]

The 16th Battalion then faced the main British assault by the three battalions of the 1st Parachute Brigade. The advance of the 1st and

46 The Last German Victory

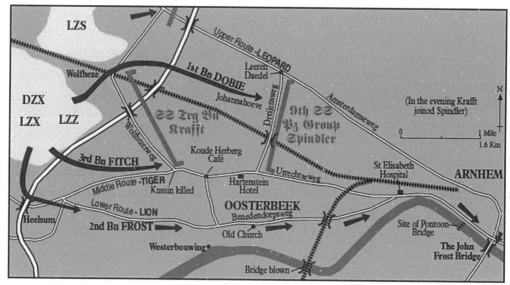

1st Parachute Brigade vs *Kampfgruppen* Krafft and Spindler, 17–18 September 1944. (*Courtesy Tonie and Valmai Holt*, Battlefield Guide to Operation Market Garden)

3rd Parachute Battalions along the northern (Amsterdamseweg) and central (Utrechtsweg) roads, respectively, quickly stalled in the face of Krafft's fire, with both being held up for several hours in a series of confused firefights and suffering fairly significant casualties in the process. Though it is impossible to accurately assess the specific casualties that Krafft's men inflicted on the British paratroops, it is likely that they inflicted the majority of the casualties suffered by the 1st Parachute Brigade on 17 September – officially recorded as at least 40 dead, 100 wounded, and 100 prisoners, but likely significantly higher given estimates for the losses of individual companies in the battalion war diaries.[27] The British 2nd Parachute Battalion, under Lieutenant Colonel John Frost, along with elements of the 1st Parachute Brigade HQ (though not the brigade commander, Brigadier Gerald Lathbury), did, however, manage to slip through to the Arnhem road bridge by nightfall on the southern river bank road. Though some authors have credited Frost's superior sense of drive and urgency with allowing him to succeed where the other battalions failed, in that he kept his men moving quickly through the limited resistance they faced from German patrols and security troops, it seems clear that his success owed at least as much to simple luck, in that he managed to draw the one largely unoccupied road for his advance and thus was able to march his battalion past the southern flank of Krafft's short line.[28]

North of Frost's breakthrough, the 3rd Parachute Battalion eventually managed to outflank Krafft's blocking line to the south, leading him to retreat towards Arnhem at dusk to avoid the looming threat of encirclement. By the time Krafft fell back, however, the first elements of a much stronger blocking force, *Kampfgruppe* Spindler of the 9. *SS-Panzer Division*, were taking up defensive positions in the Arnhem suburbs. These forces managed to bring the two British battalions to a final halt for the night and, joined by Krafft's survivors and a steady flow of reinforcements arriving throughout the night, had established a firm blocking line across all the routes to Arnhem by the morning of 18 September.[29] Krafft's rapid and aggressive response in the face of a much superior landing force thus inflicted a critical delay upon the British advance that almost entirely unravelled the 1st Airborne Division's battle plan, ensuring that only about 750 of the nearly 2,500 men that had originally set out for the Arnhem bridges on 17 September were actually able to reach them as planned.[30]

Though Krafft, an ambitious and obsequious braggart and a devoted Nazi, exaggerated the scale of his accomplishments in his after action report which he forwarded directly to *Reichsführer* of the SS Heinrich Himmler as a birthday gift, the actual achievements that he and his troops made at Arnhem were significant enough.[31] Had Krafft not chosen to engage the British advance as he did, it is quite possible that the entire 1st Parachute Brigade, along with the over 250 men of the 1st Airborne Reconnaissance Squadron, may well have been able to follow the example of the 2nd Parachute Battalion, reaching the Arnhem road bridge before the forces of the II. *SS-Panzer Korps* were able to fully mobilize and reach the city, and been able to establish a much stronger position around the bridge that may well have been able to hold out until relieved by XXX Corps. Regardless of these counterfactuals, it is notable that General Urquhart himself believed that Krafft's force was a primary factor in the 1st Airborne Division's failure on 17 September, stating that the 16th Battalion had 'done more than any other Germans to delay us'.[32] Krafft's successes were a clear and rather exemplary product of the principles of *Auftragstaktik* and dynamic leadership, in that he saw a threatening situation developing and decided to act immediately and without orders, anticipating his likely mission of defending the Arnhem bridges, working to do whatever he could with his limited resources to disrupt the enemy effort, and operating boldly in full confidence that, following the same doctrine he was, other forces would soon be advancing to his aid.

Market Garden: The German Tactical Response – Case Study Two – *Kampfgruppe* Spindler and *Gruppe* von Tettau at Arnhem

The actions of these 'other forces' of the wider German defensive response at Arnhem were also heavily characterized by *Auftragstaktik*-driven initiative and boldness. As stated above, as the various scattered alarm units and *Kampfgruppen* of the II. *SS-Panzer Korps* began to receive Bittrich's alert order, or simply saw the incoming airborne forces, they began to ready themselves for action and move towards the battle developing just west of Arnhem. General Urquhart cited the testimony of an anonymous SS major who arrived in Arnhem shortly after the landings to find the town filled with frantic activity, as various junior officers and NCOs gathered up whatever men were at hand, assembled them into their alarm units, and began leading them towards the new front.[33] *SS-Rottenführer* (Section Leader) Rudolf Trapp of the 10. *SS-Panzer Division* similarly reported his small company advancing alongside others through the streets of Arnhem in whatever transportation they could beg, borrow, or steal, eagerly seeking out the battle on their own volition: 'Morale was high … we felt we could win!'[34] A German after action report commented upon the considerable value of these small, independent alarm units in responding to the airborne incursion, noting that they could be mobilized very quickly and did so largely on their own initiative once alerted.[35] Some of these units even began to engage the British before they were fully formed up, buying time for the wider mobilization; *SS-Rottenführer* Wolfgang Dombrowski of the 9. *SS-Panzer Division*'s *Kampfgruppe* Möller, for example, reported that the four truck convoy in which he was travelling advanced straight to the outskirts of Oosterbeek where they came under fire, with his section then immediately dismounting and engaging the enemy until dark.[36]

As Bittrich and Model began to assert a greater degree of influence over the operation, these scattered alarm units were quickly consolidated into larger *Kampfgruppen*. The most notable of these groups assembled to secure Arnhem by establishing a blocking line along the city's western outskirts was the previously mentioned *Kampfgruppe* Spindler, under the command of the 9. *SS-Panzer Division* artillery regiment's commander *SS-Obersturmbannführer* Ludwig Spindler.[37] It is worth noting that, despite being deployed as an infantry battlegroup, KG Spindler fielded relatively few 'proper' infantrymen, with the bulk of its troops being drawn from the 9. *SS-Panzer Division*'s specialist and support units. At the core of the battle group were the 120 to 350 survivors (accounts vary) of Spindler's own artillerymen, who had given up their last remaining guns to the 10. *SS-Panzer Division* and operated as two infantry companies. They were joined by the division's engineers (*Kampfgruppe* Möller), its *Panzerjäger* (tank destroyer) battalion (*Kampfgruppe* von Allworden), *Kampfgruppe* Harder's dismounted tankers and fitters from the division's Panzer regiment, and *Kampfgruppe* Gropp's former flak gunners, alongside the four remaining companies of the division's two *Panzergrenadier* regiments. With most of their heavy weapons and vehicles lost on the retreat from France, or turned over to 10. *Division*, the bulk of these varied troops, like Spindler's gunners, fought as light infantry for the duration of the battle, taking advantage of their aforementioned basic tactical infantry training.[38] The battle group also incorporated reinforcements drawn from whatever other units happened to be close at hand, including training units, recruits seconded from the *Kriegsmarine* (German Navy) and an understrength battalion of *Reichsarbeitsdienst* (RAD – National Labour Service) men, all of whom were incorporated into the existing SS units under experienced officers and NCOs.[39]

In spite of the lack of infantry experience among most of its officers and men and its polyglot nature, the battle group mobilized and formed up extremely quickly, having assembled and been ordered into action by 1700 on 17 September, less than 4 hours after the landings.[40] As mentioned earlier in the chapter, the leading elements of *Kampfgruppe* Spindler had begun taking up blocking positions in the suburbs just west of Arnhem by nightfall on the 17th, and by morning Spindler had assembled a solid line of 7 or 8 weak battalions mustering over 1,500 SS troops alongside an unknown number of others.[41] This line held out in the face of every effort by the 1st Airborne Division's 1st Parachute Brigade – which was soon joined by the 4th Parachute Brigade and elements of the 1st Airlanding Brigade – to break through to their comrades at Arnhem during 18 and

19 September, with the final defensive actions and counterattacks on the 19th effectively destroying all seven British battalions involved and ending the 1st Airborne Division's offensive on Arnhem.[42] As *SS-Hauptsturmführer* Hans Möller of the eponymous *Kampfgruppe* later, and rather dramatically, noted, 'desperate attacks were repelled time after time … it was quite obvious they were probing the front for a soft spot, but their attacks failed there also, withering in the well-aimed fire of the Waffen-SS'.[43]

In the aftermath of this defensive success *Kampfgruppe* Spindler, in accordance with both German doctrine and Bittrich's overall plan, immediately transitioned to the offensive, pursuing the British parachute brigades back to the defensive perimeter forming at Oosterbeek and then keeping up a steady, if rather sporadic and often disorganized, pressure on them for the next week, pushing steadily through Oosterbeek a block at a time against an enemy that Spindler reported as 'fighting extremely tenaciously and bitterly'.[44] Though these efforts proved extremely costly to Spindler's improvised force, with Spindler reporting at least sixteen men killed and ninety-six wounded in just a single 24-hour period,

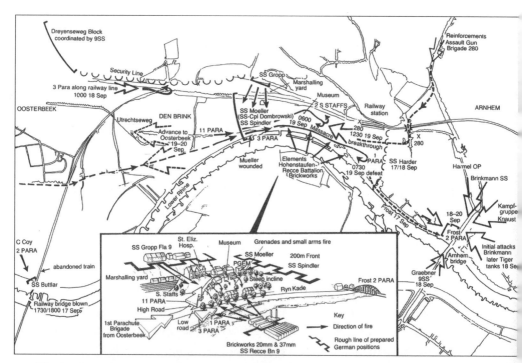

The final British assault into Arnhem, 19 September 1944. (*Courtesy Robert J. Kershaw*)

and his battle group as a whole being described as reduced to near the point of combat-ineffectiveness by 25 September, their steady advance also prevented the British airborne troops from retaking the initiative or making any significant offensive moves of their own until their evacuation on the night of 25/26 September. It is thus hardly surprising that Bittrich's after action report recognized *Kampfgruppe* Spindler as one the most critical contributors to his corps' victory at Arnhem.[45]

At the same time, on the opposite side of the British landing zones, a second improvised battle group, *Gruppe* von Tettau, initially assembled from a variety of army, SS, *Kriegsmarine*, and *Luftwaffe* (German Air Force) security, garrison, and training units drawn from the *Wehrmachtbefehlshaber Niederlande* (WB Ndl) for security duties along the Waal River, was mobilized to attack the 1st Airborne Division from the west.[46] Despite the generally low quality of its troops, which comprised mostly older men with minimal combat experience, *Gruppe* von Tettau, like *Kampfgruppe* Spindler, was mobilized within a matter of hours, and its leading units were closing on the western edge of the defensive perimeter around the British landing zones by nightfall on 17 September. The *Gruppe* probed the lines of the 1st Airlanding Brigade's 1st Battalion, the Border Regiment (1/Borders) and 7th Battalion, The King's Own Scottish Borderers (7/KOSB) through the first night of the battle and in the morning of 18 September staged a full-scale attack that made considerable progress before being forced back when the British second airlift came in behind the German force's northern flank in the early afternoon, routing a battalion of Dutch SS troops.[47]

In spite of this early setback, *Gruppe* von Tettau kept up a steady, if generally limited, pressure across the western edge of the British perimeter right up until the evacuation.[48] This pressure forced the 1st Airborne Division to keep a fairly considerable portion of their limited forces in defensive positions along the western perimeter of their landing zones and divisional headquarters throughout the battle, even as the main effort and crisis of the battle was taking place at Arnhem to the east, effectively confronting the division with a 'two-front war'. For most of the critical first two days of the battle, three airlanding battalions – over half of the British troops initially landed – were denied to the British offensive thrust, as they were needed to hold the landing zones for the second lift; even after that lift arrived on the afternoon of 18 September, releasing the 2nd Battalion, South Staffordshire Regiment (2/South Staffs) and 7/KOSB from their defensive duties, 1/Borders remained on the western perimeter, opposing *Gruppe* von Tettau, for the rest of the battle.[49]

Moreover, the fact that all the various sub-units of *Gruppe* von Tettau kept up a steady offensive pressure throughout the fighting, however tentative it was, led to one of the major German 'coups' of the battle. On 21 September, one of those units, the Worrowski Battalion of the *Hermann Göring* Training Regiment (one of several units that had been training infantry replacements for the *Luftwaffe*'s *Hermann Göring* Panzer Corps, as well as other paratroop units), attacked the Westerbouwing Heights on the northern bank of the Lower Rhine, which overlooked the ferry site at Heveadorp, the last viable crossing point over the river remaining in British hands at that time. The Worrowski battalion found those critical heights to be held only by elements of a single company (as little as a single platoon, by some accounts) from the badly overstretched 1/Borders, which it soon drove off, though, in light of its inexperience and clumsy tactics, it suffered nearly 50 per cent losses in the process.[50] The loss of these heights ensured that, although elements of the 1st Polish Independent Parachute Brigade and the British 43rd Infantry Division had managed to reach the southern bank of the Lower Rhine opposite Heveadorp by 22 September, they remained entirely unable to pass any significant force over the river to reinforce the 1st Airborne Division for the rest of the battle, as the numerous German machine guns and artillery observation posts located on the heights made crossings impossible by day and extremely difficult by night. Despite strenuous efforts by the Polish and British troops over several nights, only a few hundred men ever got over the river to the north bank, with the last effort by the 4th Battalion of the Dorsetshire Regiment (4/Dorsets) on the night of 24/25 September being a bloody disaster that saw most of those that set out killed or taken prisoner.[51] The emphasis that German doctrine placed upon units taking and maintaining the offensive whenever and wherever possible thus paid off for *Gruppe* von Tettau, allowing it to keep the forces of the 1/Borders so thinly spread that a critical opportunity simply emerged right in front of one of their attacking units, which in turn quickly took the initiative and seized the critical ground before the British could perceive the threat and reinforce the heights.

The successes of *Kampfgruppe* Spindler and *Gruppe* von Tettau were also testament to the value of the basic infantry and tactical training provided to all members of the *Wehrmacht*, enabling at least basically effective infantry units to be mustered from a mixed assortment of mostly non-infantrymen at short notice. The fact that these groups of extremely variable-quality troops were able to gain the upper hand over well-trained paratroops in intense woodland and urban fighting – though admittedly usually with the benefit of local numerical superiority and at an extremely high cost – testifies to the effectiveness of German doctrine and training in enabling German officers and troops to rise to unexpected challenges.

Market Garden: The German Tactical Response – Case Study Three – 9. *SS-Panzer-Aufklärungs-Abteilung* at Arnhem, 18 September 1944 and the Ammunition Factor

The aggressiveness of the German response to the Arnhem landings also had another unintended – but highly significant – impact upon the combat effectiveness of the 1st Airborne Division, in that it forced them into an unsustainable rate of ammunition consumption that rapidly depleted their potential firepower. One of the most significant limitations that any airborne combat force faces is the relatively limited quantity of ammunition – for both small arms and heavy weapons – that can be carried into battle. Officially, every British airborne rifleman was issued with at least a basic load of 100 rounds of .303 rifle ammunition (in 5-round stripper clips), every Sten submachine-gunner with 8 32-round box magazines, and every Bren light machine-gun team with 24 30-round magazines.[52] Support-weapon crews were generally issued with a smaller amount of ammunition for their personal weapons, due to the weight of the heavy weapons and ammunition they carried; Private James Sims, who was assigned to a 3in-mortar crew in the 2nd Parachute Battalion just before the operation, recalled that he was issued with forty rounds of rifle ammunition and four grenades (two fragmentation, one anti-tank, and one phosphorous), in addition to the six mortar shells he carried for his section's primary weapon.[53] Though most individual troopers unsurprisingly packed their equipment pouches and pockets with as many extra rounds, clips, magazines, and grenades as they could carry, this would still be a relatively limited supply for any intense and/or prolonged combat – particularly with regards to automatic weapons, which could potentially run through hundreds of rounds in a relatively short period of fighting.

Though this supply was comparable to that carried by any infantry soldier of the time, where the airborne fell short was in regards to their reserve supplies; with only a relative handful of light jeeps and trailers – flown in by gliders – to carry extra ammunition boxes, airborne forces were not able to carry as much extra ammunition to replenish that which they expended as did conventional ground forces. Though details about the 1st Airborne Division's ammunition situation at Arnhem are scarce and sometimes inconsistent, according to after action reports, the 1st Airborne Division landed a total of either 31 or 33 jeeps and trailers of the Royal Army Service Corps (RASC) to carry the division's immediate reserves of ammunition, with each combination (one per glider) apparently carrying about 16,000 rounds of .303 ammunition (it is unclear whether 9mm rounds for the Stens would been carried in place of a portion of this .303 ammo, or in addition to it).[54] Assuming the higher figure for jeeps, this means that the division had roughly 528,000 rounds of .303 ammunition for their rifles and machine guns on hand after their landings, beyond that carried by the men themselves. Though this seems a considerable quantity, it becomes much less impressive when divided among the nearly 10,000 men landed at Arnhem. Even if one reduces this number by 60 per cent to make a generous allowance for 'non-combatants' and those not armed with .303 calibre weapons, this would still mean that the brigade and divisional trains would have an average of only 132 rounds per man in reserve for each of these *c.* 4,000 riflemen and machine-gunners to refill their pouches once emptied. Such a supply might be just barely adequate to keep riflemen in action, but would struggle to keep the automatic Bren light machine guns – the central element of British squad-level firepower – in action for any significant length of time.[55]

In general, the heavy use of the maximum firepower available – and thus the rapid expenditure of large quantities of ammunition – has been and remains a standard feature of modern infantry combat. Moreover, the 1st Airborne Division generally seems to have been fairly profligate in its use of ammunition – like most airborne forces, its training sought to make up for its general lack of supporting firepower (of which more shall be said later) through the intensive use of rapid small-arms fire, particularly by automatic weapons, to maximize the shock effect of the division's light infantry forces in close combat. Lieutenant Colonel Frost, for instance, noted that running short of ammunition had been a common problem in several of his battalion's previous battles.[56] This combination of limited supply and heavy demand with regards to ammunition placed the 1st Airborne Division in a precarious position: if it could not achieve its objectives quickly it would soon find itself rendered combat ineffective, but the harder it fought to do so, the shorter this period of effectiveness would be.

At Arnhem, the 1st Airborne Division's ammunition woes were heavily exacerbated by the aggressive German defence. Confronted by both a succession of hastily advanced German defensive lines and frequent counterattacks, the British airborne troops were forced to burn through their limited ammunition supplies at a prodigious rate from the very start of the operation. Historian Peter Preston-Hough effectively illustrates this effect in his 2016 article re-examining one of the most infamous German counterattacks of the Market Garden campaign: the failed assault across Arnhem Bridge by *SS-Hauptsturmführer* Viktor Gräbner's 9. *SS-Panzer-Aufklärungs-Abteilung* (9th SS Armoured Reconnaissance Battalion or Detachment) on the morning of 18 September. This attack – prominently featured in the film version of *A Bridge Too Far* – was heavily defeated with very heavy losses of about seventy men killed and wounded – including Gräbner himself, whose body was never recovered from the charred wreckage of his command car – as well as at least eight half-tracks and armoured cars destroyed. It has often been dismissed by historians as a pointless gesture of unchecked 'berserker' aggression by fanatical SS troops, but, as Preston-Hough points out, it had a considerable effect upon the British defence of Arnhem Bridge in spite of its failure.[57]

All extant British eye-witness accounts of the action emphasize the intense 'hail' of small-arms fire that was brought to bear against the German attackers, with the various airborne troopers involved pouring in fire as rapidly as they could whenever they had anything like a clear shot throughout the battle, which lasted about 2 hours, with little evidence of control over that fire being exercised by officers or NCOs. Corporal George Cockayne, of the 1st Parachute Brigade Headquarters, later recalled that: 'I shot off nearly all of my ammunition', while Lieutenant Colonel Frost himself noted that virtually every man in the bridgehead had joined in the firing with considerable enthusiasm.[58] Preston-Hough notes that although this deluge of fire effectively shattered Gräbner's force, it also burned through the bulk of the British force's limited ammunition stocks; both Frost and Major Digby Tatham-Warter (the commander of 2nd Parachute Battalion's A Company) later recalled that the entirety of the reserve ammunition stockpile that the battalion had brought with them to the bridge was issued out to the troops later on 18 September.[59] Given that the 2nd Battalion had managed to avoid much in the way of significant combat while en route to the bridge the previous day, this means that Frost's force had exhausted the majority of its ammunition in only one major battle against a relatively small (if well-equipped) German counterattack force.

With the 1st Division unable to get any further supplies through to Frost's force in the face of the 'blockade' established by *Kampfgruppe* Spindler, the lack of ammunition quickly began to have a crippling effect upon their fighting power. By the evening of 18 September, Frost had been forced to issue orders for his men to fire only when faced with major German attacks, with sniping and general firing at whatever targets of opportunity that might present themselves being forbidden.[60] The ammunition situation thus greatly reduced the weight of the defensive fire that the British could bring to bear on the German forces opposing them, which in turn allowed the German infantry to move more freely around the British perimeter at the bridge, gradually infiltrating troops to occupy the surrounding buildings and strengthen their encirclement of the bridgehead.[61] In effect, the shortage of ammunition among the British airborne troops exercised a de facto suppressive effect upon them, allowing the Germans to steadily close in and eliminate their positions one by one while facing less return fire than might otherwise have been the case. By 20 September, the final day of resistance at the bridge, Private James Sims noted that most British troops had been reduced to scrounging whatever ammo they could from the dead and wounded of both sides and that even this barely kept the remaining troops in action; he mentions that during a final accounting of ammunition supplies just before the final breakout attempt and subsequent surrender, at least one trooper was down to just a single five-round clip for his rifle.[62] The 1st Parachute Brigade HQ's diary shows that this was far from an abnormal situation, noting that when the final breakout effort was organized, the automatic weapons available (Bren light machine guns and Sten submachine guns) had an average of only a single magazine apiece (thirty to thirty-two rounds).⁶³ It is thus hardly surprising that the breakout effort had virtually no chance of success, with the bulk of the few remaining survivors being forced to surrender in small groups throughout the rest of the day.

Thus, as Preston-Hough concludes, in spite of the clear failure of his counterattack on a tactical level, *Hauptsturmführer* Viktor Gräbner's aggressive response to the British capture of the Arnhem Bridge effectively unhinged the British defence of their prize nearly as effectively as the actions of Krafft and Spindler to the west disrupted the bulk of the British assault on Arnhem. Though his unit failed to overwhelm the British position and the effort cost him his life, by forcing the British to expend their limited resources to meet their attack, the young officer – who only the day before had been awarded the Knight's Cross (Germany's highest combat decoration) for his leadership in the Normandy campaign – effectively crippled their ability to wage a more aggressive defence.⁶⁴ Though it is impossible to know whether Gräbner's actions were motivated by fanaticism or overconfidence (as many historians have suggested) or by a simple desire (on his part or that of his superiors) to try to recapture the tactical initiative and keep the enemy off balance, the final results of his efforts serve to remind any observer that the success or failure of a combat action cannot always be easily judged from a simple comparison of casualties inflicted or received. Despite its disastrous outcome in the short term, 'Gräbner's Charge' is an example of how effectively the aggression inherent in German doctrine could disrupt the plans and intentions of their enemies even when it did not achieve immediate success on the battlefield. By forcing their opponents into rash reactions that were against their longer term interests, the German tendency to rapidly counterattack any threat could allow them to influence the battlefield situation in the long run in their favour.

This situation of immediate and intense German opposition rapidly depleting limited ammunition supplies also had a considerable impact upon the performance of the remainder of the 1st Airborne Division force at Arnhem and Oosterbeek. The effort to break through the defensive lines established by Krafft and Spindler in the early days of the battle required the British airborne troops to engage in an intense series of firefights against a determined enemy at close range and in dense wooded or suburban terrain – circumstances that ensured a very high level of ammunition expenditure.

Major Christopher Perrin-Brown of the 1st Parachute Battalion later noted that when the British troops came under any level of fire from a house, the standard response quickly became to toss grenades into the building and then storm it, with automatic weapons being used freely to overwhelm even the lightest opposition with fire.[65]

Though this practice did produce local successes against the German outpost lines, gradually forcing them back, it had dire consequences in the longer term: in the wake of the final failure of the British offensive on 19 September and the subsequent formation of the defensive perimeter at Oosterbeek, the 1st Airborne Division quickly found itself desperately short of ammunition in spite of its severely reduced complement of fighting troops. Like Frost, General Urquhart was forced to issue orders calling for 'the utmost conservation' of ammunition (as well as other critical supplies) as early as the evening of 19 September, as only limited quantities were still available in the divisional supply dumps.[66] These shortages were exacerbated by the fact that, although the planning for Market Garden had made provisions for the daily aerial delivery of key supplies – with a particular emphasis on ammunition – the rapid German follow-up of the British retreat on the 19th had overrun the designated supply drop zones.[67] Due to radio failures and the general confusion that prevailed between the 1st Airborne Division and their higher headquarters (of which more shall be said shortly), Urquhart was unable to redirect or even cancel the pre-planned supply drops, ensuring that the bulk of the materiel dropped fell into German hands.[68] Urquhart reported that, of the nearly 1,500 tons of supplies dropped to his troops, only 106 tons – about 7.4 per cent – were recovered and delivered to the divisional dumps (noting that perhaps as much as another 100 tons may have been 'unofficially' recovered and used by whatever troops happened to be nearby when the containers landed).[69]

As such, like Frost's force at the bridge, the defenders of the Oosterbeek perimeter were forced to reserve their limited remaining firepower for only the most significant threats, allowing the Germans to achieve and retain a significantly greater degree of general fire superiority than would otherwise have been the case. As in Arnhem, the German forces were able to take advantage of this weakened defensive fire to make extensive use of the infantry infiltration tactics that had been developed for and by the stormtroops of the First World War, dislocating enemy defensive positions by sneaking small groups of troops through the gaps between their strongpoints, allowing them to subject them to fire from all sides.[70] By the latter stages of the siege, British accounts make it clear that the rear areas of the perimeter were riddled with German riflemen operating as de facto 'snipers' and even machine-gun posts.[71] These infiltrators made any movement out of cover within the perimeter highly risky: the headquarters of the 1st Airlanding Brigade, for example, reported a messenger carrying orders to one of their battalions being wounded in an ambush on the night of 21 September, despite having been provided with an armed escort, while Urquhart noted that he and his fellow senior officers frequently came under sniper fire while inspecting their units. The threat posed by these infiltrators was such that the commanders of two of Urquhart's sub-units – Majors Wilson and Lonsdale – reported that they were unable to attend the final planning conference for the evacuation on the afternoon of 25 September, as there were simply too many enemy troops between them and the Divisional HQ to risk the journey.

These widespread infiltrations also forced the defenders to divert a considerable portion of their defensive efforts to rooting them out, weakening their already thin front lines. The survivors of the 1st Parachute Battalion, for example, reported spending much of the night of 24 September trying to eliminate 'large numbers' of snipers in their sector, while earlier that same day, a force of German infiltrators occupying a section of slit trenches near the 1st Airlanding Brigade's HQ proved strong enough to repel two counterattacks by the 7/KOSB and a group of glider pilots, with at least two British officers among those falling in the attempt. Thus, the aggressive stance adopted by the German forces from the very start of the operation allowed them not only to retake the initiative in the short term, but also to retain it in the longer term, reducing the already limited fighting resources available to the 1st Airborne Division and thus reducing the potential tactical options available to them to confront future German offensive efforts. Though frequently costly in terms of casualties, the intensity of the German's early efforts, including even clear tactical failures like Gräbner's attack, effectively paved the way for future successes. Though forcing higher levels of ammunition expenditure upon the British – and thus depleting their firepower in the long term – was likely not an effect specifically intended by the German commanders on the spot, it was a natural by-product of the prompt action taken in response to the Allied landings, and serves as evidence of the value of the aggressive posture that German doctrine inculcated among their soldiers, in that it restricted the enemy's scope for effective action while improving one's own.

Market Garden: The German Tactical Response – Case Study Four – 406. *Landesschützen Division* at Nijmegen, 18 September 1944

Rapidity and ferocity also characterized the German reactions to Market Garden's other airborne landings at Nijmegen and Eindhoven, and those reactions were at least as critical to the outcome for the overall battle as those at Arnhem. Both of the American airborne divisions, with the 82nd Airborne Division landing around Groesbeek, just south-east of Nijmegen, and the 101st Airborne Division landing north of Eindhoven, encountered significantly less resistance in the immediate aftermath of the landings on 17 September than did their British counterparts to the north. Like the British, the American troops encountered only scattered individuals and small groups of line of communications and security troops on or around their landing zones, who were quickly subdued or driven off.[72] Unlike the British, the Americans then managed to rapidly secure the majority of their numerous bridge objectives, though the bridge over the Wilhelmina Canal at Son and two of the four bridges over the Maas–Waal Canal were demolished by German forces before they could be captured.[73] Overall, though, the initial effort by the two American divisions almost entirely lived up to the expectations of the Market Garden plan, in that the shock of their sudden landings allowed them to capture the target bridges before any meaningful defence could be mustered.

This initial attack by the American airborne divisions left one critical objective unsecured, however: the two bridges (a road bridge and a railway bridge that could easily be modified to accommodate road traffic) over the Waal River at Nijmegen itself. This omission occurred mostly due to the presence of the Groesbeek Heights just south-east of the city, an area of high ground that rose about 300ft above the surrounding polder land, and thus overlooked the entire area, including the bridges and the main north–south road along which XXX Corps was to advance. The heights were only a short distance from the Reichswald forest along the German border to the east, which Allied intelligence from both ULTRA codebreaking and Dutch resistance sources indicated was possibly being used as a mustering point for sizeable German forces – including armoured vehicles – taking advantage of the dense tree cover to conceal their presence from Allied aerial reconnaissance. Had such forces sortied from the Reichswald and managed to capture the Groesbeek Heights, a few artillery or mortar observation posts, anti-tank guns, and machine guns atop them would have been able to completely dominate the main road with fire, preventing any advance to the north.[74] As such, both General Browning and Major General James Gavin of the 82nd Airborne Division saw securing the Groesbeek Heights as a critical element of the 82nd's mission, as all the bridges captured would be rendered effectively useless should the high ground be taken by the Germans. Moreover, the fact that the 82nd's forces had to be divided among the numerous objectives to be captured in the area (seven bridges in total, as well as the Groesbeek Heights, the city of Nijmegen itself, and a sizeable defensive perimeter around the entire area) meant that significant compromises had to be made in the plan.

In the end, Browning ordered Gavin to only try to capture the Nijmegen bridges – the last link in the chain of crossing points between the Maas and the Waal – after the heights were secured, an allocation of priorities that Gavin fully concurred with, even in his memoirs with the full benefit of hindsight.[75] Gavin, however, determined to gain control of all the objective bridges as quickly as possible, 'tweaked' his orders, ordering Lieutenant Colonel Roy Lindquist, the commander of the 508th Parachute Infantry Regiment (PIR), to send one of his three battalions to secure the Nijmegen bridges as soon as he felt the situation on the heights was under control; Gavin later admitted, however, that he perhaps did not properly clarify the importance of this supplementary instruction, as Colonel Lindquist only dispatched the force at around 1900, nearly 8 hours after the landings, and then only sent two (of three) rifle companies from his 1st Battalion.[76] This small force made its way through Nijmegen towards the bridges, but came under heavy fire at a traffic circle just south of the road bridge, which stopped their advance just 400yd short of their goal at about 2000; they then dug in to await reinforcements and resume the attack in the morning.[77]

It was at this point that German countermeasures began to have an effect on the American operation. The main German headquarters on this section of the front was *Wehrkreis Kommando* (Military District Command) VI. This was an improvised field headquarters formed from the former administrative HQ of *Wehrkreis* VI (the 6th Military District), encompassing the Westphalia and Rhineland regions, which had operated as part of the German *Ersatzheer* (Replacement Army). The *Ersatzheer* was an administrative command responsible for recruiting and training replacement troops within Germany for various associated divisions of the *Feldheer* (Field Army), as well as for overseeing general internal security and home-defence duties.[78] In early September, as the front approached the district's western borders, *Wehrkreis* VI's administrative headquarters was converted into a de facto field army headquarters and ordered to send its subordinate training and security units to occupy and begin repairing and improving the long-neglected *Westwall* defences as the tattered remnants of the *Westheer* streamed home from France.[79] To this end, the newly established *Wehrkreis Kommando* VI in turn established a corps headquarters, *Korps* Feldt, to manage its field operations. This improvised corps was named after its commanding officer, General Karl Feldt, a cavalry officer who had been deemed too old for front-line service and placed in reserve. On 12 September, *Korps* Feldt was deployed to take over the section of the *Westwall* defences that lay within the Reichswald, having only a single division under command, the 406. 'Special Administrative Division' (also described as a *Landesschützen*, or 'Home Guard' division), which had previously administered training, home guard, and POW camp guard units within the district.[80] By 17 September, this division comprised nine understrength battalions of troops, mostly training units, home guards, or march battalions assembled from various *Westheer* stragglers and recovering convalescents. These added up to a total of 6,669 men fit for duty, most with little in the way of weaponry beyond basic bolt-action rifles and only a half issue of ammunition.[81]

In spite of its limited strength and resources, *Korps* Feldt proved, much like the II. *SS-Panzer Korps* to the north, to be fortuitously positioned to oppose the Allied landings. Also like the SS formation, its forces began to mobilize as soon as the landings were spotted, even before any official orders were issued. Having been warned of the landings by some of its advance outposts in Nijmegen and on the Groesbeek Heights at 1410, the 406. *Division*'s HQ issued its initial warning order to its sub-units at 1430, ensuring that they were already in motion when Model's first orders came in at 1530 (later followed by the more detailed instructions issued across the entire army group), ordering *Korps* Feldt to attack and secure Nijmegen.[82]

The corps' advance elements on the Groesbeek Heights were rapidly overrun by the American paratroops, but its three companies in Nijmegen, under the command of a *Luftwaffe Oberst* (Colonel) named Henke, immediately set to work establishing defences around the bridges; it was these units, along with a handful of SS troops sent down from Arnhem as an advance guard for the Frundsberg *Kampfgruppe*, that repulsed the initial effort by the 508th PIR to capture the bridges on the evening of 17 September.[83] From his headquarters in the Reichswald, with the main body of his forces, General Feldt quickly realized that his troops lacked the numbers, heavy weapons, or training needed to pose a serious threat to the American parachute divisions, with their strong contingents of well-trained and experienced troops, but also recognized that he would need to buy time for reinforcements to arrive. In light of these factors, he decided that the best solution was to 'bluff' the Allied troops into a more cautious stance, acting as aggressively as possible so as to give a misleading impression of strength and force the enemy onto the defensive.[84] As Feldt later testified: 'I had no confidence in this attack, since it was almost an impossible task for 406. *Division* to attack picked troops with its motley crowd. But it was necessary to risk the attack in order to forestall an enemy advance to the east, and to deceive him in regard to our strength.'[85]

As such, though he had only about 2,000 men on hand and ready for action at the time, Feldt initiated a full-scale counterattack on the 82nd Airborne Division's airhead at 0600 on the 18 September, with a further 1,000 or so troops joining in through the course of the morning.[86] Feldt was soon shocked to find his units making rapid progress, as the 82nd Division had such a lengthy perimeter to defend that their forces were mostly divided into isolated platoon outposts at major villages and road junctions, most of which conducted a fighting retreat back towards their landing zones in the face of Feldt's attack, rather than trying to defend in place. Several outposts were cut off and surrounded, however, and Feldt's troops also overran some of the easternmost American landing zones and even seemed poised to assault the Groesbeek Heights for a time. In light of this threat, Gavin was forced to recall the 508th PIR's 3rd Battalion, which he had shortly before ordered to Nijmegen to reinforce the 1st Battalion fighting at the bridge approaches. Instead, the 3rd Battalion was directed to retake the lost landing zones before the arrival of the second airlift, and to stabilize and restore the line. However, though Feldt's attack threw the 82nd – which had not anticipated such a large-scale counterattack so soon into the operation – badly off balance at first, the veteran paratroops recovered quickly, brought Feldt's attack to a halt by about 1030, and then counterattacked, sending the German troops fleeing back to the Reichswald just as the second lift landed in the early afternoon.[87] With this, the 406. *Division*'s already limited combat power was essentially spent. Though the division still retained significant strength in simple numerical terms, having suffered the loss of about 50 dead, 400 wounded and over 100 POWs in the course of the attack, the morale of its troops – most of whom were either very young recruits or elderly militiamen, with minimal combat training – was almost completely shattered, at least for the immediate future, and 406. *Division* was unable to resume its attacks on 19 September.[88]

The efforts of the 406. *Division*, however, had not been in vain, as they imposed a fatal delay upon the 82nd's push to secure the Nijmegen bridges. The efforts of *Kampfgruppe* Frundsberg to get the bulk of its forces through to reinforce and secure Nijmegen as Bittrich had ordered had been severely hindered by Lieutenant Colonel Frost's capture of the Arnhem road bridge, as it required them to improvise a painfully slow ferry crossing at Pannerden, south-east of Arnhem, to get their troops across the Rhine.[89] However, because *Korps* Feldt's attack prevented the 82nd from dispatching a force strong enough to capture the bridges from Henke's small band of security troops throughout the 17th and 18th, KG Frundsberg was eventually able to get enough troops through to decisively secure Henke's perimeter, with at least 500 more infantrymen, along with several tanks and self-propelled guns, being in position at the German bridgehead by the morning of 19 September. Though still relatively small, this force was able to take advantage of the extensive array of pre-war Dutch concrete fortifications around the Nijmegen bridges to establish a defence that would require a further two days of set-piece attacks by the 82nd and the arriving Guards Armoured Division to overcome.[90]

Thus, although their attacks proved essentially hopeless and fairly costly at the tactical level, the very fact that *Wehrkreis Kommando* VI and its subordinate units were able to assemble, mobilize, and dispatch their forces into battle so quickly, and with such aggression, inflicted a significant operational setback on the otherwise successful 82nd Airborne Division, throwing it onto the defensive for a critical period that prevented it from securing a vital objective while it was still vulnerable to capture by their relatively lightly armed forces. This failure set Market Garden's strict timetable back by nearly 48 hours. Though the Allied forces quickly recognized the generally low quality of *Korps* Feldt's troops, the threat that they represented simply could not be ignored.

Moreover, the remnants of the 406. *Division* were soon joined by reinforcements from II. *Fallschirmkorps* (Parachute Corps) – which comprised a similarly improvised force of *Fallschirmjäger* (Paratrooper) Regiments formed around cadres of survivors from the Western Front and bulked out with fresh recruits – and together they kept up a series of attacks on the 82nd Division's eastern flank for the next few days.[91] These ongoing attacks, which at times put serious pressure on the 82nd Division and even threatened to retake some of the vital bridges, ensured that not only was the 82nd unable to spare any forces to support the advance towards Arnhem, but that the Guards Armoured Division was even forced to detach its Coldstream Guards Group on 19 September to support the 82nd along the Reichswald front until 22 September.[92] This force, which comprised a battalion of infantry and a regiment of tanks, represented fully a quarter of the Guards Division's offensive strength, strength that was thus denied to the main advance towards Arnhem for a crucial four days.

The Reichswald area remained a source of considerable anxiety for the Allied leadership throughout the rest of the operation as, even after the threat had been largely contained, they feared that the German attacks to date only presaged the arrival of larger forces from the German interior, ensuring that they kept sizeable forces in the area to meet and contain any potential attack.[93] Thus, while the German effort to hold, and later retake, the Nijmegen bridges failed, the aggressive posture of the German defenders in the area succeeded in diverting a significant proportion of the Allies' offensive strength into defensive actions along the extended flank of the corridor. These actions drew away the initiative and ensured that, even after the capture of the Nijmegen bridges, the Allied spearheads remained too weak to punch through the hastily established German defences on the so-called *Betuwe*, or 'Island' of land, between the Waal and the Lower Rhine in time to relieve the 1st Airborne Division.

Market Garden: The German Tactical Response – Case Study Five – 'Hell's Highway'

The American 101st Airborne Division, which dropped south of the 82nd around the city of Eindhoven, faced a very different reception to that which greeted their northern neighbours, but one that still bore some of the same key characteristics. Much like the 82nd, the 101st Division faced only minimal resistance to their initial landings, with only the loss of the bridge at Son to an alert German demolition party marring the successful achievement of their primary objectives.[94] With the attentions of the 1. *Fallschirmarmee* split between the landings and XXX Corps' assault out of the Neerpelt bridgehead, the 101st's sector remained relatively quiet over the next three days, apart from the capture of Eindhoven from a small German force early on 18 September and a minor skirmish to secure a secondary bridge at the town of Best that soon ballooned into a major battle as both sides continued to feed in reinforcements, even after the bridge was blown on the afternoon of the 18th.[95] Though the 101st eventually captured the town early on 19 September, with the fight having drawn in the better part of a full regiment of American troops (a third of the 101st's available strength at the time) and a squadron of British tanks, with the bridge gone, their victory gained little more than the 1,056 POWs they claimed to have taken, and the 300 or so German bodies found in the town.[96]

Instead, the main German defensive effort in this sector truly began on 21 September, when Field Marshal Model, making one of the few significant alterations to his original operational orders during the course of the battle, called for a coordinated effort by the various German formations left scattered throughout the area by the Allied assaults to sever, or at least disrupt traffic along, the Allied lines of communication leading back along the main road to their bridgehead at Neerpelt. Model hoped that such an effort would severely impede the 2nd Army's push towards the 1st Airborne Division's toehold across the Lower Rhine, allowing the forces of the II. *SS-Panzer Korps* to finally contain it short of its goal. To this end, German forces on both sides of the narrow Allied corridor were ordered to focus their efforts around the town of Veghel, about halfway along the road between Eindhoven and Nijmegen.[97] This order served to continue and consolidate the efforts of the local counterattacks that had been taking place on a smaller scale since 19 September.⁹⁸ The 107. *Panzer Brigade*, for example, which had been redirected to Holland while en route to the battle at Aachen in light of the Allied landings, and which, with its Panzer battalion mustering forty brand-new Panther tanks, was the only armoured formation of any notable strength to take part in the early stages of the battle, had made rather tentative probing attacks on the newly built Bailey bridge at Son on the evening of the 19th and morning of the 20th, being sharply repulsed both times by American paratroops and British tanks.⁹⁹

Model's order on 21 September touched off a prolonged series of attacks by German forces all along the main road in the 101st's sector, and particularly in the area around Veghel and St Oedenrode. Major General Maxwell Taylor, the commander of the 101st Airborne Division, deployed his paratroops in relatively small mobile task forces, which were shifted around as needed to rapidly counterattack any developing crisis points. Taylor later compared these operations by his division to those of the nineteenth-century US Cavalry, defending rail lines through 'Indian Country' against attacks by small groups of raiders coming from all directions; for their part, the troops of the 101st soon dubbed this hotly contested stretch of road 'Hell's Highway'.¹⁰⁰ Despite the best efforts of Taylor and his men, the sheer quantity and persistence of the German attacks left their limited forces badly overextended, as they had only so many 'fire brigades' to meet the German thrusts, meaning that countering any given attack meant opening up a gap to be exploited elsewhere. General von Zangen of the 15. *Armee*, whose advance units, having recently escaped from the Dutch coast across the Scheldt Estuary, joined in this phase of the battle, noted his surprise at the apparent lack of attention the Allies were giving to the defence of their lines of communication, commenting on the lack of concerted counterattacks against his attacking forces and suggesting that the Allies' recent victories in France had led them to severely underestimate the ability of even small German forces to threaten such a narrow lifeline. Von Zangen's criticisms clearly illustrate the scale of the task that was before the 101st Division; effectively surrounded by small, but highly active and aggressive opposing forces, the division was forced to divide and disperse its efforts. As such, individual Allied combat groups were left with only enough fighting power to hold off each immediate threat as it emerged, without achieving the concentration of strength needed to effectively counterattack and destroy those forces and decisively defeat the overall German effort.[101]

It must be noted that the well-trained and experienced troops of the 101st Airborne Division generally outclassed the mostly second-line German troops they faced, and frequently inflicted heavy and lopsided losses upon those they did engage. On 20 September, for example, a battalion of

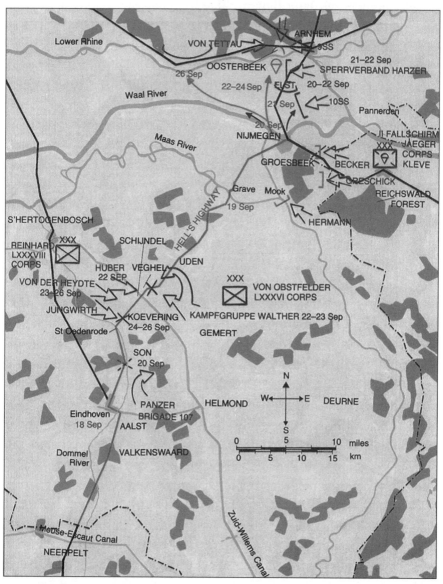

The Reichswald Flank and Hell's Highway: German attacks on the Allied lines of communication, 20–6 September 1944. (*Courtesy Robert J. Kershaw*)

the 506th Parachute Infantry Regiment engaged a battalion of German parachute trainees near Veghel with the support of a few tanks from the 44th Royal Tank Regiment, quickly driving them off and inflicting about 40 dead, 40 wounded, and taking 418 POWs, while losing only 4 of their own dead and 6 wounded.[102] The constant stream of small-scale attacks from all directions eventually paid off for the Germans though, when a further attack on 22 September by 107. *Panzer Brigade*, now operating as part of *Kampfgruppe* Walther, with support from elements of *Kampfgruppe* Huber of the 59. *Infanterie Division*, attacking from the other (west) side of the corridor, managed to find a weak point in the 101st's lines and establish a blocking force astride the road just north of Veghel.[103] This break in XXX Corps' vital lines of supply and communication forced the Allies to muster a considerable force to clear them. The Guards Armoured Division was thus ordered to dispatch its 32nd Guards Brigade, comprising the Grenadier and Coldstream Regimental Groups (each with a regiment of tanks and a battalion of infantry), along with a sizeable supporting contingent of XXX Corps' reserve artillery, to go to the 101st's aid, further depleting the strength of the corps' push towards Arnhem.[104] This brigade, joining its efforts to those of an American force of six battalions drawn from three of the 101st Airborne Division's infantry regiments, managed to reopen the corridor, but it took over 24 hours to do so, ensuring XXX Corps' supplies, particularly of vital artillery ammunition, were left badly restricted at a critical juncture in their operations to reach Arnhem. This meant that the artillery support available to both the 43rd Infantry Division's attacks on the 'Island' and the 1st Airborne Division's defence of the Oosterbeek perimeter was severely limited; the vital fire support provided to the trapped 1st Airborne Division, in particular, was limited by order of XXX Corps' artillery commander to between twenty and forty rounds per gun per day throughout the period that the road was blocked. It was such reasons that led General Horrocks to dub the day the 'Black 22nd'.[105]

Moreover, despite the heavy losses their forces suffered in both the attacks on the corridor and the Allied clearing operations, the German pressure on Hell's Highway continued. On 24 September, elements of *Kampfgruppe* Chill, the 6. *Fallschirmjäger Regiment* (*Kampfgruppe* von der Heydte), and the Jungwirth Parachute Battalion of the 1. *Fallschirmarmee* again found a weak point in the Allied lines after several probing attacks and, joined by several other small units, cut the road near Koevering, destroying a British supply convoy in the process. This relatively small blocking force clung to the road for nearly two full days in the face of attacks by elements of all four of the 101st Division's infantry regiments (the 501st, 502nd, and 506th Parachute Infantry Regiments and the 327th Glider Infantry Regiment) with British tank support, and left a large number of mines scattered across the road when they finally retreated early on 26 September as the 1st Airborne Division was evacuating across the Lower Rhine.[106]

Though most of the German units involved in these attacks were eventually shattered by the superior Allied infantry and armoured forces brought to bear against them, their efforts clearly had a strong cumulative effect on the overall strength and drive of the Allied thrust to Arnhem. It is worth noting that, given the relatively weak nature of the German forces in the Eindhoven sector, and the abysmal state of their command, control, and communications (C3) arrangements, both between the various forces, and with higher headquarters, that the Germans could not reasonably have expected any better performance from them. Though these weak, locally controlled, and poorly coordinated attacks never managed to develop the mass of fighting power that might have decisively cut off and trapped the Allied forces to the north, they still exercised a considerable influence upon the battle and contributed to the German victory. The willingness, even eagerness, of the assorted units operating under the 1. *Fallschirmarmee* to attack, largely on their own initiative and plans, and with little hope of meaningful success against heavy odds, was vital to the impact they had. Had these forces conducted themselves more passively, either defending in place or even making entirely understandable retreats in the face of the superior Allied forces, the Allies would have been able to muster considerably more fighting power at the spearhead of their advance. In such circumstances, the Allies would have been able to hold their lines of communication with only limited contingents of security troops, rather than the full strength of two airborne divisions and a considerable contingent from XXX Corps. As it was, the Allied forces deployed to defend Hell's Highway proved only just barely strong enough to keep XXX Corps from being entirely cut off from their own lines. It is worth noting that while as late as 21 September, the Allied leadership regarded the threat to their lines of communications as 'not serious', by the 23rd, General Miles Dempsey of the 2nd Army officially designated the mission of protecting these lines, and the bridgehead at Nijmegen, as the army's top two priorities, relegating the initial offensive mission towards Arnhem to a distant third.[107] The German attacks on the corridor thus effectively seized the initiative from the Allies, forcing them ever more onto the defensive and seeking to avoid a catastrophic defeat, rather than attaining their original objectives.

Overall, across the entire breadth of the Market Garden landings, the nature of the German response, characterized by rapid and aggressive reactions by units operating largely on their own initiative, with only minimal central direction, was a vital determining factor in the eventual defeat of the operation. Right from the very start, and in spite of the considerable surprise their airborne landings achieved, the Allies found themselves losing, or struggling to retain, the overall initiative in the battle, as German units reacted faster than they could put their own plans into effect. Montgomery's plans for Market Garden had been predicated around an expectation that the shock effect of the massed airborne landings – still the largest in history to this day – would produce an effective 'window' of 24 to 48 hours in which the Germans would be unable to effectively react, allowing the Allies to secure their objective crossings and thrust across the Rhine. Instead, the Germans reacted effectively within a mere handful of hours, throwing the Allied plans into total disarray from the outset.[108] After action reports by the II. *SS-Panzer Korps* in particular heavily emphasized the role that the near universal application of swift aggressive action by whatever commanders happened to be on the spot played in foiling the Allied operation.[109] This author would argue that these actions were less the product of any specific decisions made at the time, than they were of the fact that German forces had been taught, trained, and were well-versed in acting this way since not merely the days of Hans von Seeckt, but those of the Great Elector and Frederick the Great. The German victory in Holland in September 1944 was perhaps the last successful product of a long tradition of German doctrine and military thought.

Chapter 5

Fencing with a Sledgehammer: The Origins and Nature of British Tactical and Command Doctrine and its Role in Operation Garden

In direct contrast to German doctrine, the combat doctrine that was employed by British forces in late 1944 proved to be generally ill-suited to the circumstances of Operation Market Garden. In this period British doctrine centred around concepts of a 'methodical battle', in which commanders relied upon detailed and often quite rigid planning and control, meticulously set timetables, limited objectives, and carefully organized support from artillery and air power in order to effectively conduct their battles. When Market Garden was being planned, this doctrine had just proven its general effectiveness in the hands of Field Marshal Montgomery and his 21st Army Group in Normandy. In Normandy, the Germans, despite having been generally outnumbered by a significant margin, had possessed several potentially significant technological and tactical advantages over their Allied opponents, most notably in the field of armoured and mobile warfare. However, instead of the fast-moving mechanized battle of manoeuvre that the Germans had hoped to wage, they were instead drawn into an intense head-to-head war of attrition in the face of a massive Allied superiority in firepower, particularly with regards to artillery and air support. Under the cover of this blanket of fire, which effectively pinned German forces down, limiting their mobility and largely negating their qualitatively superior armoured forces, the Allies achieved a gradual, but steady progress. Though this methodical approach took a considerable amount of time and brought about very heavy losses on both sides, it was the Germans who gave out first under the pressure.[1]

In Operation Market Garden, however, Montgomery willingly, carelessly, and rather surprisingly stepped well outside the 'comfort zone' of his forces' war fighting capabilities, seeking to use shock and rapid manoeuvre to overcome German resistance rather than his more traditional approach based upon firepower and a slow, carefully managed set-piece advance. It is worth noting that several observers on both sides, such as American General Omar Bradley, *Generalfeldmarschall* Gerd von Rundstedt, and even General Urquhart, expressed shock at the degree to which Market Garden departed from Montgomery's standard combat methods and practices. Bradley perhaps put this sense of surprise at his British colleague and frequent rival's proposal the most succinctly, or at least the most colourfully: 'Had the pious, teetotalling Montgomery wobbled into SHAEF [the Supreme Headquarters, Allied Expeditionary Force] with a hangover, I could not have been more astonished ... Although I never reconciled myself to the venture, I nevertheless freely conceded that it was one of the most imaginative of the war.'[2]

However, while Montgomery may well have had the imagination to conceive of such a feat of arms, the British forces under his command did not really possess the doctrine, training, or experience that would have allowed them to execute the Market Garden plan to full effect; in fact, the plan would have required the British to operate rather like Germans to achieve the hoped for level of success. The operation demanded that all units involved act as boldly as possible to maximize the initial shock effect of the landings, seizing objectives and overcoming any resistance faced quickly and efficiently and with only limited support. Given that the airborne units would be widely separated from their higher headquarters and, at times, from each other, and that their communications equipment and procedures were known to be less than reliable, it would also demand a maximum level of individual initiative be exercised by every unit commander and soldier right down to the lowest tactical level. Such a bold plan could also naturally expect to encounter unexpected situations and setbacks, which would require local commanders to adapt and improvise their plans as events progressed. While the plans for Market Garden to some degree recognized these requirements, with most of the operational orders issued for the operation heavily emphasizing the need for all participating units to act as quickly and boldly as they could, it is one thing to simply order military units to operate in a certain way and entirely another for them to actually be capable of doing so.

In the event, the British units involved in Operation Market Garden largely failed to live up to the lofty expectations that Montgomery placed upon them with so little justification. The intended quick rapier-like thrust by XXX Corps to Arnhem and across the Lower Rhine in particular proved to be more of a ponderous series of hammer blows, with the corps advancing slowly and cautiously and frequently halting for prolonged periods to deal with even limited resistance – the advance fell well behind schedule on the first day, and this gap between intentions and reality only grew steadily thereafter. Though the operational plan called for XXX Corps to reach Arnhem inside of three days, it was still struggling to close on the southern banks of the Lower Rhine when the 1st Airborne Division was evacuated – a full nine days after the operation began. XXX Corps' failure has been widely criticized in the literature surrounding the campaign, by both historians and participants, often being attributed to an inadequate sense of urgency on the part of corps commander Lieutenant General Brian Horrocks and his troops.[3] In truth, XXX Corps' troops generally conducted themselves in full accordance with how they had been trained, and with how they had operated to date: slowly and cautiously, seeking only limited objectives in any given stage of an advance, and executing their detailed battle plans in a methodical 'step-by-step' manner. Thus, XXX Corps can hardly be faulted for its relative slowness during the campaign; it was largely the fault of Montgomery and the other Market Garden planners for presenting them with a plan that was predicated upon them operating in a manner entirely contrary to their established doctrine.

Historical Origins of British Doctrinal Principles in the Second World War

Like the Germans, or any other nation for that matter, British combat doctrine was shaped by their own philosophies of warfare and the ways that their military leadership had historically perceived and understood the nature of combat and how best to deal with its demands. Unlike the Germans, however, the British establishment as a whole never accepted the idea that war was inherently and unavoidably chaotic. Drawing upon the Enlightenment era conception that proper scientific analysis could allow mankind to understand and thus control the natural world, as well as the theories of the nineteenth-century Swiss military philosopher Henri Jomini, British military thought from the mid-nineteenth century onwards suggested that these concepts could be extended to the realm of human activities such as war; that it was possible to identify, understand, and mitigate the various factors that created Clauswitzian friction in combat and reduce them to a manageable level.[4] Thus, in contrast to the Germans, who believed that chaos was an unavoidable and inherent factor in war, the British establishment believed that it was possible (if often difficult) to make war 'orderly', that human ingenuity, willpower, and technological aids could bring the various random factors that affected the fortunes of their forces in combat under a degree of control and reduce the effects of friction to a minimum.[5]

As such, the effort to establish and maintain control over the battlefield was a central component of British doctrine in the late nineteenth and early twentieth centuries. This doctrine called for strict centralized planning and management of battles, for commanders to lay down plans in advance and in as much detail as possible, dictating the objectives of their subordinate units and the direction, speed, and timing of their movements and engagements. Senior commanders – who were seen as the only ones who would be able to obtain a full and proper overview and understanding of the overall situation, and thus have the capability to make fully informed decisions – were to endeavour to extend their control over as many aspects of the battle as possible.[6] Ideally, as circumstances at the front changed during the course of a battle, individual units would report the new situation back to the central commander, who would thus be able to adjust the plan and issue new orders as needed. In reality, as the British soon became fully aware, especially through the course of the First World War, the expanding scope and level of unit dispersion on the modern battlefield, and the limitations of contemporary means of communication between senior commanders and their units, meant that this level of fine control was an as yet unachievable ideal. Unlike the Germans, however, who sought to solve this problem through the devolution of authority to junior leaders – effectively preparing their army to operate with only a bare minimum of central control, if necessary – the British instead sought to maintain that control through a policy of rigid adherence to centrally created battle plans. In the absence of direct instructions to the contrary, units were simply to carry out their set role within the plan by rote, which would minimize any weaknesses of command and control in combat by allowing a commander to lay down plans in advance, reducing the need for back-and-forth communications between central commanders and units as the battle progressed. These subordinate units were to keep to these plans at all costs; any alterations to their actions in the face of unexpected situations would simply disjoint the overall plan, creating the confusion and chaos this doctrine sought to avoid. The maintenance of unified action was seen as vital, and to maintain this unified effort, it was believed that a full degree of initiative could only be exercised by the senior commander.

To this end, a core element of British military doctrine and training in this period was an emphasis on discipline, which would provide junior officers and men with the willpower and self-control necessary to stick to plans even in the face of setbacks and casualties; it was widely believed by the British military establishment that an opponent could simply be forced to conform to any plan, if that plan was pressed forward with sufficient determination and will.[7] Thus, the most important role for doctrine and training was to foster a strict and reflexive obedience among the troops to orders given, even when such obedience might bring considerable personal risk – junior officers and men were expected to trust that their commander knew what was best for the overall situation and simply play the roles that he assigned them, whatever the cost.[8]

Centralized Control and the Set-Piece Battle in the First World War and the Interwar Period

The peak of this doctrine of centralized control came in the First World War. Like those of most of the other combatants, the British Army's early efforts at conducting traditional manoeuvre warfare in the opening months of the conflict proved to be costly failures in the face of modern firepower, mass armies, and entrenchments. By 1916, the British Army was increasingly turning away from simple infantry assaults and instead elevating the artillery to the role of their primary offensive arm. This tendency was driven in part by the fact that artillery tactics and technology developed much more quickly than those of the infantry through the first part of the war, with gunners increasingly able to deliver faster, more accurate, and more elaborately arranged and coordinated fire missions.[9] As such, achieving fire superiority over the enemy and beating down his defences increasingly became the near exclusive task of the artillery, the infantry's role being largely reduced to conducting a final assault on an enemy battered to the point of submission by the guns – to paraphrase the French General Henri Petain, artillery was to conquer, while infantry was merely to occupy.[10] Infantry assaults were thus almost entirely predicated around elaborate artillery fire plans, including counterbattery fire against enemy artillery, the destruction of enemy strongpoints, and rolling barrages to suppress enemy defences ahead of the advancing infantry. Though British infantry tactics and firepower had certainly undergone extensive development and improvement by the end of the war with the introduction of platoon-based fire and manoeuvre tactics not far removed from those of the German stormtroops, an elaborate level of artillery fire support remained central to the planning and execution of British battles.[11] Given the complexity of these fire plans, and the importance of coordinated and unified effort within them, they were generally established centrally at the highest levels of field command, that of corps and field armies. Given that the limited state of communications in the First World War would make it very difficult to call for any changes to the fire plan once the units had left the telegraph and telephone lines in their trenches, the infantry were instead expected to conform their own actions to the plan, to 'keep up with the barrage' and conform to the set artillery timetable – or risk losing their vital support. The actions of infantry units were thus generally laid down in detail in advance, with the troops to follow those set plans and timetables to the letter.

Almost inevitably, the British soon discovered that this level of strict choreography and fire support could only be maintained for a relatively short period on the offensive. As units advanced into unknown situations in the enemy rear, they would quickly go beyond both the scope of their set plans and the range of their artillery support; many early offensives – such as the battles of Neuve Chappelle and Loos in March and September 1915, respectively – achieved a degree of initial success, but then failed as they overextended and outran their plans and support. These limitations led the British leadership to turn away from seeking deep penetrations and breakthroughs and towards what became known as 'bite and hold' tactics, which called for limited advances against set objectives relatively close to their own front lines and conducted with the full benefit of elaborate advance planning and artillery support. The achievement of these limited objectives would be followed by a period of consolidation where the artillery and reinforcements would be advanced, and new plans laid for the next stage of the battle.¹² While the defeat of the enemy's front-line forces might offer apparent opportunities to exploit and expand the initial success by carrying the advance deep into the enemy's rear areas, hard-won experience convinced British leadership that the likely risks of any such extension of their offensive efforts outweighed any potential gains, and that it was better to be content with limited gains than run the serious risk of a costly defeat by seeking an ephemeral possibility for a decisive victory. Thus, instead of a single 'flowing' advance, the British broke their efforts down into an intermittent series of smaller operations that could be planned in detail, with the maximum possible use of concentrated and coordinated mass and firepower. These methods proved extremely effective in the latter stages of the war; the decisive '100 Days Campaign' of mid to late 1918, in particular, entirely comprised a steady series of these relatively small set-piece battles, linked together into a general offensive by the British and Dominion forces. Though the gains achieved by each individual stage were limited, they eventually added up, breaching the German Hindenburg Line defences that had held off all previous efforts and leaving the German Army on the brink of total defeat, eventually bringing about the November armistice. These results compared favourably to those of the Germans' more ambitious '*Kaiserschlacht*' offensives in spring 1918, which sought to achieve decisive breakthroughs that could effectively win the war at a single stroke. Though the Germans achieved considerable early success, the fact that they continued to press their attacks even in the face of mounting resistance and waning resources, seeking ever greater results, eventually resulted in their assault forces being crippled by attrition and the failure of their final offensive.

Given the sudden and comprehensive defeat of the British Expeditionary Force alongside the French Army at the hands of the German 'Blitzkrieg' on France in 1940, the British Army has long been charged by many analysts, historians, and other commentators with having failed to make a serious effort to adapt their rigid doctrine to the rapidly changing realities of modern warfare in the wake of the First World War.¹³ The interwar British Army is often accused of being extremely conservative, even reactionary, on a social, intellectual, and institutional level, and thus largely ignoring the tactical and technological developments of the 1920s and 1930s, and even many of the lessons of the First World War, in favour of restoring a traditional way of soldiering from the heyday of the British Empire and the colonial era. There is certainly some truth to this stereotypical view, as many among the still aristocratically oriented British officer corps did remain highly conservative in their views on the conduct of war, devaluing modern developments and 'intellectual soldiering', while lacking much sense of true professionalism. However, the fact remains that the British Army did make some serious efforts to adapt its doctrine to the demands of modern war in the interwar period. Much like its German counterpart, the British Army formed several committees right after the First World War to analyse the conflict and derive useful lessons for building a doctrine suitable for a modern army.[14] The leadership of the British Army largely took the reports of these committees to heart and, though there were many bitter disputes regarding the specific details, it very quickly became widely accepted that the next major war would be mainly characterized by highly mobile mechanized combat.[15] Moreover, the British military and political leadership was all too aware that Britain could not simply plan to refight the First World War, as it was naturally assumed that the British public would never again accept the devastating level of losses that that victory had required.[16] The doctrinal and training manuals produced by the British Army in the 1920s and 1930s thus called for relatively small forces employing a high level of mechanization and firepower, as well as manoeuvre, flexibility, and combined arms cooperation, all acting as vital force multipliers to maximize the combat effectiveness of a relative handful of soldiers – concepts broadly similar to those advanced by Hans von Seeckt in Germany.[17]

This doctrine, however, was still heavily influenced by the legacy of the successful set-piece battle doctrine of the First World War. The *Field Service Regulations* of 1935 (FSR 1935), the last full revision of the overall doctrine of the British Army produced before the Second World War, still emphasized the initial, closely controlled, phase of any battle as being the most important and decisive one, with the more mobile and chaotic efforts to exploit any initial success being seen as much more difficult, with proportionally lower prospects or expectations for significant gains.[18] Similarly, a very strong emphasis remained upon the use of set-piece attacks, carefully prepared and managed in stages and centred around timed artillery fire programmes.[19]

British interwar doctrine also remained heavily wedded to practices of centralized control, heavily emphasizing the concept in spite of its general incompatibility with the ideas it espoused on modern mobile warfare. British generals, influenced by the continuing prominence of notions of hierarchy and socio-economic class within both the army and wider British society, all too often took a fairly dim view of the intelligence and abilities of their junior officers and men and were unwilling to trust them to function effectively without close direction and supervision.[20] As such, post-First World War British doctrine continued to allocate the great majority of decision-making authority to senior commanders, with subordinates generally expected to simply follow their orders without question, and to ask for further instructions in the case of any unexpected developments. In this area, the British placed considerable faith in the ability of modern developments in communications – particularly the development and widespread deployment of more reliable radio sets with significantly improved range and portability – to maintain this level of command, control, and communications under the conditions of mobile warfare.[21]

Thus, while FSR 1935 did speak of the need for low-level initiative among individual unit commanders, it also continued to heavily emphasize the dominant role of a central commander in controlling battles to the greatest degree possible and to heavily qualify any delegation of authority to subordinate commanders.[22] FSR 1935 suggests that the latter, in particular, should only be done as a matter of exception and when absolutely necessary, when circumstance rendered central control impossible. Moreover, FSR 1935 suggested that even when authority *was* delegated, the subordinate commander should keep to the original plan as much as possible, emphasizing that they should immediately report – and even ask permission – when making any changes, and that they would be held responsible should independent actions cause any disruption of the overall plan. Unlike German doctrine, which saw independent decision making and action as a standard – and indeed, desirable – practice to be fostered among junior officers and men, FSR 1935 clearly saw such independence as merely an occasional, and generally unwelcome, necessity, to be avoided whenever possible. In practice, the continuing emphasis upon strong central control within British doctrinal material, such as FSR 1935, seems to have reduced its calls for a greater degree of initiative and independent judgement among subordinate commanders to a matter of mere lip service. Throughout the Second World War, British commanders, and Field Marshal Montgomery in particular, continued to show a distinct tendency towards micromanagement of their battles, seeking to control every aspect down to the smallest tactical details.[23]

Lost Opportunities: Training and Doctrine in the British Army

The British Army also experienced great difficulties in even effectively promulgating any revisions of its doctrine among its troops. Perhaps the most critical factor in this difficulty was the simple fact that the British put much less focus and effort into the training of their officers and men than the Germans did. Despite the potentially useful revisions made to their overall doctrine through the interwar period, the training standards and regimes of the British Army remained highly traditional, based heavily around formal parade ground drills, the development of a 'proper soldierly bearing' and appearance, basic physical fitness, and the rote memorization of various manuals on tactics and weaponry. Relatively little emphasis was placed upon the practice of realistic tactics, or into the development of soldiers' intellects or sense of tactical judgement in evaluating and responding effectively to unexpected situations. In fact, British Army training all too often made concerted efforts to discourage any independent thinking or sense of initiative among the troops. Private James Sims of the 1st Airborne Division's 2nd Parachute Battalion, who started his military career in the Royal Artillery (RA), stated of his basic training: 'if you had any spirit at all the RA seemed determined to break it'.[24] Even the British Army's officer academies and Officer Candidate Training Units (OCTU) focused much more on the learning of drill, proper bearing and personal conduct, the recitation of manuals, and the ubiquitous competitive sports than it did on instructing young officers in tactics and leadership, the general assumption being that such matters would be learned 'on the job' with their units.[25] Much expectation was also placed upon the 'natural' leadership skills and decision-making abilities that were viewed as being inherent to men of the British upper class, and the idea that such men would simply be able to 'figure things out' when needed.[26]

These problems of training were further exacerbated by the limited budgets and manpower available to the British Army in the interwar period. In the aftermath of the First World War, the British armed forces were faced with extensive budget reductions, which only deepened with the onset of the Great Depression in the early 1930s. With the cash-strapped British government increasingly forced to choose between various competing priorities, the bulk of military funds and quality recruits went to the 'senior service' of the Royal Navy, or to the newer and more prestigious Royal Air Force – both of which were seen as the natural first lines of defence for the island nation.[27] The low pay, limited facilities, and arduous conditions of service that were all that the underfunded army could offer ensured that it had great difficulty recruiting many men with the level of intelligence and motivation necessary to fully comprehend and apply more than the most basic training and doctrine; all too many of the men that volunteered for the army in peacetime were those that simply had few or no other viable employment options.[28] Moreover, the army was badly hindered by a shortage of properly qualified instructors and appropriate training equipment, supplies, and facilities.[29] This ensured that field exercises on any significant scale were rare in the interwar army, and that those that were held were often very simplistic, heavily choreographed, and highly unrealistic in their conditions.[30] Given these limitations, it was much easier and cheaper for the overworked British training establishment to focus their efforts on matters such as traditional discipline and marching drills.[31] Though these budgetary limitations were naturally greatly reduced with the outbreak of the war, the British Army was forced to play 'catch-up' from years of relative neglect in developing its wartime training regimes and facilities – all while integrating a massive influx of new volunteers and conscripts and still generally being allocated the lowest priority for resources among the British services.

In addition, the promulgation of doctrine was hindered by the fact that there was no centralized authority governing standards for training within the British Army; the interpretation of official doctrine and the development of actual programmes of training were largely left up to the tastes and whims of individual divisional and battalion commanders, ensuring a wide variety of standards and practices among various units.[32] Furthermore, as historian Jeremy Krang notes, many of these middle-ranking officers were actually more conservative than the army's senior leadership. Having been more recently indoctrinated in these traditional skills and practices, and owing their advancement through the ranks to their relative proficiency in them, such officers were often quite heavily invested in them and less willing or able to take a broader or more flexible view of such matters.[33] As such, many of these officers were unenthusiastic in adopting new doctrine or practices that would effectively invalidate their own hard-earned training and experiences, forcing them to relearn everything from scratch alongside their men. This general neglect of training proved to be a critical impediment to the British Army's ability to put *any* sort of new doctrinal ideas into practice – training being the effective 'connective tissue' between the theory of doctrine and actual practice employed by armies in the field.

Montgomery and the 'Return' of the Set-Piece Battle

Thus, by the time that the Second World War broke out, the British Army was effectively caught 'mid-stream', having officially adopted a partially modernized doctrine, but having been unable to properly prepare its forces to implement it. These shortcomings were perhaps best demonstrated by the British Army's relatively clumsy early efforts to conduct mobile mechanized warfare in North Africa, a field in which it found itself badly outclassed by General Erwin Rommel's German *Afrika Korps*.[34] Though the British were able to muster significant armoured and motorized forces in the theatre, during 1941 and much of 1942 they proved largely unable to wield them as effectively as did the Germans and suffered several humiliating reversals, culminating in a crushing battlefield defeat at Gazala in May and June 1942 and the subsequent loss of the vital Libyan port town of Tobruk. The key turning point for British doctrine and fighting methods in the Second World War came with the arrival of then-Lieutenant General Bernard Montgomery in North Africa in August 1942, to take command of the struggling 8th Army in the wake of the summer disasters. Montgomery quickly came to recognize the weaknesses and limitations of the forces under his command, particularly the relatively low standards of training and tactics among his infantry and armoured troops and the general weakness of the army's officer corps in exercising effective command. Montgomery also saw that the 8th Army's most effective assets to date had been the gunnery of the Royal Artillery and the air support provided by the Desert Air Force.[35]

In light of these strengths and weaknesses, Montgomery effectively turned to a partial 'reversion' to the set-piece doctrine of 1918, updated for the prevailing conditions of 1942.[36] This traditional doctrine would play to both his army's strengths and limitations, placing as it did a heavy reliance upon artillery firepower, while making relatively limited demands upon his less-proficient infantry and armoured arms.[37] Montgomery was a particularly strong advocate of the principle of centralized control, and always sought to plan and prepare for his operations well in advance, carefully formulating a 'master plan', and then exerting as much personal control as he could over its execution, what he called keeping a 'firm grip'. In this way he sought to control as many potential variables as possible and keep close tabs on his subordinates to ensure that they did not deviate from his intentions.[38] Montgomery's revised command doctrine was thus less a truly new innovation as it was a clarification of the contradictions inherent in British interwar doctrine, largely discarding the elements on flexibility of command and mobile warfare – for which the army had proven poorly suited – and emphasizing those of firepower and meticulous central control.

The 2nd Battle of El Alamein in late October and early November 1942 quickly became the first demonstration of this reworked fighting method, a battle that 'established Monty's reputation as a master of the set-piece battle', to quote General Horrocks, who was in command of the 8th Army's XIII Corps at the time.[39] El Alamein served as a basic template for most of Montgomery's subsequent operations, in that he continued to devote considerable time before any battle to meticulously laying plans and preparing his army, made extensive use of firepower in the form of artillery and air power, and proceeded slowly and cautiously once engaged, seeking to avoid any significant risk of defeat, even at the expense of opportunities to achieve a greater victory.[40] The battle also demonstrated the limitations of this methodology, as the Axis forces, though heavily defeated, were able to successfully disengage a significant portion of their fighting strength – particularly the motorized forces of the German *Afrika Korps* – and retreat to Tunisia in the face of Montgomery's slow and meticulous pursuit, there to fight on until finally overwhelmed by the combined forces of two Allied field armies in May 1943.[41] El Alamein and the remainder of the Mediterranean campaign quickly established the set-piece battle as Montgomery's 'signature', with his efforts almost always characterized by a careful matching of his plans to the capabilities of his forces, the maximum employment of supporting firepower, and relatively limited missions being assigned to his infantry and armoured forces.[42]

Thus, when appointed as commander of what would become the 21st Army Group for the invasion of North-West Europe in January 1944, Montgomery naturally brought this successful doctrine – which was already being introduced in training throughout the British Home Forces – with him.[43] As Montgomery served as the overall commander of the Allied ground forces for the initial phases of the Allied invasion, the plans for the battle of Normandy bear the hallmark of his methods. Moreover, several of the commanders he appointed to key positions throughout the 21st Army Group, such as General Dempsey of the 2nd Army, and General Horrocks of XXX Corps, were hand-picked 'acolytes' of his from North Africa, who had largely learned their craft under his tutelage and closely followed his methods.[44] Montgomery's plans for Normandy called for a steady advance via a series of limited local attacks, backed by the full weight of Allied artillery and air power, seeking to wear down the German armies gradually, rather than with a single decisive blow, and with any decisive breakthrough and subsequent major mobile operations to take place only after the Germans had been all but defeated by this relentless attrition.[45]

The actual conduct of the campaign in Normandy closely followed these patterns, with British and American operations generally being characterized by a considerable degree of caution and meticulousness; most offensive operations were of a fairly limited scale, being planned carefully in advance with extensive provision of artillery and air support, and setting limited objectives of capturing key pieces of terrain or simply inflicting losses upon the enemy. Though many German observers criticized this approach as far too slow and wasteful of opportunities – largely due to its clear contrast with their own practices – the German Army could also muster very little in the way of a truly effective long-term response to it. Though the Germans could and did certainly win individual battles, the Allies' superiority in manpower and materiel meant that they would almost inevitably win any prolonged battle of attrition. Most significantly, the Allies' slow, cautious and meticulous approach to planning largely denied the Germans any chance to redress the numerical imbalance by inflicting any serious reverses with major counterattacks against overextended and vulnerable assault forces, as they had so frequently done to Soviet forces on the Eastern Front; though German counterattacks often stopped Allied offensives and inflicted losses, they were never able to change the overall operational or strategic situation to a meaningful extent.[46] Montgomery's conduct of the land battle in Normandy ensured that German forces were steadily pushed back and worn out, eventually allowing the American forces in the western sector of the beachhead to pierce their emaciated lines, letting the Allies break out from Normandy and eventually drive the Germans from France – though once again, the relatively slow pace of their mobile operations and pursuit, particularly in their early stages, ensured that a sizeable portion of the German *Westheer* would live to fight another day.

The Battle of Normandy thus served as a very strong testimony to the effectiveness of the set-piece battle doctrine employed by the 21st Army Group in 1944. Though there is much evidence that the German Army outclassed its Allied opponents to some degree on a unit for unit basis, the Allies' doctrine allowed them to fight in a way that maximized their strengths while minimizing their weaknesses.[47] In return, the German Army was left with no effective reply as long as the Allies remained able to dictate the pace of the fighting; the Allies' cautious approach limited German ability to bring their superiority in small-unit combat and manoeuvre warfare to bear.

British Doctrine in Operation Market Garden – Case Study One – XXX Corps

In Operation Market Garden, however, Montgomery seems to have almost entirely discarded the doctrinal tenets and practices that had brought him and his forces so much success to date, in that he prepared a plan that ran almost entirely contrary to British doctrine as it was practised in mid-1944. Most notably, his expectation that XXX Corps' armoured spearhead would be able to rapidly exploit the initial breakthrough and rush through over 60 miles of German-occupied territory along a single road to link up with the airborne forces and reach Arnhem flew in the face of the way that British forces generally operated. The operational orders for Operation Garden – the ground component of the overall operation – called for the leading brigade of XXX Corps, the 5th Guards Armoured Brigade, to reach its final objective at the town of Nunspeet on the Zuider Zee in a maximum of five days, but ideally within three, on D+2; Arnhem, and the final link up with the last of the parachute forces, was to be reached in one to three days.[48] This plan was based around the fact that the Allied leadership, drawing on optimistic intelligence estimates and their own wishful thinking, generally believed that the German forces in the path of the thrust, having been badly weakened and demoralized by their recent defeat in Normandy, would not be able to muster much resistance beyond the 'crust' of their front lines along the Meuse–Escaut Canal. The Germans were thought to have little in the way of useful reserves behind this line, and so the bulk of planning for XXX Corps' assault was focused on achieving the initial breakthrough, with the rest of the operation being seen largely as a relatively simple matter of pursuit and exploitation.[49] The presence of the new and still forming 1. *Fallschirmarmee* in the area – though known to Allied intelligence – was largely dismissed, with it being assessed – fairly accurately – as a hodgepodge force of mostly second-line forces and stragglers barely strong enough to hold a relatively thin outpost line along the canal.[50] The Allied leadership was also largely aware of the presence of the II. *SS-Panzer Korps* in the area – despite some long-standing assertions to the contrary in older accounts of the battle – but this too was largely dismissed based on the assessment, again fairly accurate, that it currently mustered only a very small fraction of its notional strength and had not yet been able to conduct its planned refits.[51]

At Operation Garden's outset, the breakout of the Guards Armoured Division from the Neerpelt Bridgehead was enabled by a typical application of massed firepower within a carefully prepared and orchestrated plan. This plan called for the Guards' path to be 'paved' by a 23-minute rolling barrage, which was to be fired by six field regiments (the 74th, 112th, 124th, 147th, and 179th) and three medium artillery regiments (the 7th, 64th, and 84th) and was to move forward at a rate of 200yd per minute just ahead of the advancing column. This curtain of fire would be supplemented by timed concentrations fired on known or suspected German strongpoints by a further three field regiments (the 86th, 90th, and 151st), one heavy battery (the 419th), a heavy anti-aircraft regiment (the 165th), and a handful of Belgian and Dutch manned batteries; in all, the preliminary bombardment would involve a total of over 300 guns firing at maximum rate.[52] This gunfire would be supplemented by the efforts of eight squadrons of rocket-armed Hawker Typhoon fighter-bombers of the 2nd Tactical Air Force's 83 Group, which would provide a relay of suppressive area strikes by eight aircraft every 5 minutes for the first 35 minutes of the attack, as well as a rotating 'cab rank' of on-call aircraft that could be directed by the Forward Air Controllers (FACs) travelling at the head of the column against any targets of opportunity encountered.[53]

In spite of its massive weight and intricacy, this fire plan failed to achieve the full effect desired. Though the bombardment knocked out the bulk of the towed German anti-tank guns covering the road in the German front line, several infantry ambush parties, armed with *Panzerfaust* handheld recoilless anti-tank weapons and concealed in foxholes dug in the ditches along each side of the road, survived and engaged the leading squadrons of the 2nd (Armoured) Battalion of the Irish Guards as they passed, quickly knocking nine Sherman tanks out of action and bringing the column to a halt.[54] Although the bulk of these ambushers were swiftly eliminated by the supporting infantry of the 3rd Irish Guards, assisted by fire from the 2nd Irish Guards' remaining tanks and strikes from the cab-rank Typhoons, in the wake of the ambush the Guards Armoured Division, true to its doctrine, training, and experience, chose to withdraw its leading elements and repeat the entire bombardment process to eliminate or suppress any further resistance before resuming the advance. This second effort proved more successful, but was then followed by another short withdrawal and the firing of a *third* barrage by the corps' medium regiments when further resistance was encountered shortly thereafter at the villages of Hoek and Heuvel.[55]

The Guards Armoured Division's reliance upon the repeated use of prolonged set-piece bombardment programmes to enable its advance ensured that, although they eventually broke through the German lines, the division had only managed to advance 7 miles out of the 13 that they had been expected to by nightfall on the first day of the offensive. The division laagered for the night at the town of Valkenswaard at a point when the plan had expected them to have already linked up with the 101st Airborne Division at Eindhoven.[56] There is no real evidence that Major General Allan Adair, commander of the Guards Division,

1. The architects of the victory. From left to right: *Generalfeldmarschall* Walter Model, commander of *Heeresgruppe B*; *Generaloberst* Kurt Student, commander of 1. *Fallschirmarmee* (just visible over Model's left shoulder); *Obergruppenführer* Wilhelm Bittrich, commander of II. *SS-Panzer Korps*; Major Hans Peter Knaust, commander of *Kampfgruppe* Knaust; and *Brigadeführer* Heinz Harmel, commander of 10. *SS-Panzer Division/Kampfgruppe* Frundsberg. (*Bundesarchiv, Bild 146-1971-033-49, Foto: o.Ang*)

2. The craftsmen of the victory. This mixed group of German troops from multiple branches is typical of the type of improvised units formed during the Market Garden battle from whatever forces happened to be at hand, usually placed under the command of the most experienced elements among them. From left to right: (foreground) a Waffen-SS NCO, three Luftwaffe *Fallschirmjäger* (Paratroops); (background) a soldier and a junior officer or NCO from the *Heer* (Army). (*Bundesarchiv, Bild 183-1991-0912-503, Foto: Pospesch*)

3. The German MG 42 *Einheitsmaschinengewehr* (General Purpose Machine Gun). This weapon, seen here being operated from an improvised field mount by a team of *Fallschirmjäger* (Paratroops) somewhere on the battlefields of Holland, was the backbone of German infantry firepower in 1944. With a cyclic rate of fire of 1,200 rounds per minute, and the ability to maintain a high practical rate of fire through the use of linkable ammunition belts and quick-change barrels, this widely issued and highly portable weapon ensured that even small or understrength German infantry units could generate a tremendous amount of killing power on the battlefield. (*Bundesarchiv, Bild 101I-590-2335-13, Foto: Zimmerman*)

4. An Sdkfz 250/1 light half-track advancing through wooded terrain in the Arnhem area past discarded British parachutes. This light AFV, and its larger cousin, the Sdkfz 251, normally used for reconnaissance or the transport of infantry in German mechanized units, were likely the most common German armoured fighting vehicles participating in the Market Garden campaign, with about seventy being available to II. *SS-Panzer Korps* at the start of the fighting. Despite being only thinly armoured, having an open-top crew compartment, and carrying relatively light weaponry (usually one or two machine guns, though some variants carried light guns or howitzers) these vehicles proved a useful source of mobile and protected firepower for the German defenders, particularly given the limited anti-tank weaponry available to the British airborne troops. (*Bundesarchiv, Bild 101II-M2KBK-771-28, Foto: Höppner, Willi*)

5. A *Sturmgeschütz* III self-propelled assault gun moving through the streets of Arnhem or Oosterbeek with infantry in support. This AFV, initially developed to provide close fire support for the German infantry, had become a 'jack of all trades' for the *Wehrmacht* by late 1944, serving in tank and anti-tank units as well as in its original role. In the decisive early days of the Market Garden fighting, a relative handful of StuGs (fielded mostly by the 280. *Sturmgeschütz Brigade*) were the principal heavy armoured vehicles available to the German forces fighting at Arnhem. When the German forces went on to the counteroffensive on 19 September, the long-range firepower provided by the 75mm guns of these StuGs proved vital in eliminating British strongpoints and easing the advance of the German infantry. (*Bundesarchiv, Bild 101I-497-3529-03, Foto: Jacobsen*)

6. The aftermath of a German ambush on the road to Arnhem. This photo illustrates the incident described in the text by *SS-Rottenführer* Alfred Ziegler of *Kampfgruppe* von Allworden (see p. 145), in which his unit ambushed a marching column of British paratroops advancing on Arnhem. The tight grouping of the at least four bodies visible shows the clear lethality of even a brief exposure to German infantry firepower – these men were cut down before they could even begin moving to the cover on the sides of the road. The cumulative effect of many such small-scale ambushes and firefights across the Arnhem/Oosterbeek battlefields upon the attacking British can easily be imagined. (*Bundesarchiv, Bild 183-R97496, Foto: Peterson*)

7. An Sdkfz 11/1 half-track mounting a 2cm FlaK 38 anti-aircraft gun. The surviving self-propelled anti-aircraft guns from the anti-aircraft battalions of the two Panzer Divisions of II. *SS-Panzer Korps*, such as this example, proved to be yet another valuable source of firepower when deployed in support of their infantry. Their mobile heavy automatic weapons played a major role in the defeat of the 4th Parachute Brigade's attack to the north-west of Arnhem on 19 September. (*Bundesarchiv, Bild 101I-590-2333-23, Foto: Appe [Arppe]*)

8. An 8.8cm FlaK 36 heavy anti-aircraft gun deployed in the ground role in the woods around Arnhem or Oosterbeek. The famous 'eighty-eight' had developed a fearsome reputation among Allied troops through the early years of the war, not for its rather average performance against aircraft, but rather for its ability to dispatch virtually any Allied tank at long range using armour-piercing shells; the high velocity and heavy projectiles required to engage high-altitude aircraft proved even more deadly against ground targets. During Market Garden there were no Allied tanks to engage north of the Lower Rhine, and so many of the heavy flak guns dispatched as reinforcements to the Arnhem/Oosterbeek were instead assigned to serve as improvised field artillery – mostly operating under *Artillerie Kommando 191*, the improvised headquarters set up by *Heersgruppe B* to coordinate all artillery operating against Allied forces on both banks of the Lower Rhine. Given its firing angle, it is highly likely this example is operating in just such a role, firing on the Oosterbeek perimeter or the British and Polish forces on the south bank. (*Bundesarchiv, Bild 101I-497-3508-12, Foto: Grosse, Helmut*)

9. A towed 6-pounder gun of the 4th Parachute Brigade at the tail end of a column of troops marching towards Arnhem on 19 September 1944. This medium anti-tank gun comprised the bulk of the 1st Airborne Division anti-tank firepower during the Market Garden battles, with a total of forty-eight guns being deployed. Though the gun itself proved reasonably effective against the German AFVs it faced during the fighting, such towed weapons proved both difficult to deploy on the offensive and highly vulnerable to enemy counterfire – only thirteen guns remained in action following the rout of the 1st Airborne Division on the 19th. (© *IWM, BU 1091, Photo: Sgt. D.M. Smith*)

10. A patrol of paratroopers from the 1st Airborne Division moving through the ruins of Oosterbeek on 23 September 1944. This photo clearly illustrates the difficult urban terrain across which much of the Market Garden fighting took place. In such terrain, encounters generally took place at very close quarters – squad-level firepower proved essential and the rate of casualties was very high, rapidly depleting the relatively small airborne battalions. Also visible is the one significant effort made by the British airborne forces to improve the firepower of their squads beyond that of standard infantry: two of the troopers carry Mk V Sten submachine guns, issued in large numbers to the airborne forces to supplement their automatic firepower. Though generally a significant and highly welcome addition to the firepower of the British troopers, they were an imperfect solution to the imbalance of infantry firepower between British and German forces. Firing a relatively low-powered 9mm pistol cartridge, they lacked both the range of German machine guns and – more significantly in the close fighting of Market Garden – adequate power for penetrating through masonry or dense vegetation. (© *IWM, BU 1121, Photo: Sgt. D.M. Smith*)

11. Four Waffen-SS POWs in the custody of British glider pilots on 18 September. Despite their exhausted and bedraggled appearance – and the apparent youth of the two men in the middle – it is well worth noting that the soldiers of II. *SS-Panzer Korps* were a highly trained and experienced force by autumn 1944, having trained in France through much of 1943 in anticipation of the Allied landings and then having fought throughout the maelstrom of the Normandy campaign before retreating to the German border shortly before Market Garden was launched. Faced with the unexpected threat of the Allied airborne landings, such veteran troops proved a critical asset in allowing the badly depleted forces of the II. *SS-Panzer Korps* to contain and then counterattack the 1st Airborne Division. Though long-established German doctrine provided the basic framework for the victory at Arnhem, it was veteran troops such as these that served as the backbone of the German response, putting theory into action and guiding their less experienced fellows through their example. (© *IWM, BU 1159*, Photo: Sgt. D.M. Smith)

12. A column of Sherman tanks (led by a 17-pounder armed 'Firefly') from the 2nd (Armoured) Irish Guards advances past the wrecks of some of their less fortunate brethren along the road towards Eindhoven on 17 September. This photo clearly illustrates the Dutch terrain that played such a role in hindering the advance of the Guards Armoured Division throughout the battle – both the elevation of the road above the surrounding terrain and the steepness of the bordering embankments are clearly visible. These factors left British tanks starkly visible targets for German gunners and generally prevented them from manoeuvring off the road to seek cover or bring the weight of their numbers to bear against any opposition. The nature of the terrain greatly limited the potential fighting power of the British armoured forces and thus exacerbated the pre-existing British reliance upon heavy artillery and aerial bombardment to pave the way for their advance. (© *IWM, BU 926, Photo: Sgt. Carpenter*)

13. A column of British paratroops from the 2nd Battalion, South Staffordshire Regiment advancing towards Arnhem on 19 September. Strung out in the open along the relatively wide main roads, and surrounded by dense woods and groups of houses and villas, columns such as this would have been very vulnerable to sudden bursts of machine-gun or mortar fire from German troops lying in ambush. (© *IWM, BU 1089, Photo: Sgt. D.M. Smith*)

14. A 75mm M1 pack howitzer of the 1st Airborne Division's 1st Airlanding Light Artillery Regiment firing on the outskirts of Arnhem on 19 September 1944. Twenty-four of these light guns, supplied by the US via Lend Lease, comprised a British airborne division's organic artillery support in late 1944. Although the 1st Airlanding Light Artillery Regiment provided invaluable support for the division's infantry brigades throughout the fighting around Arnhem and Oosterbeek, the limited number, firepower, and range of their weapons (as compared with standard foot or motorized infantry divisions) severely restricted their overall effectiveness. (© *IWM, BU 1094, Photo: Sgt. D.M. Smith*)

15. Troops from 15 and 16 Platoons of C Company, 1st Battalion, The Border Regiment, dug in along a road on the western edge of the Oosterbeek perimeter on 20 September 1944. According to the original caption for this photo, German forces were within 100yd of these positions when this photo was taken. Throughout the course of the battle, steady, if often tentative, pressure from the improvised forces of *Gruppe* von Tettau kept this battalion occupied in defence of the rear of 1st Airborne Division's landing zones and HQ area. (© *IWM, BU 1103, Photo: Sgt. D.M. Smith*)

16. Troops from the 1st Airborne Division use a discarded parachute in an attempt to signal aircraft attempting to deliver supplies to the Oosterbeek pocket on 23 September 1944. With the bulk of its designated supply drop zones having been overrun by the Germans after the disastrous defeat on 19 September and unable to contact higher HQs to request new drop sites, the great majority of supplies dropped to the 1st Airborne Division fell into German hands. Improvised signalling efforts such as this generally proved futile, as the transport pilots had been specifically ordered to ignore any signals from the ground in case of any German attempts to mislead their drops. The resulting shortage of supplies, particularly ammunition, proved a crippling hindrance for the British efforts to hold off the German counteroffensive. (© IWM, BU 1119, Photo: Sgt. D.M. Smith)

17. British outpost positions manned by men from C Troop of the 1st Airborne Reconnaissance Squadron in wooded ground somewhere near the town of Wolfheze, west of Arnhem, on 18 September 1944. A Bren light machine gun (the standard British squad automatic weapon) is visible in the background, while a trooper wielding a Projector, Infantry, Anti-Tank (PIAT) lies prone in the foreground. In light of the limited off-road mobility and vulnerability of the 1st Airborne Division's contingent of anti-tank guns, the PIAT became the division's most important and effective anti-tank weapon throughout the Market Garden fighting. During the German counteroffensive against the Oosterbeek perimeter, PIAT 'hunting' teams inflicted significant losses on the German armoured forces involved. However, the weapon's limited effective range meant that it was unable to effectively respond to tanks and self-propelled guns employing stand-off fire against British positions at long range. (© *IWM, BU 1144, Photo: Sgt. D.M. Smith*)

18. British tanks crossing the Nijmegen road bridge over the Waal River, some time after its capture by British and American forces on 20 September 1944 (the presence of seemingly casual civilian traffic would suggest that the photo was taken after the front lines had advanced further north). The three-day delay in securing this bridge – brought about in part by the determined (if futile) attacks by German forces against the Allied right flank on the Groesbeek Heights – was one of the most significant factors in preventing the forces of XXX Corps from reaching the 1st Airborne Division before its position north of the Rhine became untenable. (© *IWM, EA 44531*)

19. German Polizei (police) troops manning foxholes in sparsely wooded terrain in the Arnhem sector in September 1944. *Heeresgruppe B* relied heavily upon security and rear-area troops such as this to supplement its depleted front-line forces in the Market Garden campaign. The commonality of basic combat doctrine and training among the various branches of the German forces involved in the fighting proved a major factor in enabling German commanders to rapidly assemble an effective response to the Allied landings. (© *IWM, MH 3956*)

20. A Panzer III *Ausführung* (Version) G from *Kompanie* Mielke of *Kampfgruppe* Knaust, knocked out by British anti-tank fire on the so-called *Betuwe* ('Island') between the Waal and Nederrhin rivers and being examined by British soldiers passing through the battlefield sometime in early 1945. This particular model of the Panzer III (armed with a short-barrelled 5cm gun and with much lighter armour than later models) had been essentially obsolete since as early as 1943, and had been gradually phased out of front-line service. However, the crisis that had developed on the Western Front following the German defeat in France led to the mobilization of virtually any man or vehicle that could fight. *Kompanie* Mielke was formed from a training unit at Bielefeld, Germany just prior to the Arnhem fighting and was thus armed with eight of the outdated and worn-out Panzer III and IV tanks used to train newly recruited crews. Despite their obsolescence and limited numbers, this handful of tanks had a disproportionate impact on the fighting, playing a significant role in the destruction of Lieutenant Colonel John Frost's small force at the Arnhem Bridge before joining the prolonged fighting on the *Betuwe* against the forces of XXX Corps and the 1st Independent Polish Parachute Brigade. In the face of the heavier anti-tank firepower wielded by XXX Corps this elderly tank's relatively thin armour (by the standards of late 1944) clearly proved to be a fatal liability, as is shown by the two clearly visible penetrations – one in the centre of its bow plates and the other just above the driver's visor.

or General Horrocks of XXX Corps even considered simply taking their chances and pressing on after the wreckage from the initial ambush was cleared from the road, trusting in speed and shock effect to see them through any remaining resistance (which was, in fact, minimal after the initial ambush positions had been eliminated). This was not a matter of cowardice or exhaustion in the face of heavy losses – the casualties of the two engaged battalions were in fact relatively light, with the 3rd Irish Guards only adding another seven dead and nineteen wounded to the 2nd's nine destroyed tanks, eight dead, and a handful of wounded – but rather the fact that this was simply the way that the British Army of 1944 did things, seeking to completely overwhelm even the lightest resistance with firepower and then pausing to rest, regroup, and plan anew in the wake of a day's fighting.[57] Lieutenant John Gorman of the 2nd Irish Guards later noted, with no small amount of chagrin, that the Guards Division's decision to halt for the night after such limited progress was more a matter of ingrained practice than a conscious decision: 'habit seemed to dictate that one slept at night and worked by day'.[58] For his part, General Horrocks expressed complete satisfaction with the day's events, seeing the breakthrough attack as 'a classic example of perfect co-operation between the R.A.F. and the Army', and stating that 17 September had 'ended happily'.[59] In a similar vein, XXX Corps' Intelligence Summary for the day suggested a complete lack of concern for the delays, simply assuming that the worst was now behind them and that it would likely be a simple matter to press on and link up with the airborne the next day: 'In spite of the fact that the whole German Army in the Netherlands will be in a state of alarm, it is reasonable to hope that this evening's breakthrough will not have been sealed off by tomorrow, and that only minor opposition should prevent our columns pushing on to the airborne bridgeheads.'[60]

It is also worth noting that the Guards Armoured Division was well known for the conservative and ponderous nature of its battle tactics, even by the general standards of the British Army, with its efforts in Normandy having generally been characterized by prolonged preparations for each stage of an attack, and slow, deliberate advances against even light opposition; it was hardly a reasonable prospect to expect such a force to completely alter its entire way of waging war overnight, purely because it was ordered to do so.[61] However, it is far from clear whether any other

British division would have performed much better in the leading role for Market Garden, given the nature of the British Army's overall doctrine and training in late 1944.

This cautious, stop and start progress by XXX Corps continued throughout the campaign; when faced with virtually any degree of resistance, the Guards Division more often than not chose to halt and prepare a fully supported set-piece attack to overwhelm the defenders. Early on 18 September around the town of Aalst, for example, the Guards Division, having just resumed its advance from the previous day, encountered a German roadblock based around four 88mm dual-purpose (anti-aircraft and anti-tank) guns and a couple of self-propelled anti-tank guns. Despite the limited nature of this resistance, to which it is not clear if the Guards even lost any tanks, the Irish Guards' leading tank squadron chose to hang back and engage these guns in a prolonged and indecisive long-range firefight from cover while they waited for artillery and air support. In the end, it was after 1730 when the Guards Armoured Division finally resumed its advance, nearly 10 hours after the engagement began at 1000, after a German prisoner came in stating that the flak crews had just been ordered to abandon their immobile guns and withdraw. This prolonged delay meant that it was dusk before the division had linked up with the 101st Airborne Division at Eindhoven, with it then proceeding to Son to begin replacing the blown bridge. The Guards' cautious set-piece tactics ensured that a small German rearguard had been able to prevent nearly half a day's worth of potential progress towards Arnhem, putting the operation even further behind schedule.[62]

Perhaps the best-known act of delay on the part of XXX Corps during Market Garden came in the wake of the capture of the Nijmegen bridges in the afternoon and evening of 20 September by the combined efforts of the Guards and the 82nd Airborne Division. Here, the leading elements of the Guards Division had successfully stormed across the road bridge in the wake of a daring assault crossing of the Waal River by elements of the 3rd Battalion of the American 504th Parachute Infantry Regiment that had captured the far end of both bridges and overwhelmed most of the German defenders. In the wake of this considerable achievement, however, the British guardsmen failed to heed the increasingly heated entreaties of the exhausted American paratroops to take advantage of their shock assault to rush on through the night to Arnhem before the Germans could recover and reform their lines. Instead the Guards – rather predictably in light of their actions so far – chose to consolidate in the bridgehead they had gained, regroup, and prepare for a full-scale attack the next day.[63] This was in fact a not entirely unreasonable precaution, given the unknown state of German defences on the 'Island' between the Waal and the Lower Rhine. Though *Brigadeführer* Harmel of the 10. *SS-Panzer Division*, who had commanded the unsuccessful defence of the Nijmegen bridges from a bunker near the town of Lent on the northern bank of the Waal, later noted that there was almost nothing in the way of German forces between XXX Corps and Arnhem on the evening of 20 September, the British naturally had no knowledge of this, and every reason to expect trouble in the wake of the unexpected resistance that Allied forces had encountered all across the Market Garden battle zone so far. It is thus quite understandable that the British wanted to ensure they were well-prepared for whatever lay ahead.[64] Moreover, the Irish Guards Group (comprising the 2nd (Armoured) and 3rd Irish Guards) that had advanced into the bridgehead had only limited infantry strength and badly depleted stocks of ammunition. Though the 3rd Irish Guards (the Group's infantry component) had suffered relatively limited casualties to date in the Market Garden fighting, they had still not replaced the heavy losses they had suffered in France and the subsequent pursuit to the Dutch border; just prior to Market Garden, the battalion had been forced to disband one of its four companies to maintain the other three at even a bare minimum of effective fighting strength.[65] The tanks of the 2nd (Armoured) Irish Guards, in turn, had expended the bulk of their stocks of high-explosive and smoke ammunition for their 75mm and 17-pounder main guns while supporting the 3/504th's assault crossings with their fire earlier in the day.[66] Though they certainly could have tried to proceed, relying upon speed, shock, and what little ammunition they had left to get through – and may well have succeeded, given the gap that the Waal crossing had torn in the German lines – it was hardly a normal British practice to take such a degree of risk with their troops' lives by sending them into an unknown situation in such a poorly prepared and exhausted state. As stated above, British doctrine and experience to date meant that they generally preferred to 'play it safe' rather than take risks in pursuit of greater potential gains, a generally sound practice in the right wider context, but one entirely incompatible with an operation predicated upon speed.

Moreover, Horrock's memoirs suggest that, as after the initial breakthrough on 17 September, he believed that his corps had accomplished more than enough for a single day's fighting, having played a very creditable part in getting over the Waal, and had thus earned a brief respite before resuming their efforts the next day, a sentiment entirely consistent with British doctrine's views on the importance of conducting battles in carefully controlled and limited stages to avoid overextension – once again, though still well short of the final objective, the commander of the XXX Corps recalled that he 'went to bed a happy man'.[67] Thus, when Horrocks later responded to criticisms, particularly by General Urquhart, that he and his troops had shown very little sense of urgency or drive on the road to Arnhem by stating that 'the sense of desperate urgency was there all right', and that 'it was not for want of trying that we failed to arrive in time', it seems likely that he was being entirely sincere; certainly his troops did not move as fast as *other* troops could or might have under the circumstances, but they perhaps did advance as quickly as *they* could, given the limitations of their doctrine, training, and experience.[68] Put simply, this was what 'urgency' looked like for the British Army in 1944; a steady advance, but still one cautiously made, broken into manageable stages, and backed by careful planning and preparation and a maximum of fire support at every step of the way. In the end, the Guards Armoured Division – only partially due to their own unique faults – was just not well suited to the demands that Montgomery placed upon it for Operation Market Garden, and few other British formations in autumn 1944 would have done substantially better under the circumstances. Montgomery, who was ordinarily so conscious and accommodating of the limitations of his forces in his planning, should have been far better aware of such facts and accounted for them in making his plans for the push into Holland.

Chapter 6

No Mere Matter of Marching: The Role of British Tactical and Command Doctrine in Operation Market

The Airborne Elite?: Doctrine and Training in the 1st Airborne Division

The limitations of British doctrine and training also played a significant part in the struggles of the 1st Airborne Division at Arnhem. While most historical accounts of the famous 'Red Devils' of the British airborne forces describe them as an elite force, and one of the British Army's best trained and most effective units, there is considerable reason to believe that the general flaws and limitations of British doctrine and training applied almost as much to them as it did to their ground-bound comrades.[1] As with most airborne forces, British paratroops undoubtedly went through a longer and more intensive training regime than most 'conventional' British troops. The evidence suggests, however, that the majority of that extra training was centred either around the actual act of parachuting from aircraft, or around the development of individual skills such as marksmanship, fieldcraft, or physical fitness; there is very little evidence that British airborne troops received an unusual level or quality of tactical training at either the small- or large-unit scale.[2] The War Diary of the 1st Parachute Battalion for the month of August 1944, for example, lists only a few days of combat exercises or 'company training', but the bulk of 'normal training', carried out on most days, seems to have consisted of PT (physical training) and route marches; the records of the 2nd Parachute Battalion for the same period are quite similar.[3] Though such training was certainly necessary to ensure the high level of physical conditioning that was so critical to the effectiveness of paratroopers (who, lacking the extensive array of motor vehicles available to conventional divisions, largely relied upon their own marching speed and endurance for mobility after their initial landings), it would not on its own be enough to ensure their effectiveness in combat.

Moreover, the few exercises the airborne troops did conduct seem to have been more formal 'parade ground' manoeuvres than realistic tactical training. Exercise 'Golden Miller', conducted by the 4th Parachute Brigade's 156th Parachute Battalion on 31 August 1944, focused on practising transitions between the various textbook battalion formations, with a note emphasizing the importance of maintaining 'proper spacing' between the companies.[4] As with most other British soldiers, the inculcation of proper discipline and obedience occupied a disproportionate part of their training efforts, including practising close-order marching drill and other skills with little or no practical field application for airborne troops.[5] It is worth noting that General Browning, the effective founder of the British airborne arm and the 1st Airborne Division's commanding officer from its establishment in late 1941 to March 1943 (and thus the primary architect of its training regime), was a former member of the Grenadier Guards with a strong penchant for the Guards' traditional drill and discipline-centric training standards and a marked aversion to allowing too much freedom to his troops. Two training pamphlets he wrote for the division emphasized the importance not only of discipline, which he called 'the only road to victory', but also of proper turn out, saluting, and 'soldierly bearing'.[6] A fair proportion of the officers and men of the 1st Airborne Division were also volunteers from the Brigade of Guards, a corps well known for its discipline and toughness, but hardly for quick independent thinking or tactical innovation.[7] Overall, there is very little evidence that the standard, and fairly limited, British infantry doctrine or training was heavily modified to suit the unique requirements and challenges that airborne troops would inevitably face, particularly the relative paucity of centralized control or fire support that could be provided to their often scattered operations deep behind enemy lines. The only major advantage in training or tactics that British paratroops seem to have enjoyed over British regular infantry (beyond their superior physical conditioning – which was, to be certain, a significant advantage) was the fact that, as a new and highly prestigious special purpose force, which recruited mainly through men volunteering from other units, they tended to attract a considerable share of the most active, energetic, and aggressive officers and men within the British Army.[8] In the end, British airborne training can be said to have produced superb individual warriors, but failed to effectively provide them with the knowledge and skills necessary to combine their talents for maximum effect within combat units in the field.

General Urquhart himself later lamented that his division's training did not seem to have done enough to develop a suitable sense of initiative among its junior officers and NCOs, which proved to be a considerable hindrance at Arnhem.[9] Moreover, Urquhart himself could hardly claim any sort of specialized tactical command training or preparatory experience for the unique conditions of airborne combat. He had taken command of the 1st Airborne Division in January 1944, having previously commanded the 231st Independent Infantry Brigade in the invasions of Sicily and Italy, but without any previous airborne experience or training. He later commented in his memoirs that he saw no real distinction between the tactics required for airborne operations and those of standard 'foot' infantry combat, with the only difference being the means by which they arrived on the battlefield.[10] Moreover, the very fact that Urquhart was appointed to the command of this division, in lieu of any candidate with useful experience in airborne combat, or even theory (though admittedly there were relative few of these in 1944), suggests that the British leadership saw airborne divisions much the same way he did, as infantry divisions that just happened to ride into battle in aircraft, rather than trucks. Given that British airborne divisions had less manpower and considerably less firepower than a standard infantry division (about which more shall be said in the next chapter), this was clearly a flawed assumption.

The limitations of the 1st Airborne Division's training were further exacerbated by their relative lack of combat experience, which might well have 'smoothed out' some of the rough edges in their training and honed their tactical skills and the command abilities of their officers. Prior to Market Garden, the division had never operated as a single unit. At the battalion level, the division would appear to have been a well-seasoned one, with only one of the division's nine infantry battalions not having seen any combat prior to Market Garden – the 7th King's Own Scottish Borderers, which had only been converted to the air landing role at the beginning of 1944, after a prolonged stint of quiet garrison duties in Britain. However, though some of the division's battalions, particularly those of the 1st Parachute Brigade, had been in service since as early as 1941 and several had seen intense, if relatively brief, action in the

Mediterranean where they operated as independent battalions or brigades, its overall percentage of experienced troops at the time of Market Garden was fairly low. Most of the units that had fought in North Africa, Sicily, and Italy had suffered significant casualties which had since been replaced by fresh recruits. Moreover, as the airborne arm eventually expanded to a size of two divisions (the 1st and the 6th) and one independent brigade (the 2nd), the surviving core of veterans was diffused to form cadres for the new units, ensuring that they were fairly thinly spread by September 1944; Middlebrook estimates that perhaps only about half of the troops that landed during Market Garden had ever seen battle before, and some of these only very brief and low-intensity combat in the invasion of Italy.[11]

In addition, even the unit's veterans had not been in combat for nearly a year prior to Market Garden, as the division had been held in reserve in England throughout the Normandy fighting; this ensured not only that the experienced men's skills would have become a bit rusty in disuse, but also that they would not have been personally familiar with the many developments in weaponry and tactics that had taken place since 1943.[12] With the Normandy fighting having just concluded, there would have been very little time for the lessons learned by the troops that had fought there, including their counterparts in the 6th Airborne Division, to have been recorded and promulgated to the forces still at home. Furthermore, the fact that the division had been kept nearly constantly on standby for possible operations through much of July, August, and early September 1944 had limited the time available to the units of the 1st Airborne Division to conduct proper training.[13] Thus, despite its 'official' elite status, in September 1944 the 1st Airborne Division was a force largely new to combat and unfamiliar with the unique pressures and demands that would be placed upon an airborne division. Though the combination of experienced veterans and keen recruits may well have been welded into a very effective whole given time and experience, the sudden shock entry into combat of the Market Garden landings denied them this.

British Doctrine in Operation Market Garden – Case Study Two – 1st Airborne Division on the Offensive, 17–19 September 1944

In the event, the limitations of the overly centralized and relatively inflexible British combat doctrine, which provided little scope for the exercise of initiative or independent action, and of the 1st Airborne Division's training and experience, quickly became readily apparent during Operation Market Garden. In keeping with British command doctrine, the plan for Operation Market (Market Garden's airborne component) laid out instructions for the airborne forces, and particularly those of the 1st Airborne Division in detail, with march routes, timetables and combat sectors allocated to every sub-unit, governing all of their actions.[14] Perhaps the most defining characteristic of the tasks assigned to the 1st Airborne Division at Arnhem, in particular, was that they were almost entirely predicated around the virtual absence of German resistance of any significant scale to the division's landings and initial movements, in light of the aforementioned intelligence indications and favourable speculations about the virtual 'void' of German forces supposed to exist behind the line of the Meuse–Escaut Canal. This expectation was the main reason that General Urquhart and the other 1st Airborne commanders had accepted, if somewhat reluctantly, the later highly controversial air plan that landed the division 7 to 8 miles from its bridge objectives and in two separate waves (with a third bringing in the attached 1st Independent Polish Parachute Brigade). This plan called for only the 1st Parachute Brigade to go on the offensive towards Arnhem on the first day (as the 1st Airlanding Brigade was required to hold the landing zones for the arrival of the 4th Parachute Brigade the next day). In light of the expected lack of immediate German resistance, the 1st Parachute Brigade was instructed to more or less simply march as quickly as they could to reach Arnhem and establish defensive positions around the bridge, with virtually no indication that any notable fighting was expected en route; the 4th Parachute Brigade and the 1st Airlanding Brigade were to join them in forming a perimeter around the city on 18 September, to be further joined by the Poles on the 19th.[15]

The more detailed combat instructions for each of the division's sub-units were focused almost exclusively upon the defensive positions and areas of responsibility that each unit was expected to take up within the defensive bridgehead that would be formed around Arnhem once the bridges had been secured. In essence, it was clearly expected that the battle proper would only commence once the Germans sent in reinforcements to attack the divisional perimeter around the city, at a point when the division would be able to take advantage of a fortified position and the full concentrated and coordinated weight of its infantry and artillery forces to hold off the incoming attacks.[16] The plans effectively offered no viable contingencies for what the units of the division were expected to do should they encounter significant resistance en route to Arnhem. Though the air plan would later draw considerable criticism from both participants and historians, the officers of the 1st Airborne Division generally seem to have accepted it without much argument at the time. Only Major General Stanislaw Sosabowski, commander of the Polish Brigade, openly expressed his objections to the plan's failure to account for possible German countermeasures and his fellow commanders do not seem to have paid them much heed.[17]

Thus, Brigadier Gerald Lathbury's plan for his 1st Parachute Brigade on 17 September was more one for a route march to an assembly point than for an assault on an enemy held town, emphasizing speed over all else. To maximize this speed, Lathbury divided his three battalions (the 1st, 2nd, and 3rd Parachute Battalions) between the three main roads leading from the division's landing zones west of Arnhem into the city proper, designated, from north to south, 'Leopard', 'Tiger', and 'Lion' routes.[18] This disposition of the brigade left its three battalions too far separated from one another to provide effective support should any encounter significant resistance and, even more critically, left Lathbury without any significant force in reserve to deal with any unexpected developments.[19] Though the 1st Parachute Battalion was ordered to briefly act as a de facto brigade reserve at the outset of the operation, being held at the landing zones until the other two battalions were well on their way, it was released to its own mission within half an hour.[20] According to 1st Airborne Division veteran Geoffrey Powell, Lathbury himself later saw this failure to maintain an effective tactical reserve as one of his greatest errors on the first day of the battle.[21] Though Lathbury can certainly be justly criticized for what turned out to be a badly flawed plan, it was entirely in keeping with the information and instructions he had been given by his superiors and, given the nature of British command doctrine and training, it is hardly surprising that he made every effort to follow them to the letter.

When the 1st Parachute Brigade encountered the defensive lines of Krafft's *SS-Panzergrenadier Ausbildungs und Ersatz Battalion 16*, and later *Kampfgruppe* Spindler, Lathbury's plans, all too true to Moltke's famous adage about no plan ever surviving contact with the enemy, fell apart almost immediately. As each of the battalions along the two northern routes (with the 1st Parachute Battalion on Leopard and the 3rd on Tiger) came under heavy fire from the German defenders from about 1630, as well as numerous small-scale counterattacks, their orderly advance into Arnhem quickly degenerated into a messy series of scattered skirmishes in the woods and suburbs along the western outskirts of the city. Unable to support one another or to call upon any aid from the rear, each battalion was left to deal with whatever resistance was in front of them with their own fire and manoeuvre. Furthermore, though German accounts frequently noted the paratroops' determination and skill in marksmanship, here and throughout the rest of battle, the ability of the two battalions' field officers to manoeuvre their units tactically seems to have been limited.[22]

The war diaries of the battalions of the 1st Parachute Brigade and other records make it clear that the standard response whenever a pocket of resistance was encountered on their advance into Arnhem was for the leading company to deploy and engage the enemy, while the remainder of the battalion column sought to divert around the firefight and then continue along the route to the bridges; orders issued by the 2nd Parachute Battalion specifically stated that any resistance en route was simply to be bypassed in the interest of speed – clearly expecting to encounter only small outposts or patrols – and similar orders were issued to that battalion's brigade mates, explaining their conduct in this phase of the battle.[23] By nightfall on 17 September, for example, two of 1st Parachute Battalion's three rifle companies had already been drawn into prolonged and costly firefights at different points along the route, from which they were only able to extricate themselves under the cover of darkness.[24] Though the 1st and 3rd Parachute Battalions' commitment to their original mission was in some ways an admirable display of discipline and focus, and may well have been effective had events matched initial expectations, in the face of the widespread and deep German resistance its end result was to leave the strength of each battalion dispersed across the battlefield, leaving their commanders with little ability to coordinate, concentrate, or even control their efforts; Lathbury thus summed up the situation at nightfall on 17 September by simply noting: 'it was as this point that I realized I was losing control of the situation'.[25]

The advance thus degenerated into a confused 'stop-start' series of clashes along the roads, as each battalion was repeatedly brought to a halt as they ran into new pockets of German resistance and tried to manoeuvre around them. As Private Walter Boldock of the 1st Parachute Battalion later observed: 'We halted, then we started off again. Then we halted and dug in. Next, we moved on again, changing direction.' With each separate battalion possessing only limited offensive tactical capabilities of their own, and with no other free forces left to throw into the fray, Lathbury's lightly equipped and supported troops had no effective options for dealing with the German blocking lines beyond trying to outflank them via manoeuvre. The 1st and 3rd Parachute Battalions, however, quickly found themselves confronted by an almost continuous series of successive lines thrown across their paths, with virtually every flanking manoeuvre or hard-won penetration of the German line simply running into new German positions. In one extreme example, noted in an after action report compiled from the accounts of 1st Parachute Brigade survivors, the 3rd Parachute Battalion, having largely gone to ground in the face of heavy resistance at about 1600 on 17 September, dispatched its C Company at about 1800 to try to find a way around the German position using the cover of a nearby railway embankment. Though the company apparently succeeded in getting around that initial position, they quickly fell victim to the 'hornet's nest' developing around Arnhem; though a handful of men from the company eventually managed to infiltrate through the town and reach the 2nd Parachute Battalion's positions at the bridge, the remainder simply vanished – likely killed or taken prisoner as they manoeuvred right into the rapidly deploying forces of *Kampfgruppe* Spindler.[26] As manoeuvre became increasingly futile, each battalion simply got further and further bogged down in a costly series of frontal assaults against steadily strengthening German defences, ensuring that they made only limited progress prior to their decisive defeat on the morning of 19 September.[27] Only the 2nd Parachute Battalion, which, as mentioned previously, had fortuitously managed to avoid the German defensive line, was able to achieve its original objectives and reach the bridge.[28]

Overall, it is quite clear that the 1st Parachute Brigade's training and tactical doctrine left its units unprepared for this sort of confused, close-range, small-unit fighting, even though such fighting had been a common characteristic of most airborne operations to date; right from the very start, each battalion rapidly fragmented in the course of their efforts to employ fire and manoeuvre tactics, quickly rendering them combat ineffective. Moreover, the doctrine of central control almost entirely failed the brigade as Lathbury, even though he kept close behind the front lines, quickly lost control of any troops beyond his immediate vicinity in the prevailing confusion – a situation that was not helped by the fact that the bulk of his Brigade HQ personnel had continued along Lion Route with Lieutenant Colonel Frost's force to the Arnhem bridge when Lathbury had departed to 'briefly' inspect 3rd Parachute Battalion's progress early in the advance. Lathbury's isolation was such that he remained largely unaware of the scale of the resistance the 1st Parachute Battalion (he remained mainly with the 3rd on Tiger route during 17 September) was facing until a report got through to him early on 18 September.[29]

This rapid breakdown of the 1st Parachute Brigade under fire was only exacerbated by the general inexperience of its troops, as the largely green soldiers, increasingly deprived of the direct supervision and direction of their officers as the fighting in the close wooded and suburban terrain became increasingly confused, began to shy away from the fire that they faced, often choosing to simply take cover, returning the occasional snap shot, while waiting upon further developments, rather than taking any initiative to try to overcome the resistance themselves.[30] Urquhart later commented upon this tendency among his troops, stating that they generally proved quite 'sticky' in the advance, frequently diving for cover even in the face of just minimal fire and requiring much effort by officers – including himself – to get them up and moving again, and argued that there was a need for much better and more realistic pre-battle training in the future to properly acclimatise fresh troops to the confusing conditions of the battlefield.[31]

Clearly the failure of the British Army to develop a greater sense of initiative and tactical skill among its troops and junior officers was a considerable detriment to the planned rush to Arnhem. With the airborne troops so often falling out of the control of higher authorities, they generally tended to either devolve into a confused mass, or take cover, stay put and wait for orders and/or help – a clear contrast to the tendency of German troops to take the offensive – or at least to do *something* – whenever possible in an uncertain situation. The doctrine of central control ensured that confusion or inaction were effectively the British Army's 'default setting' in the absence of specific direction, even in their supposedly elite parachute units. Though the paratroops fought hard in these initial clashes, the failings of their doctrine ensured that their sacrifices counted for little in achieving their goals. Without an effective battle plan, or the capacity to improvise such on the fly, the 1st Airborne Division frittered away much of its fighting strength in fruitless efforts to batter a path through the German defences around Arnhem on 17 September.

The confusion and fragmentation that plagued the 1st Airborne Division at Arnhem was exacerbated still further by the fact that the division's radio communications network – which would clearly have been vital to any plan relying upon centralized control – broke down almost entirely right at the outset of the operation. The breakdown of the 1st Airborne Division's radio communications is one of the better known failures of the operation, being prominently featured in the 1977 film version of Cornelius Ryan's *A Bridge Too Far*, and has been the subject of extensive discussion by several historians, often being cited as one of the most significant factors in the division's defeat. The breakdown, which occurred due to a combination of unsuitable equipment and flawed networking procedures (the full technical details of which have been covered in some of the other works cited here, particularly that by John Greenacre, and thus will not be discussed further), was certainly a significant factor in the division's ill fortunes, but a major part of the reason it had such a crippling effect upon the division's ability to operate effectively was the fact that British doctrine relied so heavily upon centralized control.[32]

Though 1st Airborne Division's divisional communications network was rapidly set up and established soon after landing, the 1st Parachute Brigade's march towards Arnhem quickly took them beyond the limited range of the Division HQ's sets on the landing zones, ensuring that Urquhart had entirely lost contact with his forward units within an hour of them setting off.[33] In light of this breakdown, and again in full alignment with British command doctrine, which encouraged generals to keep very close supervision over their subordinates, Urquhart quickly proved unable and/or unwilling to fully trust his subordinates' ability to carry out their missions without further direction, and thus set out from his HQ in a radio-equipped jeep to try to make contact in person with Lathbury and his battalion commanders, to ensure matters were proceeding smoothly and, more usefully, to assess the overall situation at the front for himself.[34] It is worth noting that Urquhart himself stated in his memoirs that the main message that he sought to carry forward to his subordinates was to 'advance as quickly as possible to Arnhem' in light of the reported failure of the 1st Airborne Reconnaissance Squadron's *coup de main* effort – a course of action that was already clearly emphasized in the operation's orders, and which any competent officer could reasonably be expected to already be carrying out if they had read those orders.[35] All the difficulties that followed were thus the result of Urquhart's desire – justified or not – to 'double check' that his subordinates were following the relatively simple orders they had already been given. Urquhart's inspection tour quickly devolved into a mixture of comic-opera and disaster, however, as, though he soon managed to meet up with Lathbury on Tiger route, he and the brigadier quickly became caught up in the 3rd Parachute Battalion's battle with Krafft and Spindler's troops.[36] Though their presence proved, at best, superfluous to the 3rd Battalion's fight (with both Harvey and Middlebrook suggesting that the presence of the two senior officers offering their own advice and opinions on the battalion's fight was likely a source of considerable distraction and irritation for the 3rd's Lieutenant Colonel John Fitch), it further ensured that both the 1st Parachute Brigade and the 1st Airborne Division as a whole remained almost entirely bereft of the central direction that British units so depended upon – a situation that was only exacerbated when Urquhart's jeep was hit by a mortar round, leaving him without any means of contacting his own headquarters back at the landing zones.[37] The radio breakdown, and Urquhart's determined but somewhat ill-considered response to it, thus ensured his division was effectively left headless through the entirety of the critical period of fighting on 17 September, contributing to the rather spasmodic, uncoordinated and directionless nature of the division's battle.

As bad as this initial disruption was to the overall plan – dependent as this was on the surprise effect of the initial rush to the bridges – matters of command only got worse for the 1st Airborne Division. Early on 18 September, as the fighting seesawed back and forth along Tiger route, Urquhart and Lathbury soon found themselves cut off by a German counterattack, with Lathbury being seriously wounded and left with a

Dutch family to be captured a few days later, while Urquhart was forced to hide out in the attic of a house for nearly 24 hours, keeping him away from his HQ at a critical juncture in his division's battle.[38] With the arrival of the division's second airlift on the afternoon of 18 September, bringing in the three fresh battalions of the 4th Parachute Brigade, along with two stray companies from the 1st Airlanding Brigade, the 1st Airborne's Division suddenly had available not only those newly arrived forces, but also the two battalions of the 1st Airlanding Brigade freed up from their defensive duties at the landing zones (as stated previously, the 1st Borders remained in position on the western perimeter). As such, even with the 7/KOSB needing to devote at least a portion of its forces to securing further landing zones near Johannahoeve Farm for the Polish Brigade's glider landings on 19 September, the division now had at its disposal a potentially powerful reserve force of more than four fresh infantry battalions with which to try to rescue its failing battle plan.

Brigadier Philip Hicks of the 1st Airlanding Brigade, who had assumed command of the 1st Airborne Division in light of Urquhart's absence and feared death, and who had been receiving a steady flow of fragmentary reports on the continuing struggle on the outskirts of Arnhem, soon dispatched the 2nd Battalion, The South Staffordshire Regiment (2/South Staffs) from his own brigade, as well as the 11th Parachute Battalion from 4th Parachute Brigade, to proceed to Arnhem to link up with the 1st Parachute Brigade and try to make a renewed effort to push through to the 2nd Battalion force at the bridge.[39] However, Brigadier John Hackett of the 4th Parachute Brigade, who apparently resented Hick's 'dragooning' of one of his battalions, as well as the fact that Hicks had been designated by Urquhart as third in the division's line of succession (after the also missing Lathbury), despite Hackett's seniority to him in the rank of brigadier, dispatched the 11th Parachute Battalion as ordered, but effectively refused to allow the rest of his brigade to be sent into the growing fight on the edge of Arnhem, suggesting that Hicks had allowed the battle there to become 'grossly untidy'.[40] Instead, Hackett chose to all but ignore the growing crisis in the effort to get a sizeable force through to Arnhem bridge and instead decided to stick to the objectives assigned to his division in the original operational plan, which was to support the defence of Arnhem by the 1st Parachute and 1st Airlanding Brigades by securing high ground to north of Arnhem which commanded the main road into the city, along which any German reinforcements were expected to arrive.[41] Hicks, uncertain in his new command responsibilities and apparently unwilling to assert his authority over the often volatile Hackett, chose simply to acquiesce in Hackett's decision.[42] Thus, Hackett sent his two remaining battalions, the 10th and the 156th Parachute (later joined by the 7/KOSB, which Hicks transferred from the 1st Airlanding Brigade in exchange for the 11th Parachute Battalion at Hackett's insistence), well to the north of the main battle, trying once again to proceed down the 'Leopard' route that the 1st Airborne Reconnaissance Squadron and the 1st Parachute Battalion had found blocked by Krafft and Spindler the day before, thus diverting the majority of the available reserve force to an objective of minimal importance in light of the current situation.[43] Though one could certainly argue that Hackett had some justification in seeking out a new line of approach towards Arnhem, rather than reinforcing the previous failures along the central route, such dispersal of the 1st Airborne Division's relatively limited strength and firepower seems, to this author at least, ill-advised under the circumstances. Unsurprisingly, the 4th Parachute Brigade's initial probing attacks on the evening of 18 September were swiftly brought to a halt by *Kampfgruppe* Spindler's now reinforced blocking line, and a further attack on 19 September saw the 4th Brigade effectively shattered in an abortive assault on the German defences – now backed by light armour and flak guns – and by the subsequent retreat and close German pursuit back to the landing zones.[44]

At about the same time, the reinforcements sent by Hicks joined up with the depleted battalions of the 1st Parachute Brigade on the western outskirts of Arnhem. In the absence of any central plan for coordination beyond a hasty meeting between the battalion commanders early on the morning of 19 September and with two of the four battalions fresh off forced marches through the night and entering an unfamiliar situation, the subsequent attack quickly broke down into a series of uncoordinated and futile frontal assaults on the German forces dug into the buildings along the north–south streets and along high ground to the north. This attack was the 1st Airborne Division's last and largest offensive thrust towards Arnhem, with elements of four battalions taking part, but they swiftly found themselves under fire from three sides – from the heights of a railway embankment to the north and from a German-occupied factory complex across the Lower Rhine to the south, as well as from the front. With no clear commander for the overall force, the battalions proved entirely unable to coordinate their efforts or support one another. Like the 4th Parachute Brigade, these battalions, attacking largely on their own and in succession, without effective cooperation or support, were rapidly shredded by intense German fire. Suffering massive casualties and quickly being driven to cover in nearby buildings, they were subsequently routed by German counterattacks, with only a relatively few exhausted survivors reaching the main divisional area at Oosterbeek by nightfall.[45] The level of disorganization and confusion in this attack was such that the forces of *Kampfgruppe* Spindler that faced it believed it was no more than a widespread effort to infiltrate patrols into their lines, rather than a serious attack.[46]

These attacks were the last offensive actions on any scale to be undertaken by the 1st Airborne Division at Arnhem; with both the 1st and 4th Parachute Brigades, and much of the 1st Airlanding Brigade, effectively destroyed as coherent fighting units, the remnants of the division were henceforth reduced to clinging to a steadily shrinking perimeter around Oosterbeek and trying merely to survive long enough to be relieved (or evacuated, as it turned out).[47] Though General Urquhart had managed to escape from his 'imprisonment' in Arnhem, and reached the Divisional HQ just before the main attack went in, his efforts to first send a senior officer to oversee and coordinate the attack (Colonel Hilary Barlow, deputy commander of the 1st Airlanding Brigade, who never arrived, and was never seen alive again), and later to call it off, came too late to either save the four battalions on the edge of Arnhem, or further their effort to reach the 2nd Battalion's force at the bridge, which in turn succumbed to repeated German attacks on 20 September.[48]

Thus, it was not simply the failure of the 1st Airborne Division's communications network and Urquhart's prolonged absence from his headquarters that doomed the division's offensive efforts in the operation's crucial early days, but the fact that its various sub-units proved unable to operate effectively without constant supervision and instruction. Without any firm central coordination, the division was never able to effectively coordinate an effective multi-battalion attack at a single time and place. Though seven of the division's nine battalions staged determined attacks on 19 September, they did so largely as independent units, attacking mostly in succession and against separate sections of the German lines, failing to effectively support one another or concentrate their strength at any single point. Moreover, Urquhart's absence from his HQ on 18 September effectively wasted perhaps the best opportunity the division had to muster a sizeable force to make a concerted assault into Arnhem in the wake of the initial setback of 17 September and showed that his brigadiers (generally considered talented officers by most, at least in other circumstances) lacked the sense of initiative and tactical judgement necessary to modify a plan that was clearly failing to address the prevailing situation. Had Urquhart been present to assemble the five fresh battalions made available by the arrival of the second lift into a proper striking force (effectively a reinforced 4th Parachute Brigade), and sent them to the support of the 1st and 3rd Parachute Battalions still fighting in the town, the division might have had its only reasonable chance of breaching Spindler's line, reaching the 2nd Battalion at the bridge and possibly establishing the strong perimeter around the bridgehead that their entire battle plan was predicated upon. To paraphrase Benjamin Franklin's famous quote, the division's component units proved unable to 'hang together' without their divisional commander's direct guidance, and so were 'hanged separately', defeated in detail by a still fairly thin German defensive line.

The British Army's penchant for centralized control meant that, deprived of its commanding officer, the fighting capabilities of the 1st Airborne Division were effectively crippled throughout the critical phase of the operation. Though one can certainly find fault in the conduct of all four of the 1st Division's senior commanders at Arnhem, it is clear that the main source of their shortcomings and difficulties was the doctrine in which they had been trained, which designated operational, and even a large degree of tactical, command as the exclusive province of senior formation commanders, leaving the bulk of the more junior officers, NCOs, and men – those fighting at the 'sharp end' – without the training and skills they needed to fight their own battles without the closest supervision from above. Though such control could be maintained in standard set-piece battles, and often proved relatively effective there, it was entirely incompatible with the conditions inherent to an airborne operation – particularly one opposed by a foe so skilled in operating under those same conditions. In the face of unexpected resistance, the division's initial efforts quickly begin to peter out and fall into confusion as events diverged from the set plan – resulting in a 'creeping paralysis', as Ryan termed it, across the entire force.[49]

Overall, though the combat doctrine in use in the British Army of 1944, which was focused on centralized control, massed firepower, and carefully organized set-piece battles, had proven quite effective in Normandy, it was entirely unsuitable for the conditions and demands of Operation Market Garden. Montgomery's bold offensive plan required a level of speed, aggression, initiative, and flexibility that his forces simply had not been prepared for by either their training or their experience under his command. In seeking to exploit what he saw as a fleeting opportunity to win the war at a single stroke, Montgomery abandoned the cautious, meticulous fighting methods that had served him and his commands so well since El Alamein in favour of a hastily organized rush to the Rhine for which his troops proved ill-suited. Any success the operation might have achieved was entirely dependent upon the Germans not putting up any significant resistance – failing that, the forces of the 2nd Army and the 1st Allied Airborne Army found themselves in a confused, fast-moving battle at close quarters, where initiative among junior commanders and small-unit tactical training – two of the British Army's most significant weaknesses, and some of the Germans' greatest strengths – were at a premium. Though the units of these armies rose to this unfamiliar challenge as well as they could – as is clearly shown by how near they came to success in the end – and fought uniformly hard, if not always particularly well, they all too often found themselves at a critical disadvantage in the fighting that ensued. The resulting critical tactical failures or delays at key points completely disrupted a battle plan entirely dependent upon both great haste, and a near perfect rate of success in securing the vital objectives.

In the end, it was hardly a reasonable course of action for a commander to suddenly demand his forces completely alter the most basic aspects of the way in which they fought battles on the fly – particularly when those methods had proven so effective for them to date. Historian Stephen Hart has observed that Montgomery's ability to perceive, understand, and account for the limitations of his own forces – to grasp and plan for what was actually achievable in a practical sense – was typically one of his greatest strengths as a commander. In the case of Operation Market Garden, however, this skill apparently abandoned him, bringing about the only notable defeat of his career.[50]

Chapter 7

Little More than Guts and Bayonets: British Doctrine and the Role of Firepower in Operation Market Garden

As has already been touched upon in previous chapters, another central element of the combat doctrine employed by the 21st Army Group in North-West Europe was the deployment of overwhelming levels of firepower, particularly through massed artillery bombardment and air strikes, to overcome enemy resistance. This doctrine had spread across much of the British Army since the Battle of El Alamein in late 1942. By the summer of 1944, the British Army had carefully honed its ability to rapidly and accurately direct the efforts of its artillery and supporting tactical air forces onto hostile targets of all types in both attack and defence, giving them an unparalleled source of both destructive and suppressive combat power. Allied artillery and tactical airpower have often been credited by observers – both contemporary and since – as having been by far the most effective contributors to the Allied victory in France, playing the primary role in the steady attrition of German strength that eventually enabled the decisive breakout and the subsequent German rout.

However, despite their central role in the Normandy fighting, during Operation Market Garden the Allied forces proved almost entirely unable to bring these critical sources of firepower to bear effectively on their German opponents, leaving their infantry and armoured units to struggle on without the lavish level of support upon which they had long counted to help win their battles. Though the 21st Army Group still possessed most of the massive assemblage of artillery pieces that had blasted their way through Normandy, and was still ostensibly supported by the numerous Spitfire and Typhoon fighter-bombers of the 83rd Group of the RAF's 2nd Tactical Air Force, a combination of flawed planning and a doctrine for employing that firepower that proved poorly suited to the circumstances faced ensured that the Allied airborne forces and the 2nd Army entered Holland with their greatest weapons effectively blunted.

Firepower in British Army Doctrine: The World Wars

As with their tactical and command doctrine, the views of the British Army on the role and employment of firepower were shaped largely by their experience of the First World War. As previously stated, after several catastrophic experiences with massed and poorly supported infantry attacks in 1914–16, by the last years of the war, most British and Dominion offensive operations were first and foremost artillery operations. These operations centred around increasingly heavy and elaborate fire plans intended to destroy enemy strongpoints, suppress their defending troops, and allow the attacking infantry and tanks to advance onto their objectives with a minimum of casualties. This concept of warfare emphasizing the use of firepower, rather than the mass and raw numbers of infantry, became even more prominent among British military leaders in the interwar period, as they were increasingly unwilling to risk losses on the scale of the First World War in any future conflicts. As such, firepower increasingly came to be seen as the primary means by which battles should be won.[1]

Based upon this First World War experience, and their general views on the nature of command, British interwar doctrine also called for control of this firepower to be centralized as much as possible to maximize the ability of forces to concentrate and coordinate fire plans in support of their attacking elements.[2] Thus, the great bulk of the British Army's firepower in the 1930s and 1940s was concentrated in the field regiments of the Royal Artillery assigned to the various divisions, and in the assortment of field, medium, and heavy regiments placed under the control of corps and army headquarters; by the summer of 1944, about half of the total British artillery strength was concentrated in units controlled at the corps level or above.[3]

The infantry, on the other hand, was increasingly deemphasized as a source of effective firepower generation on the offensive within British interwar doctrine, being relegated almost solely to the role of conducting the final assault on an enemy position and the occupation of any captured ground.⁴ The winning of the firepower battle and the suppression of enemy defensive fire to enable that assault therefore became more and more the exclusive province of the artillery, with infantry relying on the cover of barrages, rather than their own fire and movement tactics, to reach enemy lines intact.⁵ Thus by the time the Second World War broke out, the British Army's deployment of firepower, in both theory and practice, was largely based around centrally controlled artillery fire.

The experience of the early years of the Second World War only intensified this tendency, as British tank and infantry units all too often found themselves outclassed by their generally better trained and equipped German opponents and thus relied upon their supporting artillery to make up the difference. From the famous '1,000-gun barrage' that heralded the beginning of the Battle of El Alamein onward, Field Marshal Montgomery and the British Army as a whole placed an ever-increasing reliance upon the steadily growing strength and proficiency of their artillery arm to make up for the continuing relative shortcomings of their infantry and armoured forces and win their battles.⁶ Throughout the remainder of the Mediterranean campaign Montgomery became increasingly focused on ensuring his attacks had a truly 'luxurious' level of artillery support, massing guns and stockpiling large quantities of ammunition prior to any significant offensive.⁷ This Mediterranean experience thus crystalized the leading role of artillery within British doctrine. This modified doctrine began to filter back into the doctrinal manuals and training regimes of the British Home Forces via the steady series of field reports sent home by the Mediterranean armies, ensuring that when Montgomery arrived in England in January 1944 to assume command of what would soon become the 21st Army Group, his efforts to fully standardize this artillery centric doctrine fell on a very receptive audience of officers and troops that had already begun training along those lines. It is this that the historian Stephen Hart, drawing upon a statement made by Montgomery, has aptly termed the 'Colossal Cracks' doctrine.⁸

The enthusiasm with which the 21st Army Group adopted the 'Colossal Cracks' doctrine was also driven by the fact that Montgomery and his fellow commanders were increasingly aware that Britain was facing a growing crisis of manpower after four-and-a-half years of war. By early 1944, virtually all able-bodied men in the country had been mobilized to either the fighting forces or critical industries and so, unlike the United States or the Soviet Union, almost no reserves of trained military manpower remained in Britain after Operation Overlord was launched in June.[9] The future supply of casualty replacements to the field forces would thus be largely limited to whatever new conscripts or volunteers came of age each year or, more drastically, from the cannibalization of existing formations to replace losses in others. The 21st Army Group was in fact forced to disband two of its combat divisions – the 59th and 50th Infantry Divisions – for this purpose by the end of 1944.[10] This critical shortage of manpower ensured a further degree of impetus for a battle doctrine that focused upon spending materiel rather than men; as Montgomery's chief intelligence officer, Brigadier Edgar 'Bill' Williams, put it, the British Army of 1944 preferred to 'let metal do it rather than flesh'.[11] A strategy centred around the expenditure of firepower rather than manpower also served a useful political purpose for the British government, in that it would limit any significant reduction of the forces that Britain was contributing to the conflict and thus maintain its degree of political influence over the establishment of the post-war order – something that was already declining in the face of the growing American dominance over the overall war effort in the West.[12]

As well as the growing effectiveness and prominence of the Royal Artillery, the North African campaign had also seen the tactical air forces of the RAF become an increasingly important source of additional firepower for the British ground forces. Upon his arrival in the Western Desert, Montgomery and his RAF counterparts in the Desert Air Force – particularly its commanding officer, Air Vice-Marshal Arthur Coningham – worked to develop a very close cooperative relationship, the 8th Army and DAF HQs almost invariably being set up in close proximity to one another, and all operational plans being prepared jointly by the two headquarters staffs.[13] Montgomery himself frequently expressed the view that the RAF was an integral and indispensable part of his operations in Africa and beyond, and further asserted that modern ground operations in general were entirely inseparable from the supporting efforts of air forces; an assertion that Hart argues has been largely proven in the decades since.[14] Thus, most 8th Army operations in North Africa, Sicily, and Italy from El Alamein onwards were characterized by a lavish scale of tactical air support, with fighter-bombers and medium bombers striking at both Axis front-line positions and lines of communications almost continuously and in large numbers in support of the ground battle.[15]

Perhaps most usefully for future operations, the 8th Army and the Desert Air Force worked out particularly effective systems of ground to air communications for directing close air support. They began using 'control cars' that operated with the leading troops on the ground, manned by specially trained RAF personnel – many of whom had served as pilots themselves – and used to communicate by radio directly with aircraft orbiting the battlefield at the ready in 'cab ranks', vectoring them directly onto specific targets with a much greater degree of accuracy, and lower risk of friendly fire, than had previously been possible.[16] This development made strikes by fighter-bombers a standard part of British ground battles, allowing them to be called down and directed much like artillery fire, greatly boosting the potential firepower that any given unit could have at its disposal. Thus, by the end of the campaign in the Mediterranean, artillery and airpower had clearly become the central elements of British operational doctrine and practice. Though much still remained up to the efforts of infantrymen and tankers, British battles generally turned on the ability of those supporting arms to win the firefight and suppress and disrupt Axis defences sufficiently to allow the 'closing' arms (those forces that actually closed upon the enemy in combat) to effectively assault, drive out, and defeat the enemy.

The British campaign in Normandy continued this policy of reliance upon overwhelming supporting fire from artillery (including the heavy guns of the Allied naval forces stationed offshore) and air power (including not only the tactical forces, but also frequent 'carpet bombings' of German front-line positions by the heavy bombers of RAF Bomber Command and USAAF's 8th Air Force). Accounts of the fighting, particularly from the German side, heavily emphasized the prominent role of this firepower in the Normandy fighting, with numerous German eyewitnesses describing the paralytic effects of such heavy bombardments, which left units unable to do much more than cower in whatever cover they could find and often left them physically stunned and badly demoralized, even if actual casualties were limited.[17] Though the Germans often derided Allied infantry and tank forces as being timid and unwilling to risk engaging in close combat, they almost invariably expressed a wary respect and admiration for the effectiveness of their opponents' artillery and tactical air power.[18]

114   The Last German Victory

Though the Germans naturally had good reason to explain away their defeats as being due to overwhelming Allied materiel superiority – an 'unfair' fight, as it were – even allowing for a degree of exaggeration it seems clear that this firepower played a critical role in the Allied ability to win in Normandy. The superiority of Allied artillery and air power was something the Wehrmacht of mid-1944 simply could not match in a stand-up battle of attrition. The apparent 'cowardice' displayed by Allied infantry and armoured forces was simply the result of the Allies refusing to wage their battles in the way the Germans would have wanted them to – as experience had shown that they were generally outclassed by the Germans in those categories, it was entirely reasonable for them to wield those forces cautiously, while placing the main weight of their efforts in areas in which they held the clear advantage.

British Firepower in Operation Market Garden – Case Study One – Artillery and the 1st Airborne Division

Thus, by the time of the invasion of Holland in September 1944, Allied forces rather naturally took for granted the scale of fire support that had paved their way through Normandy, expecting that at any given time, in any situation, they could call down a blizzard of artillery fire or aerial rockets and bombs upon any German force that dared to oppose them. Unfortunately for them, the Allied forces proved almost entirely unable to bring this weight of fire effectively to bear in Market Garden, leaving the infantry and armoured formations of the 1st Allied Airborne and 2nd British Armies to struggle on with only a fraction of the firepower that had been so vital to success in the Normandy fighting.

Perhaps most critical, in light of the British Army's artillery centric fighting methods, was the relative paucity of artillery support directly available to the 1st Airborne Division at Arnhem and Oosterbeek. Since their emergence in the 1930s, a relative lack of firepower had been an inherent weakness of airborne infantry forces. Given that they had to be transported entirely by air, using the relatively small and limited capacity transport aircraft and gliders of the 1930s and 1940s, they naturally could not be outfitted with the full complement of artillery pieces and towing vehicles that could be fielded by a conventional foot or motorized infantry division. Though this situation had improved somewhat by

1944 in comparison with earlier airborne efforts, as improved aircraft and cargo-glider designs were brought into service – allowing for a division to fly in with a limited complement of artillery and other support weaponry – airborne forces generally remained very weak in this category in comparison with standard ground units. A British airborne division in late 1944 fielded a single Airlanding Light Artillery Regiment (the 1st Regiment in the case of the 1st Airborne Division), which comprised three eight-gun batteries of modified American 75mm pack howitzers, for a total of twenty-four pieces – with a single battery normally being assigned to support each of the division's three infantry brigades.[19] Each howitzer was landed with its crew and a towing jeep in an Airspeed Horsa – a heavy British glider with a cargo capacity of over 7,000lb.[20] At Arnhem, two of the 1st Airlanding Light Artillery Regiment's batteries were landed in the first lift on 17 September, with the remaining battery arriving in the afternoon of 18 September, with twenty-three of the twenty-four howitzers flown in being landed and deployed intact.[21]

Though the deployment of these guns was a considerable feat for the airborne logistics of 1944, it still left airborne divisions with only a fraction of the artillery firepower that an infantry division enjoyed. The standard British infantry division of 1944 fielded three field regiments of twenty-four guns each, for a total of seventy-two tubes. Thus, in terms of raw numbers, an infantry division fielded three times as many guns as an airborne division. However, airborne divisions were even worse off in terms of relative firepower than this simple numerical comparison suggests, as each of a field regiment's guns was a considerably more powerful and effective weapon than the light pack howitzers of an airborne artillery regiment. The standard British field gun in use with the field regiments was the 25-pounder gun/howitzer, which could fire its 25lb high-explosive (HE) shells out to a maximum range of 13,400yd; by comparison, the 75mm howitzer fired a 14.7lb HE shell out to a maximum of 9,610yd. An infantry division could thus fire a weight of 1,800lb of shells in a single full salvo from its artillery regiments, more than five times the 352.8lb 'broadside' weight that an airborne division's single light regiment could muster.[22] As such, the 1st Airborne Division clearly fell well short of the high volume and reach of artillery firepower that was so central to British infantry doctrine, a standard that it is well worth noting had by no means been a guarantee of success for British infantry divisions in Normandy. Indeed, the standard artillery support available to British infantry divisions could arguably be said to be something of a minimum necessary for coping with the tactical advantages enjoyed by the Germans. Historian Maurice Tugwell describes an airborne division as a 'rapier' compared with the 'mace' that was a standard British infantry division – and to continue the metaphor, British doctrine was hardly conducive to skilled 'fencing'.[23]

In spite of its limitations, the 1st Airborne Division's 1st Airlanding Light Artillery Regiment did the best it could with its limited resources, and provided valuable service throughout the fighting at Arnhem and Oosterbeek. Despite the need to deploy and dig in its weapons, as well as to set up communications networks for fire direction, both of the two batteries landed on 17 September – at 1315 and 1345 – were conducting their first fire missions by 1700 that evening – a fairly impressive performance.[24] The Light Artillery Regiment's radio operators also proved considerably more successful in maintaining communications than their brethren with the infantry, with contact being kept up fairly reliably throughout the battle between the three batteries and their forward observers operating with each of the infantry brigades (two with each battalion), though temporary breaks were still a far from uncommon hindrance to their efforts; early on 18 September, for example, the 3rd Parachute Battalion lost heavily in the face of a sizeable German counterattack when their forward observers were unable to contact their battery to call down fire support.[25] Even the isolated 2nd Parachute Battalion force at the Arnhem road bridge was able to call down fire from its supporting 3rd Battery from the point at which communications were established on the morning of 18 September after some initial difficulties right up until the force was overrun on the 20th.[26]

However, the simple fact is that, despite the 1st Airlanding Light Regiment's best efforts, with each of the division's three brigades – plus the bridge force – fighting separate battles across a wide area around Arnhem throughout the critical offensive phase, the gunners were never able to effectively concentrate their limited firepower enough to effectively suppress the German defences and allow the infantry battalions to break through. On the critical first day of the operation, the 1st Parachute Brigade's offensive could only reliably expect the support of a single eight-gun battery for its three battalions; though the operational orders technically allowed for each brigade to call in additional support to that from their single assigned battery, the 1st Airlanding Brigade frequently called upon the Light Regiment to support its thinly stretched lines along the western edge of the landing zones against German probes throughout the evening and night of 17 September, ensuring that the two batteries landed were generally unable to concentrate their efforts in support of the struggling attack to the east, instead having to divide their efforts between multiple battalion scale battles at any given time.[27]

From 18 September, even with the landing of the third and final battery of the 1st Airlanding Light Artillery Regiment in the second lift, the dispersion of the division's fire actually became even worse. With the 1st and 4th Parachute Brigades fighting separate battles en route to Arnhem, in addition to the needs of the 1st Airlanding Brigade to the west and the separate force at the bridge – which maintained a near monopoly on the efforts of the 3rd Battery due to their particularly dire situation – only a handful of guns would be available to engage any given target, and units calling for fire often found the Light Regiment too busy to fulfill their requests at critical junctures.[28] For example, during the critical final attack on the morning of 19 September, despite the fact that the Light Regiment had been made aware of the impending effort and had sent out liaison officers and additional forward observers to maximize their ability to provide support, what fire they were able to muster proved entirely incapable of suppressing the small-arms, machine-gun, and mortar fire of the German defenders, ensuring that the advancing battalions walked into a veritable 'hurricane' of fire that all but wiped them out.[29] The fact that both the 4th Parachute and 1st Airlanding Brigades were also heavily engaged at that same time as the 1st Parachute Brigade meant that, inevitably, critical gaps in the division's fire support began to appear; the 4th Brigade's attack on the high ground north of Arnhem, and their subsequent hard-pressed retreat back to the perimeter, was left almost entirely without artillery support, contributing to both their defeat and heavy losses.[30]

During the ensuing 'siege' of the 1st Airborne Division's perimeter around the town of Oosterbeek, which formed in the wake of the defeat of its final offensive on 19 September, the Light Artillery Regiment's effectiveness was degraded still further by the fact that the retreat of the defeated infantry brigades left its gun positions only a short distance behind the patchwork front line; the Light Regiment's commander, Lieutenant Colonel William Thompson, had in fact played a significant role in halting the rout on the afternoon of the 19th, establishing a roadblock on the road just in front of his gun line to gather in and rally the defeated paratroops and glider men fleeing from Arnhem.[31] Because of this development, the Light Regiment's gunners spent the remainder of the battle dedicating a considerable portion of their efforts to defending their own gun positions with direct fire from the howitzers and their personal small arms – efforts that naturally further reduced the amount of indirect fire support they could provide to the infantry along the rest of the hard-pressed perimeter.[32] Furthermore, the regiment's losses in this fighting were such that it was soon forced to withdraw some of its forward observers from the infantry brigades to keep its howitzers crewed.[33] In the final days of the siege, the Light Regiment was frequently forced to fend off enemy tanks with armour-piercing shells fired over open sights and on the afternoon of 25 September, several of its gun positions were even temporarily overrun by a German attack.[34]

With the already badly overtasked Light Regiment being steadily reduced in effectiveness throughout the battle, only the fact that its radio operators had managed to establish radio contact with the command network of XXX Corps' 64th Medium Artillery Regiment early on 21 September ensured the survival of the Oosterbeek perimeter.[35] The 64th Regiment began firing concentrations in support of the perimeter from its positions near Nijmegen shortly after 1900 that same day, operating under the direction of the 1st Light Regiment's remaining forward observers on the perimeter, and was soon joined in this task by several other XXX Corps field and medium regiments as they came into firing range. This artillery fire, though fired at extreme range, and with an ammunition supply limited by the frequent cuts in XXX Corps' lines of communication, was cited by most observers in the 1st Airborne Division as being instrumental in the division's ability to hold the perimeter line long enough to be evacuated, breaking up several major German assaults and preventing them from ever concentrating a sufficiently strong force to overrun the perimeter, despite the much depleted strength of the defenders.[36] General Urquhart, in particular, despite his overall frustration with the inability of XXX Corps to reach his troops on time, later requested that the men of the 64th Medium Regiment be allowed to display the Airborne Forces' 'Pegasus' patch on their uniforms, as

Little More than Guts and Bayonets 119

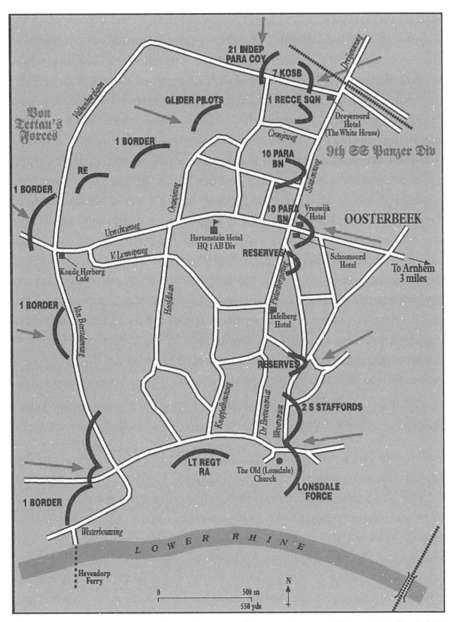

The Oosterbeek Perimeter, 20 September 1944. (*Courtesy Tonie and Valmai Holt*, Battlefield Guide to Operation Market Garden)

honorary members, for their efforts – a request that was later denied by a British high command eager to forget the entire Arnhem affair.[37]

Overall, the efforts and the fate of the 1st Airborne Division at Arnhem seem to clearly indicate the critical role of heavy artillery support in British infantry operations. With only the very limited artillery support provided by their own 1st Airlanding Light Regiment from 17 to 20 September, the infantry of the 1st Airborne Division were almost entirely unsuccessful in their offensive efforts against the German forces holding Arnhem, while, with the benefit of the more substantial support of the advance artillery of XXX Corps from 21 to 25 September, the tattered remnants of the division managed to successfully hold their perimeter against German forces that increasingly outnumbered them by a wide margin. Even the division's eventual evacuation across the Lower Rhine on the night of 25/26 September was only made possible by the intense barrier barrages fired by XXX Corps guns all around the perimeter, which kept the Germans pinned down effectively enough that most did not even realize the airborne troops had left until the next morning. Given the central role that lavish artillery support had had in most British and Allied successes to date, it seems (in hindsight at least), an extremely dubious proposition to send such a lightly equipped division into such an exposed and vulnerable position; when surprise failed, the 1st Airborne Division simply lacked the artillery firepower that British tactics relied upon to enable infantrymen to advance in the face of resistance.

British Firepower in Operation Market Garden – Case Study Two – Artillery and XXX Corps

Turning to XXX Corps, though it possessed the full range of artillery support that was so lacking in the 1st Airborne Division, its near complete tactical dependence upon this support for offensive power also proved to be a severe hindrance to their effectiveness during Operation Market Garden. Despite the fact that the Market Garden plan called for a fast-moving deep penetration and exploitation mission by the armoured and motorized columns of XXX Corps, the corps remained almost entirely bound by the combat methods dictated by its doctrine, in which it had trained and operated over the past few years. Despite the considerable organic firepower that the armoured regiments within British armoured divisions possessed in 1944, a combination of habit (dating from experiences in the desert war in 1941–2, when for much of the campaign they fielded much less capable tanks than the American-built Sherman tank that was standard issue to British armoured units by mid-1944) and the continued vulnerability of most Allied tanks to German anti-tank guns and man-portable anti-tank weapons, ensured that British tankers remained almost as dependent upon artillery support as their infantry counterparts.[38] As has already been discussed, throughout the campaign, when faced with resistance of any serious scale, the leading Guards Armoured Division generally chose to pull back, deploy its artillery and batter the opposition into submission, rather than trying to advance under cover of the fire of its own tanks and motorized infantry.

To be fair to the British tankers, this tendency was exacerbated by the terrain that confronted them throughout the operational area. This terrain – described in detail in pre-operation reports and thus hardly a surprise to British planners – consisted largely of typically flat, muddy Dutch polder land, crisscrossed with dykes and irrigation ditches as well as scattered woods and orchards; in the generally wet autumn conditions this boggy terrain was largely impassable to Allied tanks (German tanks, most of which had wider tracks and thus lower ground pressure, seem to have fared a bit better). The Allied vehicle columns were thus almost entirely restricted to the single main road, which, for considerable parts of its length, was embanked about 6ft above the surrounding terrain and bordered by deep ditches, leaving vehicles both unable to easily manoeuvre off it, and entirely exposed to any anti-tank fire from the surrounding area.

As such, between their doctrine and training and the difficult circumstances they faced, it is hardly surprising that the Guards Armoured Division's general tactical plan was to bludgeon their way through any opposition encountered, despite the mission's need for speed. Given the fact that the division's combat frontage was effectively restricted to only a single tank, and the near complete absence of any scope for tactical manoeuvre, artillery firepower was naturally viewed to be the best tool for breaking through German defences. It was for this reason that the Guards Armoured Division was assigned a strong complement of extra artillery from the corps reserves for the duration of the operation – a further seven field and three medium regiments in addition to their own three motorized field regiments.[39]

The decision of the Guards Armoured Division to halt their initial advance almost immediately after it began and repeat their preliminary barrage in the face of German anti-tank fire has already been discussed, along with the degree to which it disrupted the operation's timetable.

A similar situation occurred a few days later, and with even greater consequences, as the Guards Armoured Division advanced out of the newly established Waal bridgehead at Nijmegen onto the 'Island' between the Waal and the Lower Rhine on 21 September. With the 1st Airborne Division struggling to hold out at Oosterbeek, 2nd Army sent them a message at 0115 that morning, informing them that the Guards Division was planning to go 'flat out' to get through to them that day.[40] However, this 'flat-out' advance, starting in the early afternoon, once again quickly ground to a halt just short of the town of Elst in the face of fire from a relative handful of German towed and self-propelled anti-tank guns concealed in the nearby orchards. This fire quickly knocked out several tanks at the head of the Guards' column, obstructing the road for the remaining vehicles. With his tanks unable to advance or manoeuvre off the embanked road, and with the infantry of the 3rd Irish Guards too few in numbers to drive the German troops out of the orchards, Lieutenant Colonel J.O.E. Vandaleur of the Irish Guards Group called for artillery and air support to break through the roadblock.[41] However, traffic jams along the single road to the rear ensured that only a single battery of field artillery was within range of the combat at Elst – not nearly enough to effectively suppress the fire coming from the well-camouflaged German positions.[42]

Thus what might be seen as a simple – and all too predictable – traffic problem ensured that the Guards Armoured Division's extensively reinforced artillery complement was rendered all but useless at a critical juncture in the operation. Furthermore, though the 2nd TAF had managed to get a few cab-rank Typhoon fighter-bombers over the column to cover the advance, the failure of the column forward air controller's ground-to-air radio set meant that, though they were clearly visible overhead to the combatants, the Guards found themselves frustratingly unable to call the fighter-bombers down onto the concealed German positions, leaving the pilots with little option but to simply fly home with their ordnance undelivered soon thereafter.[43]

In the face of this check to his leading division's offensive efforts, General Horrocks made a difficult decision, effectively choosing to call off the Guards Armoured Division's advance and summoning the following 43rd Infantry Division to take over the lead in pushing to the Lower Rhine, reasoning that an infantry division would be able to operate more effectively in the difficult terrain of the 'Island'.[44] However, with the 43rd Division's three brigades scattered well back along the jammed road, it was another day before even the leading brigade was in position to resume the attack. Furthermore, once they were in position the infantry of the 43rd Division proved to need overwhelming firepower just as much as did the tanks of the Guards Armoured Division to effectively press home its attacks. Having been able to bring up only a portion of his artillery to support the three battalion attacks he had planned for 22 September, and with General Horrocks having ordered extreme economy in the use of artillery ammunition in light of the cutting of the corps' lines of communication at Veghel earlier in the day, Major General G. Ivor Thomas of the 43rd decided to concentrate the bulk of his guns in support of the attack of the 7th Somerset Light Infantry (7/SLI) on the town of Oosterhout, which lay astride a branch road leading north. Though this attack subsequently succeeded, taking over a hundred POWs while costing the 7/SLI only nineteen casualties, the less well-supported attacks by the other two battalions at Elst failed to make any significant progress in the face of a determined German defence. Similarly, ongoing attacks on the town of Bemmel by the Welsh Guards Group, in support of the 43rd Division's right flank, made little progress in light of the limited artillery support available.[45] In the end, with both the 43rd Division and the elements of the Guards Division still remaining on the 'Island' struggling to deploy the full weight of their firepower in the face of strong resistance and confining terrain, the German garrisons in Elst and Bemmel held out until the evening of 25 September before withdrawing, preventing XXX Corps from pressing forward in strength to Arnhem via the main road before the decision to evacuate the Oosterbeek perimeter was made.[46] Thus, the reliance that the forces of XXX Corps placed upon their extensive artillery firepower to overcome any opposition, combined with the corps' persistent inability to effectively deploy that firepower in a timely manner throughout the campaign due to the terrain and local circumstances, contributed greatly to the generally slow progress that the corps made towards Arnhem, and its subsequent inability to reach the 1st Airborne Division in time. The leading role that British doctrine allocated to centralized artillery firepower in defeating enemy forces thus left XXX Corps ill-equipped to carry out the mission of deep, rapid exploitation assigned to it.

The Role of Infantry Firepower within British Doctrine

A further consequence of the British Army's general reliance upon centrally controlled artillery as its main source of firepower was the resulting relative paucity of organic firepower provided to its infantry units – a situation that was, as has already been made apparent, even more pronounced in the airborne forces than it was among more conventional infantry formations. Prior to the First World War, British doctrine (like that of most nations of the era) saw infantry as the primary arbiter of battle, with all other branches working to support its efforts.[47] The experiences of the First World War and the tight military budgets of the interwar period changed this perception however, leaving infantry with a relatively limited role in post-war British doctrine, in spite of the official emphasis on combined arms warfare. British leaders saw the offensive use of infantry on any sizable scale – even employing the more effective platoon tactics developed by the end of the war – as being too costly in terms of casualties in light of ever increasing modern firepower.

The language used in the 1935 *Field Service Regulations* manual regarding the role of infantry is quite instructive – while previous doctrine had emphasized infantry as the primary means of winning battles, the 1935 manual described its role as that of merely 'confirming' victories won by an all-arms effort, by closing with the enemy to take and occupy ground.[48] Furthermore, FSR 1935 emphasized that, while strong on the defensive, where it could benefit from the use of terrain, field entrenchments, and concealment, the infantry was 'relatively weak in the attack' and that it would normally rely upon the supporting fire of artillery and tanks when on the offensive.[49] The 1935 doctrine saw only a limited role for an infantry unit's organic machine guns and mortars in supporting attacks, and suggested that infantry should only try to attack under the cover of its own weapons fire alone in the most favourable of circumstances – against a very weak or disorganized enemy – and that this would be a demanding task even then.[50] British interwar doctrine thus effectively reduced the role of infantry to that of little more than a mere 'clean-up crew' for the artillery, relying almost entirely upon preliminary artillery barrages to actually overcome the enemy's capacity to resist so that all that was left for the infantry to do was to carry out the final assault into enemy positions and occupy them.[51]

As such, little need was seen for either equipping infantry units with their own heavy weaponry or for further development of fire and movement tactics with which the infantry might suppress an enemy's resistance and then close to assault through their own means. British infantry units generally saw little improvement to, and even some decline in, their own organic firepower in the interwar period, as budget cuts severely limited initial postwar plans to expand the complement of machine guns, mortars, and other support weaponry with which infantry platoons had been so usefully equipped in 1917–18. British infantry throughout the period generally continued to depend upon their own rifles and bayonets, supplemented by a single light machine gun per squad, a 2in light mortar of limited utility in each platoon, and a few 3in mortars at the battalion level. All other heavy infantry weapons – such as heavy machine guns capable of sustained fire or heavier mortars – were held at the brigade or even the divisional level, for assignment and allocation by higher commanders as they saw fit.[52] In effect, the British infantry doctrine in use through the interwar period and much of the Second World War had actually regressed to some degree from the standards of 1918, with their heavy emphasis on platoon-based fire and manoeuvre tactics using the platoon's own Lewis machine guns and rifle-grenade launchers, reverting to a state closer to that of pre-First World War doctrine, focused on the use of aimed rifle fire and assault with the bayonet.[53] The 1935 FSR, as well as infantry manuals produced as late as 1937 and 1938, suggested that the best tactical practice for infantry was to maintain a steady advance behind the supporting rolling barrage, without any stopping to fire unless absolutely necessary, ensuring the maximum degree of order and control; these suggestions bear a rather unsettling resemblance to the practices that proved so costly at the Somme in July 1916, where the British suffered nearly 60,000 casualties on the first day of their offensive alone.[54]

The British Army thus entered the Second World War with a relatively limited doctrine for infantry combat, with their infantry being trained to operate effectively only as part of a combined arms team at the divisional level and up. Though the British were undoubtedly correct to emphasize the overall importance of combined arms warfare in their doctrine, as the proper use of combined arms tactics has often been a vital factor in military effectiveness throughout the course of recorded history, the lack of viable alternative methods for British infantry to fight effectively at the small-unit level in the absence of supporting arms was extremely problematic. In the wake of the crushing defeat of the BEF in France in 1940, some elements among the British military leadership did make concerted efforts to improve the performance of their infantry in the lull as they rebuilt their forces and awaited either a possible German invasion or the resumption of their own offensive efforts. Perhaps most notable among these efforts was the development of 'battle drills' to train British infantry in the long-neglected basic skills of fire and movement, which might enable them to engage and close with the enemy without extensive artillery support.[55]

These battle drills, which were sets of standardized patterns of fire and manoeuvre to be used in response to specific situations encountered, were developed – largely on the basis of First World War models – by various commanders and within various units through the early years of the war. By mid-1942 they were being adopted fairly widely – though hardly universally – across British forces in the Mediterranean and at home.[56] While battle drills were certainly an improvement upon the near total neglect of basic infantry tactics that had existed before, their overall impact was fairly limited. The developers of battle drill, particularly Major Lionel Wigram, the chief instructor at the British Army's central 'Battle School' established in December 1941, had intended the drills to serve merely as the basis for a deeper and broader development of tactical skills throughout the army, building a sense of tactical judgement among officers and men by helping them to understand why certain tactics worked in certain situations, knowledge which would eventually allow them to learn to mix, match, and adapt the set tactical patterns to non-standard situations as needed.[57] In practice, however, few British units were able to advance beyond the simple rote enactment of the standard drills, often in a very rigid and stereotypical manner. Though perhaps a good starting point, battle drills were adopted too late, and with too little enthusiasm and support from the British Army leadership, to develop the deeper skills of true tactical judgement they aimed at.[58]

In the field, these problems of infantry tactics quickly became a sort of vicious circle – the more inadequate British infantry tactics proved in practice, the more that British forces in the field found themselves needing to rely upon heavier and heavier artillery support. This reliance in turn ensured that little improvement was actually made in the abilities of the infantry as they learned to simply rely on the artillery to do the bulk of the work for them, effectively developing a sort of 'addiction' to artillery firepower.[59] Increasingly, when confronted with any sort of resistance, the standard response of British troops became to stop and call for fire support. From late 1942, the British Army had relatively rarely been faced with a situation where it did not have access to a lavish degree of artillery and air support for any significant amount of time – thus the potential weakness that such dependence represented was never properly perceived or understood. Though battle drills remained in use throughout the war, the rise of the 'Colossal Cracks' doctrine, and experience with its employment in the Mediterranean and Normandy, effectively confirmed the pre-existing doctrinal view of the relationship between infantry and artillery within British operational technique.

British Firepower in Operation Market Garden – Case Study Three – Infantry Firepower in the 1st Airborne Division

Though the lack of effective infantry firepower or tactics was thus not a fatal impediment for the well-supported infantry divisions of the British ground forces, it quickly proved to be a devastating weakness for the isolated 1st Airborne Division at Arnhem. Compared to even the fairly limited assets available to infantry battalions within a standard British infantry division, the infantry units of a British airborne division were severely lacking in organic firepower. Beyond the rifles, submachine guns, and Bren light machine guns of its infantry squads, and a single 2in mortar per platoon (which lacked the explosive power to be useful for much more than laying smokescreens) each battalion of a 1944 British infantry division had only a platoon of six 3in mortars to provide immediate organic fire support to its four rifle companies.[60] This firepower could be supplemented, however, by the allocation of detachments from the divisional Machine-Gun Battalion, which fielded sixteen 4.2in heavy mortars and thirty-six .303 Vickers medium machine guns.[61] In contrast, while the British Parachute Battalion of 1944 fielded its own platoon of four Vickers guns in its Support Company, its mortar platoon was reduced to only four tubes (technically the battalion was authorized eight mortars, but could only crew the extra four by swapping out the medium machine guns, which the battalions at Arnhem do not seem to have done).[62]

The airborne division's three airlanding battalions were considerably better off, with each battalion fielding a 'Mortar Group', with twelve 3in tubes and two four-gun Vickers MMG platoons.[63] This extra firepower was largely wasted in the offensive phase of Market, however, as the battalions of the 1st Airlanding Brigade remained guarding the landing zones while the lighter, but more mobile, parachute battalions of the 1st Parachute Brigade led the push towards the bridges; Urquhart later stated that the 1st Airlanding Brigade's firepower 'would have been invaluable offensively during the first twenty-four hours'.[64] Even when the 2nd Battalion, South Staffordshire Regiment was sent to join the 1st Parachute Brigade's attack on the afternoon of 18 September, most of its heavy weapons were left behind to help protect the landing zones and Divisional HQ area, depriving the assault force of what might have been a significant boost to their firepower.[65] Moreover, unlike a standard infantry division, the British airborne divisions had no pool of additional heavy infantry weapons to call upon, leaving the attacking parachute battalions almost entirely reliant upon the overburdened divisional light artillery regiment for fire support.

One area where British airborne troops were relatively well-equipped in terms of firepower was in the field of submachine guns; the British Army's development of the light and cheap – if occasionally less than fully reliable – 9mm Sten submachine gun had been heavily influenced by the need for a highly portable automatic weapon for use in the fledgling airborne force, and these forces received a generous issue of them. Whereas a standard 845-man British infantry battalion in 1944 was officially issued with fifty-six Sten guns (though units often acquired more 'unofficial' weapons), mostly for use by officers, squad commanders, and some heavy weapons crews, a 1944 Parachute Infantry Battalion was allocated a 'pool' of 300 Sten guns to be issued as needed among their 613 men, while further weapons seem to have been issued equally generously to the various divisional supporting units; Captain Eric MacKay, for example, who commanded A Troop of the 1st Parachute Squadron, Royal Engineers, noted that, of the twenty-seven men that remained under his direct command by the early afternoon of 19 September, fully fourteen were wielding Sten guns in defence of the position at the Arnhem road bridge.⁶⁶ Though it is unclear how many men in the 1st Airborne Division chose to carry Stens in place of their standard rifles during the Market Garden operation, the weapon's relative prominence in numerous accounts by survivors and the mention of Sten ammunition as one of the division's most critical requirements for resupply in administrative reports suggests that a considerable portion of the division's pool of submachine guns was indeed brought along, likely in anticipation of close-quarters urban combat in defence of the hoped for Arnhem bridgehead.⁶⁷

However, while these numerous Sten guns would indeed have been a very useful addition to the infantry firepower of the British airborne troops at Arnhem, they also would have introduced some significant drawbacks: firing as it did a relatively low-powered 9mm pistol cartridge, the Sten, like most submachine guns, would have been limited to an effective combat range of about 50 to 100yd and had only a limited ability (in comparison with rifle cartridges) to penetrate either dense vegetation or urban masonry – both of which were common in the fighting around Arnhem. Furthermore, the prevalence of automatic weapons among the airborne troopers would have contributed to the aforementioned high rate of ammunition consumption and subsequent supply difficulties. While the Sten's handiness and high rate of fire in comparison with the standard Lee–Enfield service rifle would likely have outweighed these limitations in the generally close-ranged combat at Arnhem, the widespread employment of submachine guns was far from a perfect solution to the British airborne's firepower problems.

As a result of these limitations in their armaments, British parachute battalions relied heavily upon aggressive close-range shock tactics, taking advantage of their high standards of marksmanship, fitness, discipline, and high morale to close with the enemy and overwhelm him in close combat.⁶⁸ These tactics were very prevalent at Arnhem, with numerous references throughout the documentation and literature on the battle to the widespread use of bayonet charges by the airborne troops to clear German resistance nests or counterattack penetrations of their own lines.⁶⁹ To be sure, these tactics could and did often achieve a degree of success, at least in the short term. However, they also proved extremely costly; right from the start, the British paratroops seem to have suffered heavily every time they clashed with the Germans, even in the relatively limited scale skirmishes of the first 24 hours. For example, the 1st Parachute

Battalion's R Company was reporting approximately half of its original 117 men having fallen as casualties by midnight on 17/18 September, less than 12 hours after the landings, while, in the wake of a series of assaults on German strongpoints throughout the morning of the 18th, the same battalion's T Company was reduced to a mere twenty-two men by the early afternoon.[70]

Similarly, accounts of the desperate final assault into Arnhem on 19 September describe an almost Napoleonic series of frontal assaults up the main streets of Arnhem towards the German lines located in rows of buildings along perpendicular streets – historian Robert Kershaw described it as 'the tragedy of the "Charge of the Light Brigade" in miniature'. Though the charge overran a few outlying positions, it eventually ended, as mentioned earlier, with only a handful of unwounded men even reaching the main German lines before being overwhelmed by the subsequent counterattack.[71] When a headcount was conducted of the remnants of the 4 attacking battalions on the evening of the 19th, it was found that only 116 and 40 men were left in the 1st and 3rd Parachute Battalions, respectively (from an establishment strength for a parachute battalion of 613), while the 11th Parachute Battalion and the 2nd South Staffordshires, neither of which had been engaged with the enemy before that morning, were down to 150 and 100 men respectively – the South Staffordshires having landed with a total of 779 men.[72] Though it is likely that some of the missing men had merely become separated in the chaos and may have later returned to the unit, the assault clearly left the participating units in no position to continue their offensive efforts.

Moreover, the British use of these shock tactics persisted even after the devastating losses of the 19th, with numerous German penetrations of the Oosterbeek perimeter being counterattacked at bayonet point. One such counterattack by 7/KOSB on 21 September retook a lost position (a large building dubbed the 'White House'), but achieving this minor victory reduced the already battered battalion, which had numbered 270 men the previous day, to less than 150 men fit for duty. These losses ensured that the battalion's success was an entirely pyrrhic one, as its reduced fighting strength soon forced it to abandon the recaptured position and pull back to a shorter defensive line. Furthermore, the losses suffered in this type of close fighting fell disproportionately on the small-unit leadership in the British battalions, who generally led such charges from the front; the 7/KOSB War Diary notes that the fight at the 'White House' cost them twelve officers, including the last of their company commanders, as well as the last of their company sergeant majors.[73] Clearly the 1st Airborne Division's shock tactics were a losing prospect at Arnhem, producing only limited results while rapidly inflicting a scale of casualties that rendered the division's infantry brigades almost entirely combat ineffective less than two days after they landed. Thus, lacking in either artillery or organic firepower, and not trained or equipped to fight effectively without outside support, the British 1st Airborne Division was forced into exactly the sort of costly infantry assaults that British interwar doctrine had sought to avoid, which quickly rendered the division unable to complete its mission.

Taken for Granted: Close Air Support in the Market Garden Campaign

Given the lack of firepower that was essentially inherent to airborne formations, it is perhaps not surprising that most nations that began experimenting with airborne forces through the interwar and early war period saw tactical air power as a potentially invaluable source of support for these types of operations, with bombers and fighter-bombers acting as long-range aerial artillery for the isolated and under gunned formations operating beyond the range of the conventional artillery of the main ground forces. The Germans, in particular, saw the provision of the greatest possible level of tactical air support to airborne operations as critical to their success.[74] As mentioned above, by the time of the Normandy campaign, the Allies had developed ground-air tactical cooperation into a fine art, with air attacks targeted on the German ground forces playing a prominent role in most of their operations there.[75] Like their artillery, Allied troops came to depend heavily upon the support of strike aircraft and increasingly called upon them to deal with any significant resistance; as Lieutenant General Lewis Brereton, who had commanded the American 9th Tactical Air Force in Normandy before taking command of the 1st Allied Airborne Army for Market Garden, said: 'It was an ordinary occurrence for the ground forces, held up by a strongpoint, to call on the Ninth Air Force for help.'[76] It is worth noting that the actual physical damage inflicted by such air strikes is highly debatable, with studies both at the time and since suggesting that it was usually much less than the air forces claimed, an unsurprising fact given the accuracy limitations of contemporary air-to-ground weaponry. Its morale effect, however, was considerable for both sides; German troops often panicked and scattered for cover at the mere appearance of fighter-bombers overhead, while Allied troops were usually heartened by the sheer spectacle of their strikes, if nothing else.[77] By the end of the Normandy campaign, tactical close air support (CAS) had become an integral and vital part of Allied ground combat efforts, with some observers and historians crediting it as the single most important factor in the Allied victory.[78]

Unfortunately, by the time of Market Garden, this support had been so long and so widely available that it seems that the Allied planners involved took it almost entirely for granted, forgetting the considerable degree of preparation and planning that it had taken to provide such a level of support to date. As such, the planning for the provision and direction of tactical air support for Market Garden, particularly for the airborne formations that needed it most, was generally quite poor, ensuring that the powerful Allied tactical air forces played only a limited role in the campaign.[79] Matters actually started off fairly well, with the initial pre-planned and heavily choreographed bombardment and support missions for the initial airlifts, such as fighter escort and flak suppression, proving fairly effective, ensuring that very few transport aircraft or gliders were lost to the German air defences.[80] The air support plan for XXX Corps focused largely upon the initial effort to penetrate the German lines, using rolling suppressive strikes by Typhoon fighter-bombers as discussed earlier, but the arrangements for this scale of air support extended only as far as Valkenswaard, just 7 miles beyond the initial front lines.[81] Similarly, tactical air support for the airborne divisions focused on supporting the initial landings, with pre-planned strikes on fixed targets around the various landing zones, such as flak positions and known barracks, with the operational orders emphasizing that the level of support for the airlifts was to be at the 'max scale'.[82]

The provision of ongoing close air support to the ground and airborne forces after the initial attacks, however, was much less efficiently arranged. In perhaps the first and most blatant error in the planning process, particularly in light of Montgomery's views on the 'joint' nature of modern warfare, Air Marshal Sir Arthur Coningham, the commander of the force given primary responsibility for providing close air support for the operation, the RAF's 2nd Tactical Air Force, and one of the key architects of the close air support methods developed in North Africa, was not invited to any of the planning conferences for Market Garden bar one on 16 September, only a day before the operation began; ironically, he was unable to attend this meeting when his flight was grounded by weather.[83] Similarly, though Air Vice Marshal Harry Broadhurst – commander of the 2nd TAF's 83 Group, which would provide the fighter-bombers required – and his staff were consulted by the 21st Army Group headquarters prior to the operation, this meeting came only on 15 September, leaving them with very little time to develop and enact effective plans before the operation began.[84]

This rushed planning process, with minimal effort made to coordinate effectively with the commanders who were both the ones that would be directing the air support effort and those with the best experience and knowledge to advise on the requirements and limitations of such an effort, ensured that several aspects vital to the provision of effective close air support were ignored or neglected in the Market Garden plans. Perhaps most notably, the 1st Airborne Division, which possessed no trained forward air controllers (FACs) of its own to call in and direct air strikes, had to be hastily provided with the means to communicate with supporting aircraft at almost the very last moment. Two American FAC teams, equipped with jeep-mounted Very High Frequency (VHF) SCR-193 radio sets for communication with aircraft, were thus assembled and attached to the 1st Airborne Division, but the lack of advance notice and adequate command attention meant that, rather than being properly trained and experienced FAC specialists, the two officers and eight men assigned were simply drawn from whatever US Army Air Force communications personnel happened to be available. As it turned out, no one in either team was actually familiar with the operation of the highly specialized radio equipment, nor with the proper procedures for forward air control. As such, when the men of the two parties found shortly after the landings that their SCR-193 sets had been pre-tuned to the wrong frequencies, they were entirely unable to fix the problem, and thus could not establish contact with either the 2nd Army or any aircraft; adding insult to injury, both radio sets, which were too large to be dismounted from their vulnerable jeeps, were soon destroyed by mortar fire, ensuring that, throughout Market Garden, the 1st Airborne Division never possessed the means to effectively call down and direct fighter-bombers onto identified targets. As one of the division's after action reports noted, with more than a hint of frustration, these air control parties, a vital factor in the ability to effectively wield airpower on the battlefield, proved 'quite useless'.[85] Without this means for direct contact, the 1st Airborne Division's requests for air support had to be routed up the chain of command to the 2nd Army's HQ, before being forwarded to the 2nd TAF. This was naturally a slow and laborious process, especially in the face of the division's general communications problems; for much of the operation, the only reliable connection to the 2nd Army for requesting air support was the link to the 64th Medium Artillery Regiment established on 21 September, a network that was naturally already heavily burdened with the radio traffic managing the division's requests for artillery support.[86] This slow process for requesting and directing air support meant that any support requested would usually come far too late to address whatever situation had initially prompted the call, if it came at all.

The air support effort for Market Garden was also badly hindered by the fact that the plan, laid with only minimal input from the airmen responsible for such support, failed entirely to account for the effects that the circumstances prevailing in September 1944 would have on 83 Group's physical ability to provide the air support desired. For one, the ambitious thrust across the Rhine, coming as it did at the end of the lengthy pursuit through France and Belgium, put the Allied spearhead at Arnhem at the very limits of the combat radiuses of the short-ranged Typhoon and Spitfire fighter-bombers, even when operating from the most advanced Allied air bases in Belgium. Moreover, most of these advance bases had only just been set up or captured in the last week or two, ensuring that they lacked the full range of supplies or facilities to operate more than a relative handful of aircraft. This situation was further exacerbated by the general logistical crisis that prevailed at the time, with virtually all Allied supplies still having to come over 300 miles by road from the Normandy beaches to the front lines.[87] These factors ensured that only a limited number of aircraft could be deployed in support of the operation at any one time, and that their loiter time over the battlefield would be limited, leaving them with little opportunity to search out concealed targets or make multiple attacks.

Furthermore, the unpredictable and often poor prevailing weather conditions at the time – fairly typical for a north-western European autumn – also proved a major limiting factor, with bad weather over either the airfields or the battlefield often keeping tactical aircraft out of the action for days at a time, with support operations being flown on only five of the nine days of the battle.[88] Weather was the main factor that led the RAF to turn down forty-six out of the ninety-five requests for air support it received from the airborne forces during the battle and in its immediate aftermath. XXX Corps, which was not generally plagued by the same level of ground-to-air communications problems that hampered the 1st Airborne Division, remarked in many of its daily reports upon the degree to which weather conditions severely limited what air support could be provided to their advance.[89] Montgomery himself later cited these weather conditions as one of the most critical factors in Market Garden's failure, stating in his memoirs that 'had good weather obtained, there was no doubt that we should have attained full success'.[90] Though there may be a degree of truth to this, and the weather was naturally a factor entirely beyond Montgomery's or anyone else's control, this does not mean that the Field Marshal and the other Allied leaders involved are entirely free of blame in the matter. Given that they were fully aware of the prevailing seasonal weather conditions for the region, the very fact that they chose to undertake an operation at that time of year that was so dependent upon the extensive use of airpower and thus upon a highly unlikely prolonged stretch of clear skies over both Britain and the continent, makes those planners at least partially responsible for the impact that the weather had upon the operation's level of tactical air support and thus upon denying their forces the firepower they so relied upon to operate effectively. The fact that Montgomery's Market Garden plan failed almost entirely to account for the potential effects of weather suggests a very serious lapse in judgement for the normally air-minded Field Marshal.

The critical end result of all these problems was the virtual absence of tactical air support in the skies over Arnhem and Oosterbeek throughout most of the battle. Urquhart, in particular, was bitterly disappointed by the level of air support provided, believing that, had tactical aircraft been available on the scale that had been the norm over France, his division's chances for success would have been vastly improved.⁹¹ One after action report noted simply that direct support from 83 Group to the 1st Airborne Division was 'negligible' up until 23 September. Even when the number of aircraft put over the 1st Airborne perimeter on a daily basis significantly improved thereafter, with twenty-four Typhoons dispatched on missions to the Arnhem area on the 23rd, for example, the division's complete inability to direct the efforts of those fighter-bombers that arrived over the battlefield onto specific targets severely hampered their ability to intervene in the ground battle to any significant effect.⁹² Lacking any specific details on the locations of German targets, and with their ability to seek out those targets themselves severely restricted by the heavily wooded terrain around the Oosterbeek perimeter, pilots were often forced to either turn back without engaging, or resort to simply strafing or rocketing general areas around the perimeter with little in the way of observable results.⁹³

These attacks did have significant morale value to the British defenders, however, and even some degree of more practical effect, with several 1st Airborne Division accounts noting that the mere presence of fighter-bombers overhead kept German artillery and mortars silent for fear of betraying their locations and inviting attack.⁹⁴ Urquhart later chastised the RAF for not flying more of these 'armed reconnaissance' sorties over the perimeter, arguing that 'air formations must not expect to be given pin point targets always when air support is demanded', but his view does not fully take into account the great difficulty that tactical pilots had in distinguishing friend from foe while traveling at several hundred miles per hour and at several hundred feet above the battlefield.⁹⁵ Due to a combination of luck and skill on the part of the RAF pilots, no friendly fire incidents were reported by the 1st Airborne Division, but even a single misplaced strike (an all-too commonplace occurrence during the Normandy campaign) may have inflicted considerable damage and cured Urquhart of his enthusiasm for 'blind' fire from the air. Still, the reported effectiveness of even the meagre efforts that the 2nd TAF was able to put up over the Arnhem battlefield serves as a hint to the potential difference that better planned and coordinated CAS might have had upon the outcome of the battle. Effective close air support could arguably have made a considerable contribution to Market Garden, given that it was perhaps the only means available to compensate for the 1st Airborne

Division's lack of organic firepower. But a combination of poor planning and circumstance kept perhaps the Allies' most powerful advantage over the Germans in 1944, and a cornerstone of their combat doctrine, all but grounded. With the British spearhead forces thus all but deprived of the full effect of their two most important sources of combat power, tactical air power and artillery, it is hardly surprising that they proved unable to decisively defeat their German opponents.

Chapter 8

The Thin Grey Line: German Doctrine and the Role of Firepower in Operation Market Garden

While the Allied forces participating in Operation Market Garden may have proved unable to effectively wield the considerable superiority in firepower that was at their disposal in autumn 1944, the forces of the German *Heeresgruppe B* which confronted the Allied thrust found themselves almost entirely lacking in heavy weaponry, particular with regards to the famed Panzer and motorized forces that had been the backbone of their combat capabilities since 1939. The crushing defeat suffered by the 7. *Armee* and 5. *Panzerarmee* in France, and their subsequent panicked rout back to the German border, cost these armies the great bulk of their heavy equipment. Though, as General Eisenhower later lamented, large numbers of German troops had indeed managed to escape the Allied encirclement at Falaise, the need to withdraw at speed across numerous water obstacles (with many bridges and ferries having been destroyed by Allied airpower), and under a near constant threat of air attack, meant that the retreating armies were forced to abandon most of their surviving vehicles and artillery along the way.[1] Heeresgruppe B was thus in very poor condition as September began; a message from *Generaloberst* Alfred Jodl, head of the Operations Staff of the *Oberkommando der Wehrmacht* (Armed Forces High Command), sent on 15 September acknowledged that the Army Group had been reduced to holding a 400km front with forces equating to about 12 divisions, and possessing only an estimated 64 operational tanks and self-propelled guns; they were estimated to be confronting a force of between 20 and 28 full-strength Allied divisions with over 1,700 operational tanks.[2]

As such, the main front-line forces available to *Heeresgruppe B* for the defence against Market Garden, the 9. and 10. *SS-Panzer Divisionen* of the II. *SS-Panzer Korps*, were hardly worthy of the designations of

'Panzer' or 'Division', having between them lost all but 16 to 35 of their tanks and assault guns, less than 70 variously armed half-tracks and armoured cars, and about 2 battalions worth of artillery (24 pieces).[3] As mentioned in the earlier discussion of *Kampfgruppe* Spindler, most of the 9. *SS-Panzer Division*'s vehicle and gun crews (and many of those of the 10. *SS-Panzer Division* as well) fought as infantrymen during the battle, with each division thus effectively operating as a weak light infantry brigade group, with very limited heavy support weaponry.[4] Most of the rest of the forces available to oppose the Allied airborne invasion were even less well provided with such support, comprising as they did a wide variety of small security, administrative and training units, and hastily formed march units assembled from stragglers from France. Few of these units were proper front-line divisions, and as such mostly lacked the usual array of heavy weaponry that was normally deployed in battalions and detachments at the divisional level to support a division's infantry regiments; a standard German infantry division, for example, would include an artillery regiment of four twelve-gun battalions, with a total of thirty-six 10.5cm light howitzers and twelve heavy 15cm howitzers.[5] The great majority of German forces in Holland were thus largely an assortment of what could be called light infantry and not a proper, fully balanced field army with an appropriate array of support units.

In addition to *Heeresgruppe B*'s paucity of heavy weaponry, the *Luftwaffe*, whose effective close support of the German ground forces had been so essential to those forces' widespread successes in the first half of the war, had been reduced to the status of a virtual non-entity in the ground war by the time of the Normandy invasion. Ground down in a near constant series of battles with the RAF, USAAF, and the Red Air Force through the previous years and left badly short of trained pilots and fuel, the *Luftwaffe* was only able to play a minor role in the Battle of Normandy and beyond.[6]

The *Luftwaffe*'s situation was slightly better in Holland than it had been in France, with the battlefield being closer to its bases in Germany, enabling elements of the still fairly formidable air forces held back to defend the Reich to take part; post-battle Allied intelligence analysis suggested that a total of about 300 operational fighters and/or fighter-bombers were available within operating range of the Market Garden battlefield at the outset of the campaign.[7] However, the same analysis noted that the *Luftwaffe*'s ongoing lack of fuel and pilots meant that, while more active than they were over France, the *Luftwaffe*'s efforts in Holland were still very limited, with an average of only about 130 to 180 fighter or fighter-bomber sorties over the combat area managed on a daily basis.[8] Though the Allied ground forces involved reported experiencing a number of strafing attacks by German fighters during the battle – often contrasting the surprise reappearance of the *Luftwaffe* to the relative absence of their own air support – these small-scale, scattered attacks inflicted only minimal casualties and damage and had virtually no meaningful impact upon the overall course of the operation.[9] The only notable contribution the *Luftwaffe* made during the Market Garden fighting was a raid by about 100 bombers on the city of Eindhoven on the night of 19/20 September that destroyed a number of XXX Corps logistical vehicles and added to the traffic jams along the main road.[10] The *Luftwaffe*'s contribution to the fighting power of the *Heeresgruppe B* ground forces in the fight against Market Garden was thus minimal.

The Cutting Edge: Infantry Firepower within German Doctrine and Organization

Overall, the mostly infantry based forces fielded by the Germans against Market Garden could count upon very little fire support from other branches or services. This lack of outside firepower, however, was countered by the fact that the German Army had long put a high premium on maximizing the organic fighting power of its infantry units. As was mentioned briefly in the Chapter 3, the German Army's post-First World War doctrine retained a focus on the primary role of infantry in battle; unlike the 'confirming' role assigned to it in the British field regulations of 1935, *Truppenführung* clearly emphasized that infantry remained the primary arbiter of battle and that the chief task of all other branches was to support the infantry in its mission of overcoming enemy resistance.[11] This view of the leading role of infantry in battle, combined with their experience in the effective use of infantry on the offensive in the First World War, ensured that the leadership of the German Army assigned a high priority to providing their infantry units with a strong complement of integral weaponry to maximize their independent combat effectiveness. One of the critical factors in the success of German stormtroop tactics in the latter part of the First World War had been the fact that each storm battalion had been provided with its own extensive complement of support weaponry, with each battalion possessing not only the rifles and light machine guns of its infantry platoons, but also their own heavy machine guns, trench mortars, and light infantry guns. These weapons provided the stormtroop units with a source of ready, on-call firepower under the direct control of the unit itself, which allowed them to effectively employ their own fire and movement tactics to advance, rather than relying exclusively upon the covering fire provided by centrally controlled artillery barrages.[12]

Given the considerable tactical success achieved by stormtrooper tactics in the war (in spite of the German Army's wider failures), it is not surprising that they were not only retained in Seeckt's post-war reorganization, but made into the basis of standard infantry tactics throughout the German Army, rather than merely for specialized assault units.[13] Though *Truppenführung* still emphasized that artillery was a vital source of fire support, and that cooperation between the infantry and artillery was generally essential to success, it also emphasized that infantry was expected to supplement the efforts of the artillery with their own firepower, and that they must be prepared to attack under the cover of this firepower alone should artillery support not be available, or be outrun by the advance. For both offence and defence, *Truppenführung* emphasized the importance of any infantry unit making use of its own weaponry, from mortars, infantry guns, and heavy machine guns right down to the light machine guns in each rifle squad, to suppress enemy firepower, which would in turn enable their ability to manoeuvre effectively.[14] Sub-units right down to the squad level were expected to support one another with their own fire as circumstances demanded, with each sub-unit advancing by bounds while neighbouring squads and heavy weapons covered them.[15]

As such, the infantry units of the *Reichswehr* and its successor, the *Heer* (Land Army) of the *Wehrmacht*, were superbly equipped for generating their own firepower, with a strong complement of supporting weaponry provided within their tactical units, apart from the divisional artillery complement. This tendency had only increased by 1944, as the dwindling supply of manpower available to the German Army in light of their immense casualties to date led their leadership to reorganize their units to rely ever more on the firepower generated by machine guns and heavy infantry weapons, rather than riflemen. The variations between official Tables of Organization and Equipment (TO&Es) and the reality of German units' equipment were often considerable by 1944, particularly among the improvised units that were so prevalent in Market Garden, but such documents can give a rough indication of the high level of firepower provided to even the smallest German infantry units. According to the 1944 TO&E for an infantry division, each of an infantry regiment's 2 infantry battalions was to have 13 light and 2 heavy machine guns in each of its 3 rifle companies, with another 6 heavy and 3 light machine guns in the battalion's heavy weapons company, alongside 6 8cm medium and 4 12cm heavy mortars. Added to this at the regimental level were 2 heavy (15cm) and 4 light (7.5cm) infantry guns, which were sometimes replaced on a one-for-one basis by further 12cm mortars.[16] A *Panzergrenadier* (Armoured or Motorized Infantry) Regiment, such as those in the two SS panzer divisions of II. *SS-Panzer Korps*, or the several *Panzergrenadier* training and replacement regiments fielded against Market Garden possessed even greater firepower, with a full strength battalion being allocated 18 light machine guns (with 2 in each rifle squad), 4 heavy machine guns and 2 8cm mortars in each of its 3 rifle companies, with a further 2 heavy machine guns, 4 12cm mortars and 3 7.5cm infantry guns in the battalion heavy weapons company.[17] It is worth pointing out that British infantry regiments had no equivalent of either the 7.5cm or 15cm infantry guns fielded by German units, since the British infantry was not expected to rely upon their own organic heavy weapons in the same way. In fact, the infantry guns that were in theory available to German infantry units were in many senses as capable as the pack howitzers on which the 1st Airborne Division was reliant for its artillery support.

Though most of the front-line units that participated in the battle were well under their full authorized strength, particularly the two SS divisions, the priority placed upon heavy weapons for infantry units within German doctrine meant that the bulk of a unit's heavy weaponry was generally retained as much as possible even as manpower dwindled, with riflemen being reassigned to keep the weapons manned as needed. Furthermore, machine guns and mortars were much lighter and more portable than heavier artillery; even the heavy 12cm mortar weighed only 1,234lb compared with the 4,377lb of the standard 10.5cm light field howitzer, which made it much easier for lighter vehicles to tow or carry, while 8cm medium mortars and machine guns could be man-packed.[18] This relative ease of transport ensured that a larger proportion of these weapons were retained throughout the German retreat from France than that of the heavier artillery pieces or vehicles.[19] *SS-Rottenführer* Alfred Ziegler, a member of the 9. *SS-Panzer Division Kampfgruppe* von Allworden, later recalled that 'practically every man in the unit had an MG 42' at Arnhem, with the unit having both retained its own machine guns and picked up extra weapons discarded by other units on the retreat from France.[20] Though Ziegler's comment almost certainly contains a degree of hyperbole, it does suggest that the unit went to great pains to maximize its automatic firepower, and that the various battle groups in which the two SS divisions fought during Market Garden most probably possessed a much higher volume of firepower than their simple numbers suggested.

German testimonies and British POW interrogation reports suggest that most of the improvised march companies formed by the two SS divisions from their support and service units for the battle seem to have had at least a standard allocation of machine guns and mortars. Certainly *SS-Hauptsturmführer* Hans Möller, the commanding officer of *Kampfgruppe* Möller, the company sized remnant of 9. *SS-Panzer Division*'s armoured engineer battalion that was operating as an infantry unit, reported that each of his sections (squads) was properly equipped with a light machine gun, for example, a statement that matches the information one of his men provided to his British captors on 21 September.[21] Even the various garrison, training, and improvised units that participated in the battle seem to have been allocated a reasonable amount of heavy weaponry to supplement their own small arms, with shortfalls in the standard infantry weapons often being made up through the addition of whatever heavy weapons were at hand, such as anti-tank or anti-aircraft guns, or even captured Allied weapons. Prisoners taken from a '*Panzergrenadier Regiment* 63' – apparently formed from a training unit recently sent from the German training grounds at Wuppertal – on 21 September reported that their unit possessed the standard single machine gun per section, along with four 5cm light mortars, two 5cm anti-tank guns, and 'a few' motorized light flak guns, alongside the usual assortment of rifles and submachine guns.[22]

Even the more eclectic mix of naval and garrison units assigned to the command of *SS-Sturmbannführer* Josef Krafft of the *SS-Panzergrenadier Ausbildungs und Ersatz Battalion 16* as '*Kampfgruppe* Krafft' in the wake of his successful efforts on the first day of the battle were reasonably well-armed, particularly given that most were new to the infantry role. Krafft's 23 infantry companies, formed into 6 battalions, mustered an average of 4 light machine guns per company, with the battalions between them also fielding a total of 23 heavy machine guns, 14 8cm mortars, 7 light flak guns, and 5 anti-tank guns. Furthermore, Krafft could also rely upon the support of 2 Fortress Machine-Gun Battalions, defensive units equipped with 36 heavy machine guns and 12 8cm mortars apiece, and a *Luftwaffe* flak detachment with 12 8.8cm and 8 2cm guns.[23] The example of *Kampfgruppe* Krafft shows the considerable effort that the *Wehrmacht* took to provide even the most hastily improvised infantry forces with a fairly strong complement of organic firepower.

Furthermore, the German infantry at Arnhem benefitted not only from the ubiquity of machine guns among their ranks, but also their high quality. Machine guns were the backbone of German small-unit infantry tactics through the period, as they were seen as the best way to generate a great amount of concentrated firepower with relatively few men. A German training manual for light machine guns from 1921 stated that such guns were 'the most important weapon that the infantry possesses for the conduct of fire battle', emphasizing the weapon's role as the main generator of firepower within a rifle squad, and the central factor in squad tactics.[24] Given this emphasis, the German Army had placed a high priority on developing and deploying high-quality machine guns for its infantry units. The standard German general-purpose machine guns of the Second World War, the MG 34 and its improved successor, the MG 42, were well known among Allied soldiers for their very high cyclic rate of fire – 900 rounds per minute (RPM) for the MG 34 and over 1,200 RPM for the MG 42, twice that of the standard British Bren light machine gun (600 RPM), and nearly three times that of the Vickers medium machine gun (450 RPM). Moreover, the German guns could sustain much higher rates of fire than their British equivalent, in that they could fire almost continuously using linkable fifty-round belts, stopping only to change out overheating barrels. The British Bren, by comparison, could only fire from thirty-round box magazines, ensuring the need for frequent stoppages in fire to reload.[25] The effectiveness of these machine guns meant that even a much-reduced German infantry unit could generate an impressive amount of small-arms firepower, as long as it could keep its complement of machine guns in action, and that they generally significantly outgunned their British counterparts at the small-unit level. Thus, while the German forces fighting in Holland in September 1944 could not count upon a significant amount of artillery, air, or armoured support, their infantry forces possessed a level of fighting power disproportionate to their meagre numbers.

The Steel Wall: German Infantry Firepower in Operation Market Garden

This high level of infantry firepower proved to be a decisive advantage during Market Garden, given the Allies' inability to bring their superior artillery and airpower to bear. Overall, the fighting in Holland in September 1944 – and particularly at Arnhem – was largely characterized by many small-scale scattered battles between units of infantry and a relative handful of armoured fighting vehicles with little or no higher level support. In these confused, short-range clashes in wooded and urban terrain, the German Army's superiority in infantry firepower at the small-unit level – particularly in machine guns and mortars – allowed its forces to more often than not gain the advantage in the firefights that broke out. Most British accounts of the fighting that took place during their initial push towards Arnhem on 17 and 18 September emphasize machine-gun fire as the main form of resistance encountered, with units often reporting coming under fire from multiple weapons at a time.[26] The concentrated fire from these strongpoints dominated the main roads, and allowed the Germans to engage the advancing British units in devastating close-range ambushes as they tried to break through. *Rottenführer* Ziegler of *Kampfgruppe* von Allworden, for example, reported his unit's fire catching a unit of paratroops still in a single-file marching column after having been allowed to get within point-blank range of their concealed positions, with a number of men being rapidly cut down before they were able to react, and the Germans then seizing a claimed '30 to 40 prisoners' from among the stunned survivors. Though Ziegler was almost certainly heavily exaggerating the number of prisoners his unit took in that one brief clash, given the overall losses reported by the British that day, a photo of the aftermath of this ambush taken by a propaganda photographer and published in the German Army propaganda magazine *Signal* clearly shows the bodies of several paratroops scattered along the verges of the road near a distance marker Ziegler mentioned in his narrative, suggesting there was at least some truth to his account.[27]

The number of machine guns deployed by the German infantry, combined with the high fire rate of each individual gun, ensured that even a brief exposure to their fire was deadly, making them very effective in the short, sharp, and often unexpected clashes that characterized fighting in wooded and built-up terrain. Even when the British attempted to outflank the machine-gun positions covering the roads, these moves often just served to bring them into the sights of further supporting machine-gun posts positioned throughout the woods.[28] Moreover, even if the German gunners failed to hit their marks, the blizzard of fire they put out exercised a considerable suppressive effect upon the British advance, forcing the paratroops to frequently halt their advance to take cover. Private James Sims of the 2nd Parachute Battalion reported that his platoon was repeatedly engaged and pinned down by machine-gun fire in the course of their march to the bridge on 17 September, with the German gun crews, having succeeded in delaying and disordering their opponents with their fire, often simply disengaging and moving back along the road to repeat the whole process over again.[29]

The German defenders also made effective use of their mortars in this confused early fighting, with the British reporting having been frequently targeted by accurate concentrations of mortar fire, particularly at the numerous crossroads that provided natural points of reference for German forward observers and gunners. For example, at about 1800 on 17 September, the 3rd Parachute Battalion came under an intense barrage of highly accurate mortar fire at a crossroads, which inflicted several casualties and forced the paratroops – along with the accompanying Brigadier Lathbury – to take cover for some time in a series of nearby trenches dug by the Germans for field exercises. Urquhart, who joined Lathbury shortly after this bombardment while the 3rd Battalion was still pinned down, later noted the severity of the delaying effect this fire had upon the advance. With the light failing and the battalion still scattered and confused, Urquhart, Brigadier Lathbury, and Colonel

Fitch soon decided to keep the battalion where it was and dig in for the night.[30] Beyond the disruptive and suppressive effect this fire had, it also allowed the Germans to inflict significant casualties upon the British forces within a very short amount of time; as previously mentioned, both of the parachute battalions involved in this fighting reported significant losses the first 24 hours, with at least two companies being reduced to below 50 per cent strength.[31] Even the 2nd Parachute Battalion, which had a relatively easy D-Day, facing only scattered skirmishes with German patrols and outposts on the way to the bridge along the relatively undefended Lion Route, reported having suffered about sixty casualties by the morning of 18 September.[32] Clearly even relatively small numbers of German infantry had the firepower necessary to put up a very tough and effective defence.

This firepower was a central factor in the effectiveness of the delaying action waged by *Sturmbannführer* Krafft's force on the afternoon of 17 September, serving as a very effective force multiplier. Though only fielding a handful of companies with an initial total of just over 300 men, who were spread thinly across more than a mile of front between the 2 main roads to Arnhem, the firepower wielded by Krafft's relative handful of trainees allowed their thin line to all but stop cold the advance of 2 full-strength battalions of the 1st Parachute Brigade (with a strength of around 600 men each), as well as the 1st Airborne Reconnaissance Squadron (with about 270 men), for several critical hours. Krafft's report later singled out his battalion's heavy weapons as having played a central role in the unit's defensive victory.[33] Krafft's firepower ensured that the 1st Parachute Brigade was never able to effectively break through his defensive front and was only able to continue the advance when the 3rd Battalion managed to bypass his dangling southern flank, forcing him to retreat to avoid being encircled.[34]

Once the bulk of *Kampfgruppe* Spindler got into position in the outskirts of Arnhem during the night of 17/18 September, establishing a near continuous firing line from the Ede–Arnhem railroad in the north to the banks of the Lower Rhine in the south, it became all but impossible for the 1st Airborne Division's attack to make any further progress. Even the strongest attacks by the paratroopers usually netted only a block or two of gains at best, and usually only at considerable cost. Brigadier Lathbury later reported that, after spending the 18th trying to break through the German lines in the face of severe machine-gun and mortar fire from elevated positions along a railway embankment, the 1st and 3rd Parachute Battalions managed to advance only about 300yd, while being reduced to about 150 men apiece.[35] The final push on the morning of 19 September by the 1st, 3rd, and 11th Parachute Battalions, along with the 2nd Battalion, The South Staffordshire Regiment, quickly ran into what Private James Edwards of the South Staffs described as a 'shooting gallery', and historian Wilhelm Tieke as a 'steel wall'.[36] With *Kampfgruppe* Spindler having established machine-gun and mortar positions in and around fortified buildings all along the main north–south road passing through western Arnhem, as well as on high ground to both the north and the south, this allowed them to engage the British battalions both frontally and with enfilading fire from both flanks, rendering every street and open space between the buildings a virtually impassable 'no man's land'. Private Edwards later described his own D Company as having become pinned down almost immediately after the attack began, with the company's commander and second in command both trying, with limited success, to get the attack moving again before both being hit themselves; when the remnants of the company fell back to rally in the cover of nearby buildings shortly thereafter, Edwards reported that only about 20 per cent of the men that had started the attack were present to answer the roll call.[37] Thus, the high level of firepower allocated to German infantry units – a result of their doctrinal emphasis on infantry being able to operate independently if needed – allowed the depleted forces of the II. *SS-Panzer Korps* to throw up a virtually impenetrable barrier of firepower around Arnhem with only a few weak infantry units, despite the near total absence of heavy artillery or air support. After the first night of fighting, not a single British unit managed to effectively penetrate this line and their continuing efforts to do so effectively destroyed them within two days of their landings.

This firepower continued to be used with considerable effect even as the initiative shifted in the wake of the failed British attacks and the German forces took up the offensive themselves. With the surviving British airborne troops having rapidly entrenched themselves in a tight perimeter around the Arnhem suburb of Oosterbeek, the German forces north of the Lower Rhine – under *Obersturmbannführer* Walter Harzer of the 9. *SS-Panzer Division* on the eastern side of the British perimeter and

General Hans von Tettau to the west – faced a considerably more difficult task in 'digging them out' and destroying the pocket before it could be relieved. After a few costly early infantry assaults on the pocket, the German commanders realized that the bulk of their hastily improvised forces lacked the level of training and unit coherency needed to conduct such an assault in a cost-effective manner and thus largely turned instead to bombarding the British into submission.[38] As already mentioned, the German forces in the area had only a relatively limited complement of artillery to support such a 'siege' action, but the German command proved quite effective in making the most of that which it did have. By 20 September, every available gun, including numerous heavy flak guns brought up from the Reich's air defences, had been concentrated under a single central headquarters, *Artillerie Kommando* (*Arko*) 191, to direct and coordinate the bombardment of Oosterbeek.[39] Despite having relatively few guns – with an initially reported 18 10.5cm howitzers later rising to a claimed total of 30 10.5cm and 4 15cm howitzers, 20 heavy flak guns, 12 heavy (15cm) infantry guns, 10 heavy mortars, and 10 heavy Nebelwerfer rocket launchers – *Arko* 191, backed by a plentiful supply of ammunition secured by the logistical efforts of *Heeresgruppe B*'s headquarters, proved a significant force in the latter part of the fighting around Arnhem, Oosterbeek, and the 'Island'. It later reported to have to have fired between 800 and 2,100 rounds per day during the latter stages of the battle, and to have successfully engaged numerous targets and usefully supported the efforts of *Kampfgruppe* Spindler with their fire.[40] *Kampfgruppe* Spindler, in turn, commented on the value of this concentrated artillery support in their efforts to crush the Oosterbeek perimeter, reporting that *Arko* 191's fire had suppressed or destroyed several British strongpoints that were holding up their advance.[41] *Arko* 191 was thus among the units General Bittrich later singled out for praise in his after action report, citing it as one of the most effective elements of his forces.[42]

However, given *Arko* 191's relatively limited complement of artillery pieces, the humble, but ubiquitous, infantry mortar became the primary means by which the German bombardment of the Oosterbeek perimeter was carried out. Despite their relatively small size, simplicity (being essentially just a tube with an attached baseplate and some sort of elevating mechanism), and relatively short range, mortars were extremely efficient and effective weapons, being cheap to produce in quantity, easy to use, and capable of putting out a considerable volume of high explosive firepower.[43] The standard German 8cm *Granatwerfer* (literally 'shell thrower') 34 medium mortar could fire its 7.5lb bombs at a rate of about fifteen per minute, while the 12cm *schwere* (heavy) *Granatwerfer* 42, copied from a Soviet design, fired 34.83lb bombs (heavier and more powerful than the 32.66lb shell of the standard 10.5cm field howitzer) at a similar rate.[44]

By this stage of the war, the German Army was already well known among the Allied forces for the number of its mortars and the skill of their gunners. Interviews conducted in the wake of the Normandy campaign found that Commonwealth medical officers attributed about 70 per cent of the wounds they treated to mortar blast and fragments, while another study conducted in Tunisia in 1943 concluded that the experience of mortar fire was responsible for about 40 per cent of the total psychological casualties suffered in that campaign.[45] An account from the King's Company of the 1st (Motor) Battalion of the Grenadier Guards noted that being subjected to heavy, accurate mortar fire was 'a persistent feature of all our attacks' in Normandy.[46]

As mentioned above, German mortars, often as the only 'artillery' available at the time, were prominent in the defence against the initial British offensive. They would play an even larger role in the subsequent German counteroffensive, with the entrenched British forces being subjected to heavy mortar barrages several times daily from a point almost immediately after the initial formation of the perimeter on the evening of 19 September. Descriptions of these steadily intensifying daily mortar barrages (called the 'morning hate' by the British troops, a term that harkened back to the daily bombardments of the First World War) on the 1st Airborne Division's positions are conspicuous throughout the war dairies of all the units present during the siege.[47] Beyond the general area bombardments, the German forces also used their mortars for observed fire against strongpoints identified by forward observers, as well as for harassing the Allied forces on the south bank of the Lower Rhine and their efforts to establish a crossing; the mortar observation posts also kept in close contact with *Arko* 191, allowing them to call down heavier fires when needed.[48]

Though this shelling did relatively little physical damage to the well-dug-in airborne troops, considering the heavy weight of fire, it still had a considerable impact on the defence. For one, the frequent barrages kept the British troops largely pinned within their entrenchments for the majority of the siege, effectively preventing much in the way of counteroffensive action or manoeuvre on any notable scale during the daylight hours, with even the simplest of actions, such as digging or improving trenches, severely hindered by the shelling.[49] As such, the 1st Airborne Division was forced to conduct an almost entirely passive defence, with its various sub-units doing little more than holding their own trench and foxhole lines, and making occasional local counterattacks, while the Germans were able to manoeuvre their forces relatively freely around the perimeter to make attacks at various points. Though the Germans made only slow progress, without any capacity for effective manoeuvre or counterattack, the 1st Airborne Division was deprived of any real possibility of defeating or breaking out of the encirclement, ensuring that their own defeat was just a matter of time.

Furthermore, the bombardments also had a considerable cumulative effect upon the defenders. Several British accounts and war diaries conceded that the steady rain of mortar fire quickly began to have a psychological effect upon the British airborne troops, even with their superb morale and discipline, with many noting soldiers exhibiting significant signs of severe mental strain and exhaustion after a few days under the intense shelling.[50] In light of this acute mental stress, it is hardly surprising that the 1st Airborne Division began to suffer from the loss of a steadily increasing stream of men who had simply 'had enough', and began to leave the front lines to seek shelter with the wounded in local cellars, or simply wander around the woods in a shell-shocked daze.[51] Though some of these men were rallied and returned to the line by the efforts of officers and NCOs, others were simply too burnt out to fight on. On top of this, the sheer volume of flying fragments ensured that, even considering the strong defensive positions the British had constructed, the mortar fire took a steady toll of British strength each day. Particularly hard hit were the division's officers, who had to spend more time in the open moving between their various sub-units; Brigadier Hackett and Lieutenant Colonel Thompson were among the large number of officers put out of action by mortar fire, with both falling to severe stomach wounds – Thompson on 21 September and Hackett on the 24th.[52]

Beyond these casualties, the bombardment also inflicted a significant amount of meaningful material damage upon the 1st Division, igniting several ammunition dumps, crippling communications within the perimeter by cutting cable lines and damaging the battery charging stations for the unit's radios, and destroying the bulk of the Royal Army Service Corps jeeps that were used to distribute the already limited and steadily dwindling supplies of ammunition.[53] This steady rain of fire from the numerous mortars available to the German infantry units at Arnhem thus played a significant role in crippling the 1st Airborne Division's fighting power throughout the fighting around Oosterbeek; though the Germans were unable to quickly finish off the still-determined British troops, their efforts greatly reduced their effectiveness as combat units. Furthermore, the fact that the bombardment of the Oosterbeek pocket relied primarily upon mortars rather than heavy guns limited the ability of the British to effectively counter their firepower with their own artillery. Even with the significant firepower of the 64th Medium Artillery Regiment and other XXX Corps guns available from 21 September onwards, the 1st Airborne Division was unable to effectively direct their fire onto the German mortars, as their forward observers were unable to locate the small weapons – which could easily be dug into concealed pits and produced a relatively limited muzzle flash – particularly given that the 1st Airborne Division lacked the specialized mortar detection units available to conventional British forces.[54]

A similar situation to that at Oosterbeek also took place in the 'last stand' of the smaller British force at Arnhem Bridge. There too the Germans turned to a steady mortar bombardment once their initial infantry attacks were repulsed, with the shelling keeping Lieutenant Colonel Frost's troops pinned within the buildings they had fortified, and inflicting a steady trickle of losses despite that strong cover. Frost himself was seriously wounded by a mortar burst early in the afternoon of 20 September, as was Private Sims.[55] On the whole, the firepower possessed by the German infantry units that fought against Operation Market Garden proved a more than adequate substitute for their shortage of artillery or air power. On both the defensive and the offensive, the Germans' large numbers of high-quality machine guns and mortars allowed them to almost invariably achieve a degree of fire superiority over their British opponents in the numerous small-unit clashes that characterized the fighting, particularly with the British unable to effectively compensate for the superiority of German infantry firepower by calling upon their own advantages of artillery and airpower, as they had done so successfully in Normandy. With both sides largely denied the effective use of heavy weapons or air support in the circumstances that prevailed during Operation Market Garden, the superior firepower allocated to German infantry by a doctrine that continued to see infantry as having a decisive rather than merely supporting role in modern warfare proved to be a vital advantage.

A Strong Supporting Cast: The Role of German Armour in Operation Market Garden

This infantry firepower was also usefully supplemented by the limited German armoured forces deployed to the battle. Though the Germans had relatively few tanks or other heavy armoured fighting vehicles (AFVs) at their disposal through the majority of the Market Garden fighting, with less than 100 in the entirety of *Heeresgruppe B* at the start of the operation, they did manage to effectively use those they did have by deploying them to provide direct fire support to their infantry forces.[56] As stated earlier in the chapter, the Normandy fighting left the II. *SS-Panzer Korps* fighting at Arnhem with only a handful of AFVs, about 16 to 35 tanks and *Sturmgeschütze* (StuGs – assault guns – essentially turretless tanks with their main guns in a limited traverse hull mounting), and about 70 assorted half-tracks and armoured cars. Only limited armoured reinforcements became available to join this SS armoured force through the early days of the battle, with the only sizeable German armoured unit close at hand – the newly formed 107. *Panzer Brigade*, with forty Panther tanks – being sent, as previously mentioned, to join the effort to cut off the Allied corridor to the south in the 101st Airborne Division sector. The understrength 280. *Sturmgeschütze Brigade*, with only about ten operational StuGs, arrived at Arnhem and joined the SS force west of Arnhem on 19 September, while on the same day the small handful of tanks and half-tracks operating with *Kampfgruppe* Brinkmann (a mixed battle group centred on the former reconnaissance battalion of the 10. *SS-Panzer Division*, though attached to the 9. *SS-Panzer Division*) around Arnhem Bridge were reinforced by the eight mostly older model

Panzer III and IV tanks of *Kompanie* 'Mielke' of *Kampfgruppe* Knaust. These tanks had been drawn from a tank-crew replacement training unit at Bielefeld and were crewed by the young students of that school; *Gefreiter* (Corporal) Karl-Heinz Kracht, a loader in one of the company's Panzer III tanks, noted that at 19, he was one of the oldest men in the company.[57] Field Marshal Model did later manage to get a full heavy tank battalion – the newly refitted 506. *schwere Panzer Abteilung*, equipped with forty-five powerful and factory fresh Tiger II heavy tanks – assigned to the II. *SS-Panzer Korps*, but this only arrived on 24 September, after much of the decisive phase of the fighting was already over.[58]

Lacking the effective numbers to conduct anything like the massed, sweeping German Panzer offensives of the early war, most of the armour available to II. *SS-Panzer Korps* for Market Garden was parcelled out to provide close support to the various infantry battle groups, with a few being attached to each group; the StuGs of 280. *Brigade*, for example, were attached to the various sub-groups of *Kampfgruppe* Spindler.[59] During the British offensive, these AFVs provided a valuable source of mobile and protected firepower, able to manoeuvre to various 'crisis points' as they developed and add the fire of their own guns, cannon, and machine guns to that of the infantry. During their advance on 17 and 18 September, the troops of the 1st Parachute Brigade reported being frequently engaged by small groups of tanks, armoured cars, and half-tracks conducting hit-and-run attacks along the main roads, which inflicted losses and slowed the advance, as was the case with German machine-gun and mortar fire.[60]

These armoured 'fire groups' proved even more critical to the Germans' defensive success on 19 September. On the 4th Parachute's Brigade's front along the northern route, the presence of a contingent of reconnaissance and flak half-tracks bearing 20mm automatic cannon played a central role in the defeat of the attack by the 10th and 156th Battalions, decimating two companies of the 156th Battalion and pinning down the 10th to such an extent that they were effectively taken out of the fight.[61] Similarly, half-tracks of the 9. *SS-Panzer-Aufklärungs-Abteilung*, which had taken up positions in the yards of a brickworks on the south bank of the Lower Rhine in the wake of their failed attack across Arnhem bridge on 18 September, found themselves ideally positioned to fire in enfilade into the open right flank of the main British attack along the river bank on 19 September, inflicting devastating casualties on the 1st and 3rd Parachute Battalions while they in turn were utterly unable to effectively reply. Lieutenant Leo Heaps, a Canadian liaison officer who accompanied the 1st Parachute's Battalion's Headquarters during the attack, suggested that this flanking fire was the deadliest threat the paratroops faced during this attack and the source of the bulk of their casualties, stating that: 'the German guns blew up our men on the lower slopes almost at will'.[62]

In the subsequent German counteroffensive against the 1st Airborne Division, these small armoured forces served largely as a mobile source of direct-fire artillery, standing off from the British forces and using the superior range and firepower of their guns to engage their defensive positions with relatively little risk of retaliation. Such fire proved particularly effective given that the British troops made heavy use of local structures as defensive positions; the sturdy stone and brick-built Dutch houses generally proved quite resistant to small-arms fire and even mortar bombs, but quickly collapsed under sustained direct fire from tanks or self-propelled guns.[63] This AFV fire played a decisive role in the defeat of the 2nd Parachute Battalion force at Arnhem Bridge. From the morning of 19 September onwards, the tanks and other AFVs of *Kampfgruppen* Knaust and Brinkmann methodically shelled and destroyed the buildings occupied by the force of paratroops around the north end of the bridge one by one; SS trooper Horst Weber, who fought as an infantryman at the bridge, gave a brief but evocative description of the tanks' efforts: 'It was the best, most effective fire I have ever seen. Starting from the rooftops, buildings collapsed like doll houses. I did not see how anyone could live through this inferno. I felt truly sorry for the British.'[64]

With these anti-structure efforts by the German armour joining the steadily increasing artillery and mortar bombardment, as well as the use of incendiaries by the infantry, by the end of the siege the British had been driven back almost entirely into a single building, the eventual loss of which to fire effectively put an end to meaningful resistance at the bridge.[65]

The effectiveness of the fire of German tanks and StuGs against structures was also a central factor in the eventual success of the German counteroffensive against the main body of the 1st Airborne Division. The StuGs of 280. *Sturmgeschütze Brigade* were prominent in the German counterattack on 19 September that effectively routed and destroyed the

British attack force that had stalled in the face of *Kampfgruppe* Spindler's fire. When the surviving British troops were driven to take cover in the local houses by the German infantry's machine-gun and mortar fire, the StuGs were able to advance along adjacent streets and blast these improvised 'strongholds' with fire from their 7.5cm main guns, quickly forcing most of the British troops to surrender or flee for their lives.[66] In the following German push against the Oosterbeek perimeter, the AFVs attached to each German *Kampfgruppe* once again directed the bulk of their fire against the various structures that the troops of the 1st Airborne Division had occupied as strongpoints within the position. This fire soon rendered the numerous sturdy houses and villas scattered through the Oosterbeek area almost entirely untenable as defensive positions, as they were easily spotted and engaged from long range, and provided virtually no protection against high-velocity shells.[67] Brigadier Hackett later described these structures as having been a 'snare' for the defenders: seemingly tempting as fortified positions, but actually a liability.[68] Similarly, Lieutenant Colonel Thompson noted that his men were only able to properly rest and recover their morale when stationed outside the buildings in the trenches and foxholes.[69]

The relatively meagre force of armour that joined the offensive efforts of II. *SS-Panzer Korps* against the Oosterbeek perimeter were thus able to almost entirely deny a considerable potential defensive asset to the 1st Airborne Division by eliminating a large number of 'ready made' strongpoints that could have provided the British infantry with a considerable degree of additional protection against the small-arms and mortar fire of the German infantry. As such, though largely unable to make an independent contribution to the battle, the few AFVs available to the German forces at Arnhem added considerably to the offensive capabilities of the infantry forces into which they were integrated.

Part of the reason for this effectiveness of such a small German armoured force was the relative ineffectiveness of the 1st Airborne Division's anti-tank forces. This vulnerability was not simply due to any lack of materiel, however. In spite of the limitations imposed by the need for air-portability, by 1944 the British Army had put considerable effort into providing their airborne forces with a sizeable arsenal of effective anti-tank weapons. The 1st Airborne Division flew out a total of fifty-two towed 6-pounder anti-tank guns during Market Garden in standard Airspeed

Horsa transport gliders, with forty-eight of these being successfully landed and deployed.[70] Though these guns were relatively small-calibre compared with more modern pieces (the 6-pounder had first been deployed in the summer of 1942), the provision of the newly developed tungsten-cored Armour Piercing Discarding Sabot (APDS) ammunition ensured that they remained fairly effective against the armour of most German tanks, particularly at close range or when targeting their less well-armoured sides or rear.[71] Furthermore, these were usefully supplemented by a contingent of sixteen heavy 17-pounder anti-tank guns flown in using the massive General Aircraft Hamilcar glider, though difficulties with landing these huge and ungainly machines ensured that five guns were lost in landing accidents.[72] These 17-pounders were among the most powerful anti-tank weapons fielded in the Second World War and could reliably defeat the armour of all but the heaviest German tanks at relatively long range.

Despite its potential on paper, the performance of this airborne anti-tank arsenal in the fighting around Arnhem was mixed, largely due to problems inherent in the tactical deployment of towed artillery. Though fairly effective when they could actually be brought to bear, the 1st Airborne Division's 6-pounder guns proved quite unwieldly in offensive action, being restricted to the main roads and relatively slow to unlimber and deploy from their towing jeeps. On the first days of the battle, they often proved unable to deploy quickly enough to effectively counter the various hit-and-run attacks made by German AFVs along the roads. For example, Lieutenant James Cleminson of the 3rd Parachute Battalion described an attack upon his platoon on the afternoon of 17 September in which a German self-propelled gun advancing along the road managed to knock out his platoon's supporting 6-pounder before it could even be unlimbered from its jeep. Having temporarily neutralized the local anti-tank threat (Cleminson described one of his troops, lacking any other options, reduced to trying to scare the gun's crew by firing flares at them) and inflicted a few casualties on the paratroops with its fire, the SPG and its supporting infantry then managed to gather up 'about half a dozen prisoners' before falling back.[73] The 1st Parachute Brigade's after action report specifically mentioned such difficulties in deploying their 6-pounders into action as being a critical disadvantage for their forces when on the offensive, stating that a tank or self-propelled gun on the defensive in dense terrain would 'beat the [towed] A/Tk gun every time'.[74]

The restricted mobility of the 1st Airborne Division's 6-pounder guns proved to be an even more costly flaw when the division was forced into headlong retreat in the wake of its failed attacks on 19 September. Restricted to roads jammed with fleeing men and with their towing jeeps highly vulnerable to damage and becoming stuck in rough terrain, the bulk of the guns that had accompanied the assault battalions towards Arnhem was lost in the scramble back to Oosterbeek; when the battered division took stock of its remaining assets on 20 September, only thirteen of the forty-eight 6-pounder guns that had originally been brought into action were still available.[75] The case of the even larger and more unwieldly 17-pounder guns was fairly similar; though about half of the eleven guns that survived the landings were retained to defend the divisional HQ and base area, not one of the five or six (the surviving records are uncertain) 17-pounders that accompanied the 1st and 4th Parachute Brigades towards Arnhem returned to the Oosterbeek perimeter.[76]

Moreover, while the division's anti-tank guns proved more effective on the defensive, playing a significant role in the defence of both the Oosterbeek perimeter and the Arnhem Bridge, they proved vulnerable even then. Being relatively large weapons (compared with small-arms and machine guns), and producing a sharp flash and report upon firing, they quickly became priority targets for German fire, and with only relatively small and thin gun-shields for protection, their crews suffered accordingly. At the bridge, the four 6-pounders that had accompanied Frost's force and proved so effective in repulsing *Hauptsturmführer* Gräbner's armoured attack across the bridge on the morning of 18 September had been effectively silenced by the 19th. Though all remained relatively undamaged and functional, with German infantry infiltrating ever closer in around the British positions, the weight of machine-gun and small-arms fire directed upon the gun's positions became such that even trying to man them became a suicidal task for their dwindling crews, forcing them to leave their pieces abandoned in the streets, even with German armour closing in in ever greater numbers.[77] The gun crews in the Oosterbeek perimeter faced a similar experience, even with the better cover and concealment provided by the field fortifications constructed to protect their positions. During the aforementioned battle for the 'White House' on the north-eastern corner of the perimeter on 21 September, 7/KOSB reported one of their supporting 6-pounders being silenced after its entire crew was cut down by machine-gun fire, with the gun only returning to action after being laboriously dragged to a more secure position and recrewed after the fighting died down.[78]

Given the limitations thus imposed upon the effectiveness of their towed anti-tank guns, the backbone of the 1st Airborne Division's anti-tank defence lay in the PIAT (Projector, Infantry, Anti-Tank), a man-portable 'bomb-thrower' that had been issued to British infantry from early 1943. Despite an overly complicated and, at times, unreliable cocking and launching mechanism, the PIAT fired a fairly effective High Explosive Anti-Tank (HEAT) shaped charge bomb that could penetrate about 75mm of steel armour – enough to pierce the side or rear armour of most German tanks – though its targets tended to be only damaged and forced to retreat more often than destroyed outright.[79] With an effective range of only about 100yd, however, the PIAT was almost entirely a 'point defence' weapon; though it could keep German tanks from assaulting British infantry positions directly, it lacked the range to engage any armour that simply chose to stand off and engage with long-range fire, as German tankers at Arnhem quickly learned to do. Though British 'stalking parties' equipped with PIATs achieved several successes against isolated German AFVs during the siege, particularly under cover of night, they proved unable to seriously impede the German armoured forces attacking the Oosterbeek pocket.[80]

The 1st Airborne Division's determined defence did force German armour crews to be more cautious in how they operated and inflicted fairly heavy losses in spite of the limitations of their anti-tank weaponry. A British report from 22 September confirmed the destruction of at least 6 tanks, 6 armoured personnel carriers (likely half-tracks), 1 armoured car, and 2 self-propelled guns (likely StuGs) around the Oosterbeek perimeter, with other successes being reported but not verified.[81] Though no comprehensive record of German AFV losses in the Market Garden campaign exists, Robert Kershaw, drawing upon the fragmentary German sources and testimonial evidence from survivors, estimates that approximately half of the AFVs committed by the Germans in the Arnhem area were disabled or destroyed during the battle – a considerable total given the relative weakness of the British opposition and a testimony to both the intensity of British resistance and the inexperience of many of the German vehicle crews.[82] These losses did not, however, prevent the German armour from making an effective contribution to the gradual reduction of the Oosterbeek pocket. Overall, the German Army proved extremely effective in making the best use of the firepower resources it had at hand during Operation Market Garden, with even badly weakened, hastily improvised, or second-rate troops able to employ the numerous machine guns and mortars with which they were equipped to decisively defeat almost every British offensive effort towards Arnhem. These forces were then, with the assistance of a handful of tanks and self-propelled guns, able to effectively retake the initiative and commence a counteroffensive that decisively defeated their opponents. Though remnants of the 1st Airborne Division were eventually able to escape, the fact that only 2,163 men remained out of the nearly 10,000 that had originally landed west of Arnhem serves as a testament to the level of firepower that was brought to bear against them by the German defenders.

Chapter 9

Conclusions

Almost as soon as the few exhausted survivors of the 1st Airborne Division had returned across the Lower Rhine, many among the Allied leadership began a concerted effort to whitewash the Market Garden campaign, arguing notable positive results had been achieved almost everywhere except at Arnhem, and that the campaign had advanced the Allied front lines nearly 60 miles across several major waterways, putting them in a much stronger position to resume the campaign in the new year than they had been before it was launched. Montgomery himself famously declared the operation as having been 'ninety per cent successful', emphasizing the considerable strategic value of the bridgehead obtained at Nijmegen and later assuring Urquhart that the 1st Airborne Division's fate was not a defeat, but rather a noble and courageous sacrifice that had in turn enabled valuable successes elsewhere, a sentiment echoed by Generals Dempsey, Horrocks, and Browning in their own 'consolation letters'.[1] Montgomery further argued that the operation had only failed due to factors entirely beyond his control, citing the weather and its effects upon air operations as the primary cause of the failure, a sentiment that was later echoed by Eisenhower himself, who said: 'The attack began well and unquestionably would have been successful except for the intervention of bad weather.'[2]

General Lewis Brereton similarly asserted that the operation had been an almost unbroken series of victories for his 1st Allied Airborne Army, calling it a 'brilliant success'. Brereton noted that the transport commands had been entirely successful in dropping the largest airborne force ever assembled safely and accurately on the planned landing zones, and that the American airborne divisions, at least, had secured all the objectives assigned to them (conveniently downplaying the setbacks at Son, Best, and Nijmegen). Brereton argued that the only dark cloud on the operation's silver lining was fact that the ground forces of the 2nd Army had been unable to make the final link-up with the 1st Airborne Division

– with regards to his own air and airborne forces, he claimed that matters had gone entirely according to plan and with fewer losses than expected.[3]

In spite of these sunny assertions by the senior Allied leadership, the simple fact was that Market Garden had entirely failed to achieve the principal operational and strategic objective for which it had been laid down. Without the sought-after bridgehead over the Rhine, all the Allies had won was a salient into Holland that greatly extended their front lines and exposed the troops holding it to further German counterattacks. Persistent German attacks on this salient through October and into November ensured that Montgomery had to keep the two American airborne divisions in the front line for over a month (in spite of the general policy of avoiding the waste of such highly trained and expensive specialist forces in extended service as mere foot infantry), during which time they suffered more casualties than they had during Market Garden itself.[4] Moreover, adding insult to injury, when the Allies did eventually cross the Rhine, in the spring of 1945, they did not do so from out of the hard-won Nijmegen bridgehead, but rather well to the south, around the German town of Wesel. As historian Michael Reynolds notes, the thrust that had been intended to obtain a highway into the heart of the Reich, in the end, 'led nowhere'.[5]

Moreover, the Allies paid a stiff price to achieve these meagre results. According to the official post-operation counts, Market Garden cost the 1st Airborne Division 281 men killed, 135 wounded and evacuated, and a shocking 6,041 missing, most of whom would spend the rest of the war as German prisoners. To these can be added 59 dead, 35 wounded, and 644 missing British glider pilots – nearly all of whom fell while fighting on the ground as infantry after the landings – and 47 dead, 158 wounded, and 173 missing from the 1st Independent Polish Parachute Brigade, which dropped just south of the Lower Rhine on 21 September in a gallant, but futile effort to link up with the 1st Airborne Division. The American 82nd and 101st Airborne Divisions added another 530 dead, 2,038 wounded, and 974 missing to this grim tally, a clear testament to the ferocity of their own battles. XXX Corps lost a further 1,480 men killed, wounded, and missing, while the VIIIth and XIIth Corps suffered nearly 4,000 further casualties in the course of their own efforts to support XXX Corps' exposed flanks. Finally, the Allied air transport forces also suffered significant losses: 144 aircraft were destroyed, along with 30 aircrew (14 RAF and 16 USAAF) and 12 USAAF glider pilots killed; 238 aircrew (34 RAF and 204 USAAF) and 36 USAAF glider pilots wounded; and 328 aircrew (246 RAF and 82 USAAF) and 74 USAAF glider pilots missing. Overall, Market Garden cost the Allies a grand total of over 17,000 killed, wounded, and missing soldiers and airmen to all causes.[6] Though the Americans could and did replace their losses with relative ease, the fact that the bulk of the butcher's bill for Market Garden fell upon British troops made the failed offensive a harsh blow to a nation already at the very limits of its manpower, particularly as it failed to shorten the war as Montgomery had hoped. Whatever the precise cost of Market Garden, it proved to be a poor bargain.

Furthermore, though several participants and commentators have argued that the potential gains of the operation justified the high risks inherent to the plan and the eventual losses it suffered, it is quite questionable whether the operation could ever have achieved the lofty goals assigned to it.[7] Even if the 2nd Army had managed to reach Arnhem and establish the planned bridgehead on the banks of the Zuider Zee, it simply would not have been able to move immediately and decisively into the Ruhr as Montgomery had wished. With the Allied logistical situation still in dire straits, and the 2nd Army over a hundred miles further from its supply bases than it had been at the start of the operation, it likely would have been left all but crippled by shortages of ammunition and fuel in the aftermath of the initial thrust, leaving it hard-pressed just to defend itself and hold the ground it had won, much less continue the offensive. Furthermore, with the Germans beginning to build up the powerful force that would later conduct the Ardennes offensive, such an isolated and overextended army would have represented a very tempting target for a counterattack that may well have succeeded where the 'Battle of the Bulge' failed.[8] In the end, even under the best circumstances, the Allies would still have needed to prepare a large-scale offensive effort to break out of whatever defensive cordon the Germans would have placed around the Zuider Zee bridgehead in the spring – much as they actually had to do to cross the Rhine in Operations Plunder/Varsity and Flashpoint in March 1945. With such considerations in mind, Operation Market Garden begins to look less like a bold offensive gamble for the very highest of stakes, and more like an ill-considered and reckless effort to grasp at an opportunity that was never really there to begin with.

Even General Horrocks, generally a staunch defender of Montgomery's decision to launch the operation, admitted that his forces may well have faced even greater difficulties had they gotten across the Rhine in light of the potential risks: 'Instead of 30 Corps fighting to relieve the 1st Airborne Division, it would then have been a case of the remainder of the 2nd Army struggling desperately to relieve 30 Corps cut off by the Germans north of Arnhem. Maybe in the long run we were lucky.'[9]

Market Garden's failure also had other unfortunate consequences, both strategic and humanitarian. With the 21st Army Group's efforts and resources diverted from Eisenhower's original intention for it to fully secure and clear access to the port of Antwerp, it took more than a month of further hard fighting for the 1st Canadian Army to open the Scheldt Estuary on its own and bring Antwerp into operation, ensuring the continuation of the post-Normandy supply crisis throughout much of the remainder of 1944, contributing to the vulnerability of the Allied forces to the German counterattack in December. Even more serious were the consequences that Market Garden had for the people of the still-occupied portions of Holland. In the wake of the Allied advance, and the support it received from the Dutch population and Underground, the German authorities enacted a severe reprisal policy, cutting food supplies to the people of western Holland, leading to the 'Hunger Winter' that saw approximately 25,000 lives lost to starvation. It was therefore not merely Allied soldiers that paid the price of Market Garden's ambitions.[10]

Regardless of what came after, or what could or could not have been achieved, the simple fact is that Market Garden was defeated, and that this outcome was at least as much a matter of German success as it was of Allied failure. Though the specific decisions made by the commanders on both sides in the lead up to and during the course of the battle unquestionably had a considerable effect upon its conduct and outcomes, in many ways the results of Operation Market Garden should have been entirely predictable. Given the nature of the fighting that would result from such a plan, involving as it did deep operations by poorly supported airborne forces and an ostensibly bold and fast-moving mechanized advance, and the differing ways in which the opposing forces had been indoctrinated and trained to understand the nature of combat and conduct their battles, it is hardly surprising that, in the fighting in

Holland in September 1944, the Germans excelled while the Allies, and particularly the British, struggled.

Possessing as they did a long-standing military doctrine and culture that accepted the generally chaotic nature of battle and emphasized the vital role of bold, aggressive leadership and the independent exercise of initiative in mitigating the potential friction that such chaos could inflict upon combat operations, the Germans proved very well prepared for the surprise arrival of nearly 20,000 Allied airborne troops deep behind their already badly depleted lines. Guided by the principles of *Auftragstaktik* – which called upon subordinate commanders, and even individual junior officers, NCOs, and soldiers, to take action in the face of unexpected opportunities or threats on the battlefield, even in the absence of orders from above – the German forces in south-eastern Holland mobilized and began to move to block or counterattack the Allied incursion with a speed that exceeded any Allied expectations. This ensured that the airborne forces at Arnhem, in particular, were entirely unable to carry out their set battle plans. In the face of this unexpected and disruptive level of resistance, the 1st Airborne Division's offensive towards Arnhem fragmented into a series of confused small-unit battles. In these battles the Germans – better trained, equipped, and prepared for such situations – seized and retained the upper hand, first blunting the British thrust before decisively defeating it within 48 hours of the initial landings, in spite of the arrival of sizeable Allied reinforcements on the second day of the fighting. All along the corridor formed by the Allies' airborne 'carpet' similarly prompt and aggressive German reactions rapidly pushed the American troops further south onto the defensive. Such actions prevented the 82nd Airborne Division from capturing the critical bridges at Nijmegen for three crucial days, and kept the overstretched forces of the 101st Airborne Division tied down fighting what was often a losing battle to keep the Allied forces' vital lines of supply and communication open. The fact the German forces had long been trained to take action in the face of confusion and to seek out and confront the enemy wherever he could be found, even in the absence of specific instructions to do so, meant that the Allies were never able to take full advantage of the offensive initiative that their airborne drops had created. Instead, the efforts of their forces were diverted to self-defence, slowing their offensive drive to a badly weakened crawl.

These German efforts were further enhanced by the fact that their doctrine had ensured that the infantry units that made up the great majority of the defending forces were very well provided with firepower. With their doctrine emphasizing the need for infantry to be able to conduct offensive operations without an extensive level of support from the artillery, German infantry units – down to even the level of individual companies, platoons, and squads – were extensively equipped with their own machine guns and mortars to allow them to engage, suppress, and defeat their enemy with their own firepower and manoeuvre. These weapons, supplemented by the effective employment of *Heeresgruppe B*'s very limited supply of armoured fighting vehicles, proved to be a critical advantage for the German forces at Arnhem, allowing them to rapidly and effectively suppress and inflict crippling casualties upon the lightly armed and poorly supported British paratroops throughout the fighting. Consequently, within two days of setting out, the 1st Airborne Division was reduced to a fraction of its original strength and forced entirely onto the defensive. Overall, Market Garden presented the German forces with a battle almost ideally suited to their particular talents.

Conversely, Market Garden proved almost entirely unsuited to the doctrine and capabilities of the British forces involved, despite the fact that it was their plan and in spite of what might be seen as their best efforts. Tied to a doctrine based upon carefully planned set-piece battles conducted slowly and cautiously, and relying heavily upon the support of large centrally controlled artillery forces and airpower to generate offensive power, the British ground forces of XXX Corps proved entirely incapable of advancing with the alacrity that was required to reach the 1st Airborne bridgehead and jump the Rhine in a timely fashion. In light of their training and experience, the standard reaction of the British ground forces to even a modest degree of resistance was to stop and call down the full weight of their firepower upon the defenders, an action that often succeeded in overwhelming and driving out the Germans, but only after a time-consuming deployment and execution of a fire plan. With hours being taken to eliminate virtually every German roadblock, it is hardly surprising that the Germans proved able to gather in reinforcements to continuously renew their lines ahead of the Allied advance; by the time one position was successfully overwhelmed and the British advance resumed, another German force had usually moved in behind it, forcing the entire process to be repeated again and again. Though this doctrine was certainly capable of maintaining a steady, implacable forward pressure, it could not achieve the rapid breakthrough and exploitation in depth that Market Garden required.

Furthermore, Market Garden was characterized by the inability of the Allied forces to effectively deploy or employ the overwhelming advantage in artillery and aerial firepower that was perhaps their greatest advantage over their German foes. With their spearhead assault force, the 1st Airborne Division, severely lacking in both artillery and infantry firepower, and with the potentially decisive equalizer of the powerful Allied tactical air forces all but negated due to a combination of both circumstances and poor planning, the British simply found themselves unable to win the critical firefights at the decisive point of the battle. With the immense artillery resources of the Allied ground armies too far away (for the most part) to provide much more than a nominal (if still valuable and much appreciated) level of support to the isolated and trapped 1st Airborne, they were all too quickly overwhelmed by the better armed German infantry forces.

Overall, Market Garden offered the German Army perhaps its last opportunity to win a truly 'German' victory; to employ the skills of leadership, flexibility, and proficiency in rapid tactical manoeuvre that it had developed so diligently in the long years (and decades, and centuries) prior to the Second World War to achieve more than a local, purely tactical success. Such opportunities were few and far between by 1944; with both the Western Allies and the forces of the Soviet Union conducting offensives that – for the most part – skillfully wielded their immense superiority in both manpower and materiel to considerable effect, the Germans were left with few opportunities for the sort of fighting at which they excelled, in which human factors such as leadership, boldness, and quick thinking under pressure mattered more than raw firepower or mass. As long as the Allies stuck to the methods that had proven so successful for them in the recent past, the Germans were unable to muster an effective response. When Field Marshal Montgomery departed from this methodology (which he himself had honed to a very high level of efficiency and effectiveness through the fighting in Normandy), seeking to take advantage of an ephemeral – but naturally very compelling – opportunity to end the war with a single blow, he exposed his forces to defeat by a German counteroffensive. Montgomery, of all people, should have had more respect for German fighting capabilities. Though Montgomery's 'Colossal Cracks' had won a convincing victory in Normandy, and would eventually see the Allies through to final victory in the West in 1945, in the prevailing circumstances of the fighting that took place in Holland in September 1944, it was German combat doctrine that proved the superior.

It is critical to note, however, that this last German victory, however impressive it may have been in the details of its conduct, was an entirely pyrrhic one. At the conclusion of the battle, *Generalfeldmarschall* Model reported that his forces had suffered approximately 3,300 casualties in defeating the Allied drive through Holland, with about one-third of these losses being fatal.[11] However, historian Robert Kershaw, analysing the extremely fragmentary German casualty records, as well as a variety of testimonial evidence, in considerable detail, has concluded that Model grossly understated *Heeresgruppe B*'s losses. From these studies, Kershaw has estimated that *Heeresgruppe B* likely lost between 2,500 and 5,000 men in the Arnhem/Oosterbeek area alone, with a total loss of between 6,300 and 9,000 men across the entire operation – 2 to 3 times Model's figures.[12] These were losses that the German forces, having already suffered through the catastrophic twin blows of Operation Overlord in the West and Operation Bagration in the East that summer, could ill afford; even a 2 or 3 to 1 loss ratio against the Allied forces' numerical superiority was unlikely to achieve victory in the long run. Moreover, these losses were made all the worse given that Germany was now effectively 'grinding its seed corn', throwing half-trained recruits and half-recovered convalescents straight into battle in a desperate effort to stabilize the tactical/operational situation, even when their combat effectiveness in the long run would have been far greater had they been allowed the time to complete their training or recovery. With even training units and instructors being mobilized, Germany was increasingly choosing to mortgage its strategic future in the interest of immediate operational demands.

Such short-sighted focus on battlefield success over long-term planning was arguably at least as much a defining characteristic of German doctrine and military thought and culture as was *Bewegungskrieg* or *Auftragstaktik*. The First World War had been lost largely through the inability of German leaders such as von Schlieffen, Moltke the Younger, von Falkenhayn, or Ludendorff to look beyond simply winning the next battle to actually formulating a practical long-term strategic plan to achieve Germany's specific political goals; in focusing upon details, they entirely lost sight of the larger picture. The Second World War, of course, proceeded and concluded in a largely similar fashion, with the Germans able to win many impressive battlefield victories, but utterly incapable of either keeping up such a level of success, or linking the successes they did achieve together into a meaningful and lasting strategic victory.

Thus, the successful German defence against Operation Market Garden serves as an example not only of the continuing tactical and operational proficiency of the German Army, and its ability to win battles against the odds, but also of that army's wider and much discussed strategic failings, which ensured that it was entirely unable to convert its battlefield victories into a lasting and meaningful advantage over its opponents. The German Army's single-minded focus upon achieving battlefield victory ensured a significant neglect of other, equally important, aspects of waging war, which enabled its less tactically proficient enemies to win out in the end, despite numerous defeats on the scale of Arnhem or worse. In this sense, the Battle of Arnhem was, indeed, a very 'German' victory.

Notes

Chapter 1
1. Quote from Field Marshal The Viscount Montgomery of Alamein, *El Alamein to the River Sangro/Normandy to the Baltic* (New York: St Martin's Press, 1948), p. 324.
2. WO 205/873 *Report on Operations 'Market' and 'Garden', September to October 1944*, pp. 2–3.
3. WO 171/366 *War Diary HQ 1st Airborne Corps – Operation Market Operation Instruction No. 1*, pp. 1–6.
4. WO 205/873 *Report on Operations 'Market' and 'Garden', September to October 1944*, pp. 1–2; Montgomery, *El Alamein to the River Sangro/Normandy to the Baltic*, pp. 312–14.
5. Montgomery, *El Alamein to the River Sangro/Normandy to the Baltic*, p. 281.
6. Sir Brian Horrocks, *A Full Life* (London: Collins, 1960), pp. 195, 203.
7. Montgomery, *El Alamein to the River Sangro/Normandy to the Baltic*, pp. 303–4; Dwight D. Eisenhower, *Crusade in Europe* (Garden City, NY: Garden City Books, 1952), p. 326; Horrocks, *A Full Life*, pp. 203–4; A.D. Harvey, *Arnhem* (London: Cassell & Co., 2001), pp. 18–19; Cornelius Ryan, *A Bridge Too Far* (New York: Pocket Books, 1974), pp. 68–70.
8. Eisenhower, *Crusade in Europe*, pp. 257, 260, 329; Horrocks, *A Full Life*, p. 193; Guy LoFaro, *The Sword of St. Michael: The 82nd Airborne Division in World War II* (Philadelphia, PA: De Capo Press, 2011), pp. 279–80.
9. Montgomery, *El Alamein to the River Sangro/Normandy to the Baltic*, pp. 290–2, 303; Ryan, *A Bridge Too Far*, pp. 61–5; Horrocks, *A Full Life*, p. 192.
10. Montgomery, *El Alamein to the River Sangro/Normandy to the Baltic*, p. 290.
11. Montgomery, *El Alamein to the River Sangro/Normandy to the Baltic*, p. 290; Geoffrey Powell, *The Devil's Birthday: The Bridges to Arnhem, 1944* (London: Buchan & Enright, 1984), pp. 22–3.
12. Ryan, *A Bridge Too Far*, p. 62.
13. Eisenhower, *Crusade in Europe*, p. 329.
14. LoFaro, *The Sword of St. Michael*, pp. 282–3; James M. Gavin, *On to Berlin: Battles of an Airborne Commander, 1943–1946* (New York: The Viking Press, 1978), pp. 134–5.
15. Eisenhower, *Crusade in Europe*, p. 328.
16. Montgomery, *El Alamein to the River Sangro/Normandy to the Baltic*, p. 294; Ryan, *A Bridge Too Far*, p. 66.
17. Eisenhower, *Crusade in Europe*, pp. 344–6; Gavin, *On to Berlin*, p. 136.
18. WO 205/873 *Report on Operations 'Market' and 'Garden,' September to October 1944*, p. 5; Martin Middlebrook, *Arnhem 1944: The Airborne Battle, 17–26 September* (Barnsley: Pen & Sword Military, 1994), p. 437.
19. Sebastian Ritchie, *Arnhem – Myth and Reality: Airborne Warfare, Air Power and the Failure of Operation Market Garden* (London: Robert Hale Limited, 2011).

Chapter 2
1. Ryan, *A Bridge Too Far*.
2. Montgomery, *El Alamein to the River Sangro/Normandy to the Baltic*, p. 324.
3. 'Lions led by donkeys' refers to a perspective (now largely discredited by historians, though still quite prominent in popular perceptions) on the British effort in the First World War, first popularized by Prime Minister David Lloyd George, that exalted the fighting qualities of the common fighting man while blaming apparently 'incompetent' generals for the deadlock and heavy losses suffered on the Western Front.
4. Middlebrook, *Arnhem 1944*; Peter Harclerode, *Arnhem: A Tragedy of Errors* (London: Arms & Armour Press, 1994); Harvey, *Arnhem*.
5. Robert J. Kershaw, *'It Never Snows in September' The German View of MARKET-GARDEN and the Battle of Arnhem, September 1944* (Hersham: Ian Allan Publishing Ltd, 2004).
6. Ritchie, *Arnhem – Myth and Reality*.
7. John Buckley and Peter Preston-Hough (eds), *Operation Market Garden – The Campaign for the Low Countries, Autumn 1944: Seventy Years On* (Solihull: Helion & Company Limited, 2016).
8. Robert M. Citino, *The Path to Blitzkrieg: Doctrine and Training in the German Army, 1920–1939* (Boulder, CO: Lynne Rienner Publishers, 1999); James S. Corum, *The Roots of Blitzkrieg: Hans von Seeckt and German Military Reform* (Lawrence, KS: University Press of Kansas, 1992).
9. Jeremy A. Krang, *The British Army and the People's War 1939–1945* (Manchester: Manchester University Press, 2000); David French, *Raising Churchill's Army: The British Army and the War Against Germany 1919–1945* (Oxford: Oxford University Press, 2000); Timothy Harrison Place, *Military Training in the British Army 1940–1944: From Dunkirk to D-Day* (London: Frank Cass, 2000).
10. Stephen Ashley Hart, *Montgomery and 'Colossal Cracks': The 21st Army Group in Northwest Europe, 1944–45* (Westport, CT: Praeger Publishers, 2000).
11. Martin Samuels, *Command or Control? Command, Training and Tactics in the British and German Armies, 1888–1918* (London: Frank Cass, 1995).

Chapter 3
1. Samuels, *Command or Control?*, pp. 2, 283; Ola Kjoerstad, 'German Officer Education in the Interwar Years: Frei im Geist, fest im Charakter', MA Thesis (University of Glasgow, Scotland, 2010), p. 34.
2. Carl von Clausewitz, *On War* (New York: Penguin Books, 1968), pp. 164–7.
3. Bruce Condell and David T. Zabecki (eds), *On the German Art of War: Truppenführung: German Army Manual for Unit Command in World War II* (Mechanicsburg, PA: Stackpole Books, 2009), p. 17; Robert M. Citino, *The German Way of War: From the Thirty Years' War to the Third Reich* (Lawrence, KS: University of Kansas Press, 2005), pp. 61, 144–5; Trevor N. Dupuy, *Understanding War: History and Theory of Combat* (New York: Paragon House, 1987), p. 23.
4. Condell and Zabecki (eds), *On the German Art of War: Truppenführung*, pp. 9, 17; Corum, *The Roots of Blitzkrieg*, p. xv; Matthias Strohn, *The German Army and the Defence of the Reich: Military Doctrine and the Conduct of the Defensive Battle 1918–1939* (Cambridge: Cambridge University Press, 2011), pp. 14, 114; Williamson Murray, *German Military Effectiveness* (Baltimore, MD: The Nautical & Aviation Publishing Company of America, 1992), p. 206.
5. Kjoerstad, 'German Officer Education in the Interwar Years', p. 38; Samuels, *Command or Control?*, pp. 5, 13–15.

6. Citino, *The German Way of War*, pp. 32, 89, 152; Samuels, *Command or Control?*, p. 11; Corum, *The Roots of Blitzkrieg*, p. 5.
7. Citino, *The German Way of War*, p. 152; Corum, *The Roots of Blitzkrieg*, p. 5; Murray, *German Military Effectiveness*, p. 203.
8. Condell and Zabecki (eds), *On the German Art of War: Truppenführung*, p. 18; Kjoerstad, 'German Officer Education in the Interwar Years', pp. 52–3.
9. Condell and Zabecki (eds), *On the German Art of War: Truppenführung*, p. 4; Samuels, *Command or Control?*, p. 15; Murray, *German Military Effectiveness*, p. 203.
10. Citino, *The German Way of War*, pp. xiii–xiv; Murray, *German Military Effectiveness*, pp. 2–3.
11. Samuels, *Command or Control?*, p. 8; Strohn, *The German Army and the Defence of the Reich*, pp. 25–8.
12. Murray, *German Military Effectiveness*, p. 202; Condell and Zabecki (eds), *On the German Art of War: Truppenführung*, p. 19; Stephen Bull, *World War II Infantry Tactics: Squad and Platoon* (Oxford: Osprey Publishing, 2004), p. 51; Jürgen Förster, 'The Dynamics of Volksgemeinschaft: The Effectiveness of the German Military Establishment in the Second World War', in *Military Effectiveness, Volume 3: The Second World War*, ed. Allan R. Millett and Williamson Murray (New York: Cambridge University Press, 2010), p. 206.
13. Citino, *The German Way of War*, pp. 89, 152, 159, 172–3.
14. Simon Millar, *Zorndorf 1758: Frederick faces Holy Mother Russia* (Oxford: Osprey Publishing, 2003), pp. 63–7.
15. Condell and Zabecki (eds), *On the German Art of War: Truppenführung*, p. 2; Kjoerstad, 'German Officer Education in the Interwar Years', p. 22; Samuels, *Command or Control?*, p. 31; Strohn, *The German Army and the Defence of the Reich*, pp. 26–7.
16. Citino, *The German Way of War*, p. 236; Kjoerstad, 'German Officer Education in the Interwar Years', p. 22.
17. Samuels, *Command or Control?*, p. 61; Kjoerstad, 'German Officer Education in the Interwar Years', pp. 22, 35.
18. Corum, *The Roots of Blitzkrieg*, pp. 8–9; Trevor N. Dupuy, *The Evolution of Weapons and Warfare* (New York: Bobbs-Merrill, 1980), p. 225; Samuels, *Command or Control?*, pp. 88–93.
19. Citino, *The Path to Blitzkrieg*, p. 145; Corum, *The Roots of Blitzkrieg*, pp. xii–xiii, 25, 199.
20. Corum, *The Roots of Blitzkrieg*, pp. 37–9; Strohn, *The German Army and the Defence of the Reich*, pp. 107–8.
21. Corum, *The Roots of Blitzkrieg*, pp. 2–3.
22. Citino, *The German Way of War*, p. 240; Corum, *The Roots of Blitzkrieg*, p. 40; Citino, *The Path to Blitzkrieg*, p. 14.
23. Condell and Zabecki (eds), *On the German Art of War: Truppenführung*, pp. 3, 7, 10; Corum, *The Roots of Blitzkrieg*, pp. 49, 199–200.
24. Condell and Zabecki (eds), *On the German Art of War: Truppenführung*, p. 5.
25. Condell and Zabecki (eds), *On the German Art of War: Truppenführung*, pp. 17–18.
26. Condell and Zabecki (eds), *On the German Art of War: Truppenführung*, p. 37.
27. Condell and Zabecki (eds), *On the German Art of War: Truppenführung*, p. 19.
28. Condell and Zabecki (eds), *On the German Art of War: Truppenführung*, pp. 105–7.
29. Citino, *The German Way of War*, p. 242; Kjoerstad, 'German Officer Education in the Interwar Years', p. 71.
30. Samuels, *Command or Control?*, pp. 159, 167, 196; Strohn, *The German Army and the Defence of the Reich*, pp. 49–58; Murray, *German Military Effectiveness*, p. 20.

31. Condell and Zabecki (eds), *On the German Art of War: Truppenführung*, pp. 119, 128, 131.
32. Corum, *The Roots of Blitzkrieg*, pp. xvi, 205.
33. Corum, *The Roots of Blitzkrieg*, p. 10; Philip Haythornthwaite, *Frederick the Great's Army (2) Infantry* (Oxford: Osprey Publishing, 1991), p. 11; Murray, *German Military Effectiveness*, pp. 207–8.
34. Strohn, *The German Army and the Defence of the Reich*, pp. 95–6; Corum, *The Roots of Blitzkrieg*, p. 74; Samuels, *Command or Control?*, p. 284; Antulio J. Echevarria, 'Auftragstatik in its Proper Perspective', *Military Review* 66. No. 10 (1986), pp. 52–3; Citino, *The Path to Blitzkrieg*, pp. 17–18; Kjoerstad, 'German Officer Education in the Interwar Years', p. 38.
35. Corum, *The Roots of Blitzkrieg*, pp. 78–81, 201.
36. Though it was, of course, quite common in virtually all armies for NCOs to at least temporarily assume command of platoons or even companies, in combat due to losses among officers, the German Army was unusual in assigning NCOs to such posts as an ordinary measure. Corum, *The Roots of Blitzkrieg*, pp. 77, 94, 201.
37. Citino, *The Path to Blitzkrieg*, pp. 105–6; Corum, *The Roots of Blitzkrieg*, pp. 73–4.
38. Bull, *World War II Infantry Tactics: Squad and Platoon*, p. 13; Murray, *German Military Effectiveness*, pp. 210–11.
39. Corum, *The Roots of Blitzkrieg*, pp. 72–3; Echevarria, 'Auftragstatik in its Proper Perspective', p. 51.
40. French, *Raising Churchill's Army*, p. 59.
41. Citino, *The Path to Blitzkrieg*, pp. 82, 96.
42. Bull, *World War II Infantry Tactics: Squad and Platoon*, p. 10; Corum, *The Roots of Blitzkrieg*, p. 71; French, *Raising Churchill's Army*, p. 58.
43. Echevarria, 'Auftragstatik in its Proper Perspective', p. 54; French, *Raising Churchill's Army*, p. 21; Samuels, *Command or Control?*, pp. 10, 15.
44. Citino, *The German Way of War*, p. 287.

Chapter 4
1. BA/MA RS 2-2/34 Reg. Tgb. Nr. 917/44, Generalkommando II SS Pz Korps, Ic, 4th October 1944, p. 1; Kershaw, *'It Never Snows in September'*, p. 68; Ryan, *A Bridge Too Far*, pp. 186–7.
2. WO 171/366 *War Diary 1st Airborne Corps HQ, Appendix J – Summary of Statement by Lt. D.J. Simpson, RE, 1st Parachute Battalion*, 23rd September 1944; WO 171/1248 *War Diary 21st Independent Parachute Company, September 17th to 28th*, p. 1.
3. Horrocks, *A Full Life*, p. 213; R.E. Urquhart, *Arnhem* (London: Cassell & Co., 1958), pp. 202–3; Powell, *The Devil's Birthday*, pp. 92–3; Kershaw, *'It Never Snows in September'*, p. 41.
4. Ryan, *A Bridge Too Far*, pp. 90–1; LoFaro, *The Sword of St. Michael*, p. 306.
5. BA/MA RH 19 IV/56 *OB West Fernschreiben*, 15th September 1944; Harclerode, *Arnhem*, p. 35.
6. Ryan, *A Bridge Too Far*, pp. 53, 124; LoFaro, *The Sword of St. Michael*, p. 326.
7. BA/MA RH 19 IV/56 *Meldung Heeresgruppe B, Oberst i.G. von Templehof*, 1640, 17th September 1944; Harvey, *Arnhem*, p. 64.
8. BA/MA RS 2-2/32 *Zusammengefaßter Bericht des II. SS-Pz. Korps über die Kämpfe in Raume Arnheim, mit 3 Kartenskizzen*, 10.9–15.10 1944, p. 1.
9. Michael Reynolds, *Sons of the Reich: II SS Panzer Corps – Normandy, Arnhem, the Ardennes and on the Eastern Front* (Barnsley: Pen & Sword Military, 2009), pp. 91, 102; Kershaw, *'It Never Snows in September'*, pp. 16, 38–9.

10. Divisional titles, though almost unheard of among regular German Army divisions, were common among the units of the Waffen SS: 'Hohenstaufen' referred to an influential German dynasty that had ruled the Holy Roman Empire in the twelfth and thirteenth centuries, while 'Frundsberg' paid homage to Georg von Frundsberg, a general who had commanded *Landsknecht* mercenary forces for the self-same Empire in the Italian Wars of the late fifteenth and early sixteenth centuries; Ritchie, *Arnhem – Myth and Reality*, p. 128.
11. Wilhelm Tieke, *In the Firestorm of the Last Years of the War: II. SS-Panzerkorps with the 9. and 10. SS-Divisions 'Hohenstaufen' and 'Frundsberg'* (Winnipeg, MN: J.J. Fedorowicz, 1999), p. 4; Kershaw, *'It Never Snows in September'*, p. 41.
12. Quoted in Kershaw, *'It Never Snows in September'*, p. 41.
13. BA/MA RS 2-2/32 *Zusammengefaßter Bericht des II. SS-Pz. Korps über die Kämpfe in Raume Arnheim, mit 3 Kartenskizzen*, 10.9–15.10 1944, p. 7; Harclerode, *Arnhem*, p. 37; Tieke, *In the Firestorm of the Last Years of the War*, p. 230; Ritchie, *Arnhem – Myth and Reality*, p. 128.
14. BA/MA RH 19 IX/5 *Fernschrieben von Oberkommando der Heeresgruppe B an II. SS-Panzer Korps*, 1345, 9th September 1944; BA/MA RH 19 IX/5 *Fernschrieben von Oberkommando der Heeresgruppe B an II. SS-Panzer Korps*, 2200, 13th September 1944; Kershaw, *'It Never Snows in September'*, pp. 39–40; Tieke, *In the Firestorm of the Last Years of the War*, p. 223.
15. BA/MA RS 3-10/4 *Fernschreiben von 9. SS-Panzer Division 'Hohenstaufen,' Abt. Ia, an General Kommando der II. SS-Panzer Korps, Ia, 'Erfahrungen über Abwehr von Fallschirmtruppen bei Arnheim'*, 28th September 1944, p. 2; Reynolds, *Sons of the Reich*, p. 115.
16. Harvey, *Arnhem*, p. 80; Kershaw, *'It Never Snows in September'*, p. 11; Reynolds, *Sons of the Reich*, p. 121; Ryan, *A Bridge Too Far*, pp. 199, 255.
17. BA/MA RH 19 IV/56 *Meldung von Hauptmann Raeßler*, 1315, 17th September 1944; BA/MA RH 19 IV/56, 'Notiz,' 1550, 17th September 1944.
18. BA/MA RS 2-2/32 *Zusammengefaßter Bericht des II. SS-Pz. Korps über die Kämpfe in Raume Arnheim, mit 3 Kartenskizzen*, 10.9–15.10 1944, pp. 1–2, 4; BA/MA RH 19 IV/56, *Meldung von Heeresgruppe B Oberst i.G. von Templehof*, 1640, 17th September 1944; Kershaw, *'It Never Snows in September'*, p. 75; Tieke, *In the Firestorm of the Last Years of the War*, p. 233.
19. BA/MA RH 19 IX/5 *Fernschrieben von Oberkommando der Heeresgruppe B, Ia an II. SS-Panzer Korps*, 2315, 17th September 1944; BA/MA RS 2-2/32 *Zusammengefaßter Bericht des II. SS-Pz. Korps über die Kämpfe in Raume Arnheim, mit 3 Kartenskizzen*, 10.9–15.10 1944, p. 2.
20. BA/MA RH 19 IV/56 *Orientierung durch Ia Heeresgruppe B*, 17th September 1944; BA/MA RH 19 IX/5 *Fernschrieben von Oberkommando der Heeresgruppe B Ia an WB Ndl.*, 2215, 17th September; BA/MA RH 19 IX/5 *Fernschrieben von Oberkommando der Heeresgruppe B, Ia an II. SS-Panzer Korps*, 2315, 17th September 1944; BA/MA RH 19 IX/5 *Fernschrieben von Oberkommando der Heeresgruppe B Ia an Wehrkreis-Kommando VI*, 2315, 17th September; BA/MA RH 19 IX/5 *Fernschrieben von Oberkommando der Heeresgruppe B Ia an Fallschirm AOK 1*, 2315, 17th September 1944.
21. Gustav-Adolf von Zangen, *Battles of the Fifteenth Army Between the Meuse-Scheldt Canal and the Lower Meuse*, MS # B-475 (Allendorf: US Army Historical Division, Foreign Military Studies Collection, 1947), p. 18.
22. Von Zangen, *Battles of the Fifteenth Army*, p. 46.
23. Ryan, *A Bridge Too Far*, p. 222; Tieke, *In the Firestorm of the Last Years of the War*, p. 247; Kershaw, *'It Never Snows in September'*, p. 228; Reynolds, *Sons of the Reich*, p. 142.

24. WO 205/1124 *Battle of Arnhem, SS Panzer Grenadier Depot & Reserve Battalion 16 – German War Diary*, p. 1; Middlebrook, *Arnhem 1944*, p. 118.
25. WO 205/1124 *Battle of Arnhem, SS Panzer Grenadier Depot & Reserve Battalion 16 – German War Diary*, pp. 2–5.
26. WO 171/393 *War Diary HQ 1st Airborne Division, 1st Parachute Brigade Operational Order No. 1 – Operation Market, Annexure D – JA Hibbert, Brigade Major of 1st Para Bde*, 13th September 1944; WO 171/406 *Original War Diary 1st Airborne Recce Squadron, War Diary, C Troop*; Harclerode, *Arnhem*, pp. 69–71; Middlebrook, *Arnhem 1944*, pp. 123–6.
27. Middlebrook, *Arnhem 1944*, p. 162.
28. Harvey, *Arnhem*, p. 78.
29. WO 205/1124 *Battle of Arnhem, SS Panzer Grenadier Depot & Reserve Battalion 16 – German War Diary*, pp. 10–15.
30. Middlebrook, *Arnhem 1944*, p. 162.
31. WO 205/1124 *Battle of Arnhem, SS Panzer Grenadier Depot & Reserve Battalion 16 – German War Diary*, pp. 13–14; Harvey, *Arnhem*, p. 68; Powell, *The Devil's Birthday*, p. 96.
32. Urquhart, *Arnhem*, p. 47.
33. Urquhart, *Arnhem*, p. 41.
34. Cited in Kershaw, *'It Never Snows in September'*, pp. 90–1.
35. BA/MA RS 2-2/34 *Reg. Tgb. Nr. 917/44, Generalkommando II SS Pz Korps, Ic*, 4 October 1944, pp. 2–3.
36. Kershaw, *'It Never Snows in September'*, p. 91; Ryan, *A Bridge Too Far*, pp. 222–3; Tieke, *In the Firestorm of the Last Years of the War*, pp. 233–4, 237.
37. BA/MA RS 2-2/32 *Zusammengefaßter Bericht des II. SS-Pz. Korps über die Kämpfe in Raume Arnheim, mit 3 Kartenskizzen*, 10.9–15.10 1944, pp. 3–4.
38. Kershaw, *'It Never Snows in September'*, pp. 103–4; Harclerode, *Arnhem*, p. 80; Reynolds, *Sons of the Reich*, pp. 116, 118–19.
39. Harvey, *Arnhem*, p. 103; Ryan, *A Bridge Too Far*, pp. 266–7; Tieke, *In the Firestorm of the Last Years of the War*, pp. 244, 249.
40. BA/MA RS 3-9/45 *Funkspruch Nr. 182*, 1700, 17th September 1944.
41. Kershaw, *'It Never Snows in September'*, p. 165; Harclerode, *Arnhem*, p. 90; Harvey, *Arnhem*, p. 103.
42. Reynolds, *Sons of the Reich*, p. 130.
43. Quoted in Kershaw, *'It Never Snows in September'*, p. 108.
44. BA/MA RS 3-9/45 *Ia-Tagesmeldung, Kampfgruppe Spindler an SS-Panzerdivision Hohenstaufen, vom 23.9, 1830 bis 24.9.44, 1900*; BA/MA RH 19 IV/56 *Fernschreiben*, 20th September 1944; BA/MA RH 19 IX/10 *Tagesmeldung 25.9 von Heeresgruppe B, Ia an OB West*.
45. BA/MA RS 2-2/32 *Zusammengefaßter Bericht des II. SS-Pz. Korps über die Kämpfe in Raume Arnheim, mit 3 Kartenskizzen*, 10.9–15.10 1944, p. 9.
46. BA/MA RH 19 IX/5 *Fernschreiben von Oberkommando der Heeresgruppe B Ia an WB Ndl.*, 2215, 17th September; BA/MA RH 19 IV/56 *Tagesmeldung 17.9.44*, p. 3; WO 205/1124, *Battle of Arnhem, SS Panzer Grenadier Depot & Reserve Battalion 16 – German War Diary*, pp. 1–2; Kershaw, *'It Never Snows in September'*, pp. 35–7; Harvey, *Arnhem*, p. 84. LoFaro, *The Sword of St. Michael*, p. 305.
47. BA/MA RH 26-604/1 *Divisions-Befehl Nr. 10, Führungs und Ausbildungsstab WBN, Anlage 1*, 19th September 1944; WO 171/393 *War Diary HQ 1st Airborne Division – Report on Operation 'Market', Arnhem 17–26 Sept. 1944*, pp. 9–10; WO 171/1323 *War Diary 7th (Galloway) Battalion, King's Own Scottish Borderers*, 17th September to

18th September; Harvey, *Arnhem*, p. 99; Harclerode, *Arnhem*, pp. 87–8; Kershaw, *'It Never Snows in September'*, pp. 113–14.
48. BA/MA RH 19 IV/56 *OB West Mittagsmeldung vom 19.9.44*; BA/MA RH 19 IV/56 *OB West Mittagsmeldung vom 20.9.44*; BA/MA RH 19 IX/10 *Tagesmeldung vom 23.9.44 von Heeresgruppe B an OB West*, p. 2; BA/MA RH 26-604/1 *Divisions-Befehl Nr. 11, Führungs und Ausbildungsstab WBN, Anlage 2*, 20th September 1944; BA/MA RH 26-604/1 *Divisions-Befehl Nr. 13 für die Fortsetzung des Angriffes am 21.9.44, Führungs und Ausbildungsstab WBN, Anlage 4*, 20 September 1944; BA/MA RH 26-604/1 *Divisions-Befehl Nr. 16 für die Fortsetzung des Angriffes am 24.9.44, Führungs und Ausbildungsstab WBN, Anlage 7*, 24th September 1944; BA/MA RH 26-604/1 *Divisions-Befehl Nr. 17 für die Fortsetzung des Angriffes am 25.9.44, Führungs und Ausbildungsstab WBN, Anlage 9*, 25th September 1944.
49. WO 171/393 *War Diary HQ 1st Airborne Division – 1 Air Landing Bde – Operation Market, 17th to 26th Sept 1944, Annexure O.2*, pp. 2–7.
50. WO 171/589 *War Diary HQ 1st Airlanding Brigade, Appendix A – Operation Market*, p. 2; WO 171/393 *War Diary HQ 1st Airborne Division – 1 Air Landing Bde – Operation Market, 17th to 26th Sept 1944, Annexure O.2*, p. 9; Kershaw, *'It Never Snows in September'*, pp. 235–6; Middlebrook, *Arnhem 1944*, pp. 341–2.
51. WO 205/1126 *21 Army Group – Operation 'Market Garden' – 17–26 September 1944*, p. 64; WO 171/366 *War Diary HQ 1st Airborne Corps – Appendix R: Message from 130 Brigade HQ to Phantom Air Corps Detachment, 0700, 25th Sept 1944*, pp. 1–2; WO 171/660 *War Diary HQ 130 Infantry Brigade*, 24th September to 25th September 1944; RH 19 IX/10 *Tagesmeldung 25.9 von Heeresbruppe B, Ia an OB West*.
52. Peter Preston-Hough, 'The Viktor Graebner Assault, 0900 hrs Monday 18th September 1944', in *Operation Market Garden – The Campaign for the Low Countries, Autumn 1944: Seventy Years On*, ed. John Buckley and Peter Preston-Hough (Solihull: Helion & Company, 2016), p. 145.
53. James Sims, *Arnhem Spearhead: A Private Soldier's Story* (London: Sphere Books, 1980), p. 50.
54. WO 171/393 *War Diary HQ 1st Airborne Division – Report on Operation 'Market', Arnhem 17–26 Sept. 1944*, 10th January 1945, pp. 28, 33; Preston-Hough, 'The Viktor Graebner Assault', pp. 145–6.
55. Bull, *World War II Infantry Tactics: Squad and Platoon*, p. 27.
56. John Frost, *A Drop Too Many* (London: Cassell & Co., 1980), p. 194.
57. Preston-Hough, 'The Viktor Graebner Assault', pp. 142–3, 145; Stephen Bull, *World War II Infantry Tactics: Company and Battalion* (Oxford: Osprey Publishing, 2005), p. 51; Frost, *A Drop Too Many*, pp. 219–20; Ryan, *A Bridge Too Far*, pp. 286–8.
58. Preston-Hough, 'The Viktor Graebner Assault', pp. 146–7; Frost, *A Drop Too Many*, p. 220.
59. Preston-Hough, 'The Viktor Graebner Assault', p. 148; Frost, *A Drop Too Many*, p. 222.
60. Frost, *A Drop Too Many*, p. 222; Urquhart, *Arnhem*, p. 99.
61. WO 171/393 *War Diary HQ 1st Airborne Division – Report on Operation 'Market', Arnhem 17–26 Sept. 1944*, 10th January 1945, p. 12.
62. Sims, *Arnhem Spearhead*, pp. 113, 115.
63. WO 171/592 *War Diary HQ 1st Parachute Brigade, Appendix A: Operation 'Market', Story of 1 Parachute Brigade, Consolidated Report by Brigadier Lathbury*, 31st October 1944, p. 7.
64. Ryan, *A Bridge Too Far*, p. 170.
65. Harvey, *Arnhem*, p. 95.

66. WO 171/393 *War Diary HQ 1st Airborne Division – Report on Operation 'Market'*, Arnhem 17–26 Sept. 1944, 10th January 1945, p. 41.
67. WO 205/1126 *21 Army Group – Operation 'Market Garden' – 17–26 September 1944*, pp. 14–15.
68. Urquhart, *Arnhem*, pp. 89–90, 111.
69. WO 171/393 *War Diary HQ 1st Airborne Division – Report on Operation 'Market'*, Arnhem 17–26 Sept. 1944, 10th January 1945, p. 35.
70. Reynolds, *Sons of the Reich*, p. 65.
71. Urquhart, *Arnhem*, pp. 117, 122; WO 171/393 *War Diary HQ 1st Airborne Division – Report on Operation 'Market'*, Arnhem 17–26 Sept. 1944, 10th January 1945, pp. 23–4; WO 171/393 *War Diary HQ 1st Airborne Division, Report on German Troops in the Arnhem Area 17–23 Sep 44, Capt PAH Hodgson, 1st AB Div IO*, 27th September 1944, p. 2.
72. CAB 106/1056 *82nd Airborne Division – Operation Market Historical Data*, p. 4; WO 171/366 *War Diary HQ 1st Airborne Corps – Appendix E: Message from 82nd Airborne G-2 to 1st Airborne Corps HQ*, 1810, 17th September.
73. Gavin, *On to Berlin*, pp. 155–60; CAB 106/1056 *82nd Airborne Division – Operation Market Historical Data*, p. 2; WO 205/871 *A Graphic History of the 82nd Airborne Division: Operation 'Market,' Holland 1944, Map Plate #1 – D-Day through D+1*.
74. Gavin, *On to Berlin*, pp. 147–8; Russell A. Hart, 'Mission Impossible? The Mobilization of the German Replacement Army and its Role in the Thwarting of Operation Market Garden', in *Operation Market Garden – The Campaign for the Low Countries, Autumn 1944: Seventy Years On*, ed. John Buckley and Peter Preston-Hough (Solihull: Helion & Company, 2016), p. 111.
75. WO 171/366 *War Diary HQ 1st Airborne Corps – Operation Market Operation Instruction No. 1*, p. 2; Gavin, *On to Berlin*, p. 149; LoFaro, *The Sword of St. Michael*, pp. 292–3; Powell, *The Devil's Birthday*, pp. 75–7.
76. Gavin, *On to Berlin*, pp. 150–1; Powell, *The Devil's Birthday*, p. 77.
77. CAB 106/1056 *82nd Airborne Division – Operation Market Historical Data*, p. 4; LoFaro, *The Sword of St. Michael*, p. 331.
78. Ernst F. Faeckenstadt, *The Activities of the Western Wehrkreis/commandos (military area headquarters) VI and XII and their cooperation with the front in the defensive combat of OB West from September 1944 to March 1945*. MS # B-665 (Allendorf: US Army Historical Division, Foreign Military Studies Collection, 1947), p. 2; WO 171/376 *War Diary HQ Guards Armoured Division, Intelligence Summary No. 64, Appendix A, Part II: 'The Structure of the German Replacement System'*.
79. Franz Mattenklott, *Rhineland, Part 3: 15 Sept 44–21 March 45*. MS # B-044 (Königstein: US Army Historical Division, Foreign Military Studies Collection, 1950), p. 5; Faeckenstadt, *The Activities of the Western Wehrkreis/commandos*, pp. 21–2.
80. Hellmuth Reinhardt, *The Commitment of the 406th Division against the Allied Air Landing at Nijmegen in September 1944*. MS # C-085 (Königstein: US Army Historical Division, Foreign Military Studies Collection, 1950), pp. 6, 8, 15–16; Mattenklott, *Rhineland, Part 3*, p. 6.
81. Reinhardt, *The Commitment of the 406th Division*, p. 8, 16; BA/MA RH 19 IV/56 *Unterrichtung Chef Wehrkreis VI über Maßnahmen des Wehrkreises*, 18th September 1944; Hart, 'Mission Impossible', p. 113.
82. BA/MA RH 19 IX/5 *Fernschreiben von Oberkommando der Heeresgruppe B Ia an Wehrkreis-Kommando VI*, 2315, 17th September; Hart, 'Mission Impossible', p. 114.
83. The SS force was actually part of the Reconnaissance Battalion from the 9th SS Division, which had been transferred en bloc to the 10th as part of the II SS Panzer Korps' reorganization; Kershaw, *'It Never Snows in September'*, pp. 99–101.

84. Reinhardt, *The Commitment of the 406th Division*, pp. 16–17.
85. Kershaw, *'It Never Snows in September'*, p. 120.
86. Kershaw, *'It Never Snows in September'*, pp. 121–2; Hart, 'Mission Impossible', pp. 118–19; Reynolds, *Sons of the Reich*, p. 134.
87. Gavin, *On to Berlin*, p. 165; CAB 106/1056 *82nd Airborne Division – Operation Market Historical Data*, p. 5; Reinhardt, *The Commitment of the 406th Division*, p. 18.
88. Harclerode, *Arnhem*, p. 103; LoFaro, *The Sword of St. Michael*, p. 340; Hart, 'Mission Impossible', p. 121.
89. BA/MA RS 2-2/32 *Zusammengefaßter Bericht des II. SS-Pz. Korps über die Kämpfe in Raume Arnheim, mit 3 Kartenskizzen*, 10.9–15.10 1944, p. 5; Kershaw, *'It Never Snows in September'*, pp. 139–41.
90. Kershaw, *'It Never Snows in September'*, pp. 40–1; CAB 106/1054 *A Short History of 30 Corps in the European Campaign 1944–1945*, p. 33; CAB 106/1056 *82nd Airborne Division – Operation Market Historical Data*, p. 6; WO 171/341 *War Diary HQ 30 Corps, Intelligence Summary No. 504*, 2359, 20th September 1944; WO 171/376 *War Diary HQ Guards Armoured Division, Intelligence Summary No. 71*, 19th September 1944; WO 171/638 *War Diary HQ 32nd Guards Brigade, Brigade Intelligence Summaries, starting from 1st Sept 1944: No. 47*, 21st September 1944; Powell, *The Devil's Birthday*, pp. 131–3.
91. Ernst Blauensteiner, *Employment of the II Fallschirm Korps Between the Maas and Rhine Rivers, 19 September 1944 to 10 March 1945*. MS # B-262 (Allendorf: US Army Historical Division, Foreign Military Studies Collection, 1946), pp. 1–2; Eugen Meindl, *II FS Corps, part III: Rheinland (15 Sep 44 to 21 Mar 45)*. MS # B-093 (Königstein: US Army Historical Division, Foreign Military Studies Collection, 1950), pp. 1–5; Reinhardt, *The Commitment of the 406th Division*, pp. 10, 18.
92. WO 205/871 *A Graphic History of the 82nd Airborne Division: Operation 'Market,' Holland 1944, Map Plate # 2: D+2 through D+4 (19th through 21st Sept)*; WO 171/366 *War Diary 1st Airborne Corps HQ, 82nd Airborne G-3 Periodic Report*, 21st September 1944, p. 1; CAB 106/1056 *82nd Airborne Division – Operation Market Historical Data*, pp. 6–8; WO 171/1250 *War Diary 1st (Armoured) Battalion Coldstream Guards*, 20th to 21st September 1944; WO 171/1252 *War Diary 5th Battalion Coldstream Guards*, 20th to 21st September 1944.
93. WO 171/341 *War Diary HQ 30 Corps Intelligence Summary No. 504*, 2359, 20th September 1944, p. 2; WO 171/341 *War Diary HQ 30 Corps Intelligence Summary No. 505*, 21st September 1944, pp. 1–2; WO 171/341 *War Diary HQ 30 Corps Intelligence Summary No. 507*, 2359, 24th September 1944; WO 171/366 *War Diary 1st Airborne Corps HQ, Intelligence Summary No. 7*, 24th September 1944.
94. Maxwell Taylor, *Swords and Plowshares* (New York: W.W. Norton & Company, 1972), p. 88; WO 205/871 *Report of Airborne Phase (17–27 Sept., 44) Operation 'Market' 101st Division*, 12th October 1944, pp. 1–2.
95. WO 171/366 *War Diary HQ 1st Airborne Corps, 101st Airborne Division G-3 Periodic Report*, 20th September; WO 205/873 *Report on Operations 'Market' and 'Garden,' September to October 1944*, p. 8; Donald R. Burgett, *The Road to Arnhem: A Screaming Eagle in Holland* (Novato, CA: Presidio Press, 1999), pp. 77–8; Harclerode, *Arnhem*, p. 99.
96. WO 205/873 *Report on Operations 'Market' and 'Garden,' September to October 1944*, p. 9; Harclerode, *Arnhem*, p. 99; Burgett, *The Road to Arnhem*, p. 77.
97. BA/MA RH 19 IX/5 *Fernschrieben von Oberkommando der Heeresgruppe B, Ia an Fallschirm AOK 1, Luftflotte 3, AOK 15, WB Ndl, AOK 7, Wehrkreis-Kommando VI*, 21st September 1944, pp. 1–2.

98. BA/MA RH 19 IV/56 *OB West Tagesmeldung*, 20th September 1944, pp. 1–3; BA/MA RH 19 IV/56 *OB West Tagesmeldung*, 19th September 1944, p. 2.
99. Taylor, *Swords and Plowshares*, p. 91; BA/MA RH 19 IV/56 *OB West Morgenmeldung vom 20.9.44*, pp. 1–2; WO 171/341 *War Diary HQ 30 Corps*, September 20th 1944; WO 205/1126 *21 Army Group – Operation 'Market Garden' – 17–26 September 1944*, pp. 45, 48.
100. Taylor, *Swords and Plowshares*, p. 91; Burgett, *The Road to Arnhem*, p. 89.
101. Von Zangen, *Battles of the Fifteenth Army*, pp. 18–19.
102. Powell, *The Devil's Birthday*, p. 154.
103. WO 171/341 *War Diary HQ 30 Corps*, 22nd September 1944; WO 205/873 *Report on Operations 'Market' and 'Garden,' September to October 1944*, p. 14; Walter Poppe, *2nd Commitment of the 59th Infantry Division in Holland; 18 September–25 November 44*. MS # B-149 (Allendorf: US Army Historical Division, Foreign Military Studies Collection, 1946), pp. 5–6; WO 171/341 *War Diary HQ 30 Corps Intelligence Summary No. 506*, 2359, 22nd September 1944; Harclerode, *Arnhem*, pp. 138–9; Reynolds, *Sons of the Reich*, pp. 163–4.
104. CAB 106/1054 *A Short History of 30 Corps in the European Campaign 1944–1945*, p. 37; WO 171/638 *War Diary HQ 32nd Guards Brigade*, 22nd to 23rd September 1944.
105. CAB 106/1054 *A Short History of 30 Corps in the European Campaign 1944–1945*, p. 37; WO 171/1252 *War Diary 5th Battalion Coldstream Guards*, 22nd to 23rd September 1944; WO 171/1253 *War Diary 1st (Motor) Battalion Grenadier Guards*, 22nd to 23rd September 1944; WO 205/873 *Report on Operations 'Market' and 'Garden,' September to October 1944*, p. 15; WO 171/393 *War Diary HQ 1st Airborne Division, Annexure R: Report by CRA 1 Airborne Division on Operation Market, Appendix C to Part 1: 30 Corps Artillery Support*, p. 3; Horrocks, *A Full Life*, p. 126.
106. Friedrich August von der Heydte, *6th Fallschirm Jaeger Regiment in Action against US Paratroopers in the Netherlands in September 1944*. MS # C-001 (US Army Historical Division, Foreign Military Studies Collection), p. 8; Von Zangen, *Battles of the Fifteenth Army*, pp. 21–2; Poppe, *2nd Commitment of the 5th Infantry Division in Holland*, pp. 7–8; WO 171/341 *War Diary HQ 30 Corps Intelligence Summary No. 507*, 2359, 24th September 1944; WO 171/1252 *War Diary 5th Battalion Coldstream Guards*, 24th to 26th September 1944; Burgett, *The Road to Arnhem*, pp. 89–90.
107. WO 205/1126 *21 Army Group – Operation 'Market Garden' – 17–26 September 1944*, p. 53; WO 171/366 *War Diary 1st Airborne Corps HQ, Appendix L: Message from 2nd Army TAC HQ to 30 Corps and Airborne Corps*, 2020, 23rd September 1944.
108. WO 205/873 *Report on Operations 'Market' and 'Garden,' September to October 1944*, p. 20.
109. BA/MA RS 2-2/34 *Reg. Tgb. Nr. 917/44, Generalkommando II SS Pz Korps, Ic*, 4 October 1944, pp. 4–5.

Chapter 5

1. Hart, *Montgomery and 'Colossal Cracks'*, pp. 1–2, 9–10.
2. Ryan, *A Bridge Too Far*, pp. 87–8, 246; Urquhart, *Arnhem*, p. 1.
3. Lewis H. Brereton, *The Brereton Diaries: The War in the Air in the Pacific, Middle East and Europe, 3 October 1941–8 May 1945* (New York: Da Capo Press, 1976), p. 360; Urquhart, *Arnhem*, pp. 119, 203–4; Middlebrook, *Arnhem 1944*, p. 444; Powell, *The Devil's Birthday*, pp. 87, 239–40.
4. David French, 'Doctrine and Organization in the British Army, 1919–1932', *The Historical Journal*, 44, No. 2 (2001), p. 502; French, *Raising Churchill's Army*, pp. 16–17; Murray, *German Military Effectiveness*, pp. 212–13.

5. Samuels, *Command or Control?*, p. 2; French, 'Doctrine and Organization in the British Army', p. 504.
6. French, 'Doctrine and Organization in the British Army', p. 505.
7. Samuels, *Command or Control?*, pp. 118–19; French, 'Doctrine and Organization in the British Army', p. 504.
8. Samuels, *Command or Control?*, pp. 58–9, 63.
9. French, *Raising Churchill's Army*, p. 27; French, 'Doctrine and Organization in the British Army', pp. 498–9.
10. Samuels, *Command or Control?*, pp. 107–10, 113; Frederick Myatt, *The British Infantry 1660–1945: The Evolution of a Fighting Force* (Poole: Blandford Press, 1983), pp. 181, 186.
11. Place, *Military Training in the British Army 1940–1944*, pp. 36–41; Samuels, *Command or Control?*, pp. 113–14.
12. French, *Raising Churchill's Army*, p. 24; Strohn, *The German Army and the Defence of the Reich*, pp. 58–9; Myatt, *The British Infantry 1660–1945*, pp. 182–3.
13. French, 'Doctrine and Organization in the British Army', pp. 497–8.
14. Krang, *The British Army and the People's War*, pp. 1, 21, 37–9; Williamson Murray, 'British Military Effectiveness in the Second World War', in *Military Effectiveness, Volume 3: The Second World War*, ed. Allan R. Millett and Williamson Murray (New York: Cambridge University Press, 2010), p. 91; French, 'Doctrine and Organization in the British Army', pp. 498, 501–2; French, *Raising Churchill's Army*, p. 28.
15. French, 'Doctrine and Organization in the British Army', pp. 499, 512–13; French, *Raising Churchill's Army*, p. 12.
16. Bull, *World War II Infantry Tactics: Squad and Platoon*, p. 11; French, *Raising Churchill's Army*, pp. 14–16.
17. French, 'Doctrine and Organization in the British Army', pp. 404–5; French, *Raising Churchill's Army*, pp. 18–19.
18. British General Staff, *Field Service Regulations, Vol. II. Operations – General (1935)* (London: His Majesty's Stationery Office, 1935), Section 57, pp. 115–17.
19. British General Staff, *Field Service Regulations, Vol. II. Operations – General (1935)*, Section 63, pp. 128–9; British General Staff, *Field Service Regulations, Vol. III. Operations – Higher Formations (1935)* (London: His Majesty's Stationery Office, 1935), Section 18–19, pp. 37–44.
20. French, 'Doctrine and Organization in the British Army', pp. 513–14; French, *Raising Churchill's Army*, p. 129.
21. French, *Raising Churchill's Army*, p. 23.
22. British General Staff, *Field Service Regulations, Vol. II. Operations – General (1935)*, Section 13, p. 27, Section 14, p. 28; British General Staff, *Field Service Regulations, Vol. III. Operations – Higher Formations (1935)*, Section 14, p. 30.
23. Hart, *Montgomery and 'Colossal Cracks'*, p. 131.
24. Krang, *The British Army and the People's War*, pp. 75–6, 79; French, *Raising Churchill's Army*, pp. 48, 55–6; Sims, *Arnhem Spearhead*, p. 15.
25. French, *Raising Churchill's Army*, pp. 58–9, 75; Samuels, *Command or Control?*, pp. 44–7; Place, *Military Training in the British Army 1940–1944*, pp. 46, 48–9.
26. French, *Raising Churchill's Army*, pp. 21, 47.
27. French, *Raising Churchill's Army*, pp. 12, 64–5; John Peaty, 'Operation MARKET GARDEN: The Manpower Factor', in *Operation Market Garden – The Campaign for the Low Countries, Autumn 1944: Seventy Years On*, ed. John Buckley and Peter Preston-Hough (Solihull: Helion & Company, 2016), p. 70.
28. French, *Raising Churchill's Army*, pp. 49–50, 64–5.

29. Krang, *The British Army and the People's War*, p. 83; French, 'Doctrine and Organization in the British Army', p. 513; French, *Raising Churchill's Army*, p. 55.
30. Corum, *The Roots of Blitzkrieg*, pp. 203–4; Place, *Military Training in the British Army 1940–1944*, pp. 28, 32–4.
31. French, *Raising Churchill's Army*, p. 57; Samuels, *Command or Control?*, pp. 118–19.
32. French, 'Doctrine and Organization in the British Army', p. 514; French, *Raising Churchill's Army*, p. 22; Murray, 'British Military Effectiveness in the Second World War', p. 112.
33. Krang, *The British Army and the People's War*, pp. 139–41.
34. French, *Raising Churchill's Army*, pp. 215–20, 232, 239; Murray, 'British Military Effectiveness in the Second World War', pp. 110–12, 118–19.
35. Montgomery, *El Alamein to the River Sangro/Normandy to the Baltic*, p. 9; Horrocks, *A Full Life*, pp. 132–4; Murray, 'British Military Effectiveness in the Second World War,' p. 113.
36. French, *Raising Churchill's Army*, p. 240.
37. Montgomery, *El Alamein to the River Sangro/Normandy to the Baltic*, pp. 16, 20; Hart, *Montgomery and 'Colossal Cracks'*, pp. 7–8.
38. French, *Raising Churchill's Army*, pp. 246, 249; Hart, *Montgomery and 'Colossal Cracks'*, pp. 38–9, 84–5.
39. Horrocks, *A Full Life*, p. 137.
40. Montgomery, *El Alamein to the River Sangro/Normandy to the Baltic*, pp. 20, 24–8, 31–4, 46; French, *Raising Churchill's Army*, p. 250; Horrocks, *A Full Life*, pp. 124–5.
41. Montgomery, *El Alamein to the River Sangro/Normandy to the Baltic*, pp. 34–7; Horrocks, *A Full Life*, pp. 140–1.
42. Montgomery, *El Alamein to the River Sangro/Normandy to the Baltic*, pp. 56–8, 63, 126–31; Horrocks, *A Full Life*, pp. 148–50; Eisenhower, *Crusade in Europe*, pp. 205–6; Hart, *Montgomery and 'Colossal Cracks'*, pp. 5–6.
43. Montgomery, *El Alamein to the River Sangro/Normandy to the Baltic*, pp. 153–4; Hart, *Montgomery and 'Colossal Cracks'*, pp. 8, 79–80.
44. Horrocks, *A Full Life*, pp. 99, 126, 180–2; Powell, *The Devil's Birthday*, p. 82.
45. Hart, *Montgomery and 'Colossal Cracks'*, pp. 10–11, 92–5, 98–100.
46. Hart, *Montgomery and 'Colossal Cracks'*, pp. 99–100.
47. The relative effectiveness of Allied and German forces in the Second World War has been and remains the subject of prolonged and often rather rancorous debates among historians. However, this author would argue that Niklas Zetterling's examination of the overall debate as it pertains to the Normandy campaign fairly effectively shows that the Germans *did* generally enjoy a degree of qualitative superiority, at least with regards to infantry and armoured combat at the tactical level, even if the magnitude and consistency of such superiority remains very uncertain and highly debatable. Niklas Zetterling, *Normandy 1944: German Military Organization, Combat Power and Organizational Effectiveness* (Winnipeg, MN: J.J. Federowicz, 2000), pp. 87–98; French, *Raising Churchill's Army*, p. 273; Murray, 'British Military Effectiveness in the Second World War', p. 129.
48. WO 171/605 *War Diary HQ 5th Guards Armoured Brigade, Operational Order No. 1 – Operation 'Garden'*, p. 2; WO 171/341 *War Diary HQ 30 Corps, Operational Instruction No. 24 – Operation 'Garden', 15th September 1944*, p. 6; WO 205/873 *Report on Operations 'Market' and 'Garden,' September to October 1944*, p. 1.
49. WO 171/376 *War Diary HQ Guards Armoured Division, Intelligence Summary No. 68*, 16th September 1944; WO 171/638 *War Diary HQ 32nd Guards Brigade – Brigade Intel Summaries, Starting from 1st Sept 1944 No. 45*, 17th September 1944, p. 2;

WO 171/1252 *War Diary 5th Battalion Coldstream Guards*, 17th September 1944; WO 205/873 *Report on Operations 'Market' and 'Garden,' September to October 1944*, pp. 1, 6; Kershaw, *'It Never Snows in September'*, pp. 33–5; Roger Cirillo, 'Market Garden and the Strategy of the Northwest Europe Campaign', in *Operation Market Garden – The Campaign for the Low Countries, Autumn 1944: Seventy Years On*, ed. John Buckley and Peter Preston-Hough (Solihull: Helion & Company, 2016), p. 44.

50. WO 171/638 *War Diary HQ 32nd Guards Brigade – Brigade Intel Summaries, Starting from 1st Sept 1944 No. 42*, 11th September 1944; LoFaro, *The Sword of St. Michael*, p. 306.
51. Ryan, *A Bridge Too Far*, pp. 89, 129, 134–5; Ritchie, *Arnhem – Myth and Reality*, pp. 125, 129–30, 142–3; Harvey, *Arnhem*, pp. 31–4; Powell, *The Devil's Birthday*, pp. 40–5.
52. This opening barrage did not include the Guards Armoured Division's two organic field artillery regiments (the 55th and the 153rd (Leicestershire Yeomanry)), as they were to advance with the rest of the divisional column at H-Hour. WO 171/1253 *War Diary 1st (Motor) Grenadier Guards – Royal Artillery Guards Armoured Division Task Table*, 16th September 1944, pp. 1–3; CAB 106/1054 *A Short History of 30 Corps in the European Campaign 1944–1945*, p. 32; WO 171/605 *War Diary HQ 5th Guards Armoured Brigade – 'Future Ops'*, 15th September 1944; WO 171/605 *War Diary HQ 5th Guards Armoured Brigade, Operational Order No. 1 – Operation 'Garden'*, p. 4.
53. WO 171/605 *War Diary HQ 5th Guards Armoured Brigade, Operational Order No. 1 – Operation 'Garden'*, p. 4; WO 205/1126 *21 Army Group – Operation 'Market Garden' – 17–26 September 1944*, p. 36.
54. Horrocks, *A Full Life*, p. 212; WO 171/1256 *War Diary 2nd (Armoured) Battalion Irish Guards*, 17th September 1944; WO 171/1257 *War Diary 3rd Battalion Irish Guards*, 17th September 1944; Kershaw, *'It Never Snows in September'*, pp. 79–80.
55. WO 171/341 *War Diary HQ 30 Corps, Battle Logs Sept 1944: Sitreps from 1535 to 1810*, 17th September 1944; WO 171/1256 *War Diary 2nd (Armoured) Battalion Irish Guards*, 17th September 1944; WO 205/1126 *21 Army Group – Operation 'Market Garden' – 17–26 September 1944*, p. 37.
56. Ryan, *A Bridge Too Far*, pp. 217, 292.
57. WO 171/1257 *War Diary 3rd Battalion Irish Guards*, 17th September 1944; Reynolds, *Sons of the Reich*, pp. 124–5.
58. Ryan, *A Bridge Too Far*, p. 292.
59. Horrocks, *A Full Life*, p. 213.
60. WO 171/341 *War Diary HQ 30 Corps Intelligence Summary No. 502*, 2359, 17th September 1944, p. 2.
61. Peaty, 'Operation MARKET GARDEN: The Manpower Factor', pp. 65–6; Place, *Military Training in the British Army 1940–1944*, p. 121; Ritchie, *Arnhem – Myth and Reality*, p. 238.
62. WO 171/376 *War Diary HQ Guards Armoured Division, Intelligence Summary No. 70*, 18th September 1944; WO 171/638 *War Diary HQ 32nd Guards Brigade – Brigade Intel Summaries, Starting from 1st Sept 1944, No. 46*, 19th September 1944; WO 171/1256 *War Diary 2nd (Armoured) Battalion Irish Guards*, 18th September 1944; Ritchie, *Arnhem – Myth and Reality*, p. 239; Ryan, *A Bridge Too Far*, pp. 292–3.
63. Gavin, *On to Berlin*, pp. 181–2; WO 205/873 *Report on Operations 'Market' and 'Garden,' September to October 1944*, p. 12; LoFaro, *The Sword of St. Michael*, pp. 389–90; Ryan, *A Bridge Too Far*, p. 403.
64. Ryan, *A Bridge Too Far*, p. 399; Kershaw, *'It Never Snows in September'*, pp. 221–4.
65. Peaty, 'Operation MARKET GARDEN: The Manpower Factor', p. 65.
66. Harclerode, *Arnhem*, p. 118; Powell, *The Devil's Birthday*, pp. 162–3.
67. Horrocks, *A Full Life*, p. 221.
68. Urquhart, *Arnhem*, pp. 119, 203–4; Horrocks, *A Full Life*, p. 230.

Notes   183

Chapter 6
1. The sobriquet of 'Red Devils' for British paratroops was apparently coined by their German opponents in the North African campaign, referring to their red (actually maroon) berets and their dogged persistence in combat; Sims, *Arnhem Spearhead*, p. 85; Harvey, *Arnhem*, p. 193; Harclerode, *Arnhem*, p. 11; Powell, *The Devil's Birthday*, p. 62.
2. Sims, *Arnhem Spearhead*, pp. 16–17, 21; Frost, *A Drop Too Many*, pp. 195–6; Peter Harclerode, *Wings of War: Airborne Warfare 1918–1945* (London: Cassell & Co., 2005), pp. 214–16, 225.
3. WO 171/1236 *War Diary 1st Battalion The Parachute Regiment*, August 1944; WO 171/1237 *War Diary 2nd Battalion The Parachute Regiment*, August 1944.
4. WO 171/1247 *War Diary 156th Battalion The Parachute Regiment, Appendix B: Order for Exercise 'Golden Miller'*, 31st August 1944.
5. Sims, *Arnhem Spearhead*, pp. 33–4, 41.
6. Sims, *Arnhem Spearhead*, pp. 17–18; LoFaro, *The Sword of St. Michael*, p. 411; Powell, *The Devil's Birthday*, pp. 37–8.
7. Middlebrook, *Arnhem 1944*, p. 22.
8. Peaty, 'Operation MARKET GARDEN: The Manpower Factor', p. 68.
9. Urquhart, *Arnhem*, p. 124.
10. Urquhart, *Arnhem*, pp. 13–15; Frost, *A Drop Too Many*, p. 194; Middlebrook, *Arnhem 1944*, p. 21.
11. Middlebrook, *Arnhem 1944*, pp. 23–4, 26–8.
12. WO 205/873 *Report on Operations 'Market' and 'Garden,' September to October 1944*, p. 2; Middlebrook, *Arnhem 1944*, p. 39.
13. WO 171/1323 *War Diary 7th (Galloway) Battalion The King's Own Scottish Borderers*, 1st to 10th September 1944.
14. WO 171/366 *War Diary HQ 1st Airborne Corps – Operation Market Operation Instruction No. 1*, pp. 1–6.
15. WO 171/393 *War Diary HQ 1st Airborne Division, 1st Air Landing Brigade Operational Order No. 1, Annexure F*, 13th September 1944; WO 171/393 *War Diary HQ 1st Airborne Division – Report on Operation 'Market', Arnhem 17–26 Sept. 1944*, 10th January 1945, pp. 2–3; WO 171/393 *War Diary HQ 1st Airborne Division, Annexure C: 1st Airborne Division Op instruction No. 9 – Confirmatory Notes on GOC's Verbal Orders*, p. 1; WO 171/393 *War Diary HQ 1st Airborne Division, 1st Parachute Brigade Operational Order No. 1, Annexure D*, 13th September 1944, pp. 3–4; WO 171/594 *War Diary HQ 4th Parachute Brigade, Appendix B: Operation 'Market,' 4th Parachute Brigade Operational Order No. 1*, 13th September 1944, pp. 1–4.
16. Urquhart, *Arnhem*, pp. 10–11; WO 171/393 *War Diary HQ 1st Airborne Division – Report on Operation 'Market', Arnhem 17–26 Sept. 1944*, 10th January 1945, p. 3; WO 171/393 *War Diary HQ 1st Airborne Division, 1st Parachute Brigade Operational Order No. 1, Annexure D, Trace Map of Lines of Approach, Gun Posns, Rough Lines of Main Defensive Line and outer outpost line in Arnhem*, 13th September 1944; WO 171/594 *War Diary HQ 4th Parachute Brigade, Appendix B: Operation 'Market,' 4th Parachute Brigade Operational Order No. 1*, 13th September 1944, pp. 1–4; WO 171/1243 *War Diary 10th Battalion The Parachute Regiment, Intelligence Summary No. 1: Operation Market*, 16th September 1944.
17. Urquhart, *Arnhem*, pp. 6–7, 198; Harvey, *Arnhem*, pp. 38–42; Cirillo, 'Market Garden and the Strategy of the Northwest Europe Campaign', pp. 46–7; Middlebrook, *Arnhem 1944*, pp. 15–18; Powell, *The Devil's Birthday*, pp. 33–7; Ritchie, *Arnhem – Myth and Reality*, pp. 17–18, 178–9, 193–203; Maurice Tugwell, *Arnhem: A Case Study* (London: Thornton Cox, 1975), pp. 24–6.

18. WO 171/592 *War Diary HQ 1st Parachute Brigade, Appendix A: Operation 'Market', Story of 1 Parachute Brigade, Consolidated Report by Brigadier Lathbury*, 31st October 1944, p. 1; WO 171/393 *War Diary HQ 1st Airborne Division, 1st Parachute Brigade Operational Order No. 1, Annexure D*, 13th September 1944, pp. 1–2; WO 171/592 *War Diary HQ 1st Parachute Brigade, Operation Market: Outline of Events, 1st Parachute Brigade*, pp. 1–3.
19. Ritchie, *Arnhem – Myth and Reality*, pp. 184–6.
20. Harvey, *Arnhem*, p. 62; Powell, *The Devil's Birthday*, p. 64.
21. Harvey, *Arnhem*, p. 62; Powell, *The Devil's Birthday*, p. 64.
22. Kershaw, *'It Never Snows in September'*, pp. 106–8, 170, 183; Ryan, *A Bridge Too Far*, pp. 263–5.
23. WO 171/592 *War Diary HQ 1st Parachute Brigade, Appendix A: Operation 'Market', Story of 1 Parachute Brigade, Consolidated Report by Brigadier Lathbury*, 31st October 1944, pp. 2–3; WO 171/592 *War Diary HQ 1st Parachute Brigade, Appendix B: Diary of Events, 1st Parachute Battalion*, September 1944, p. 1; WO 171/592 *War Diary HQ 1st Parachute Brigade, Appendix D: Diary of Events, 3rd Parachute Battalion*, September 1944, pp. 1–2; WO 171/1237 *War Diary 2nd Battalion The Parachute Regiment, Operation Market, Operational Order No. 1*, 16th September 1944, p. 3; WO 171/592 *War Diary HQ 1st Parachute Brigade, Appendix E: Comments on Operation Market*, September 1944.
24. WO 171/592 *War Diary HQ 1st Parachute Brigade, Operation Market: Outline of Events, 1st Parachute Brigade*, p. 2.
25. Quoted in Ryan, *A Bridge Too Far*, p. 234.
26. WO 171/592 *War Diary HQ 1st Parachute Brigade, Operation Market: Outline of Events, 1st Parachute Brigade*, p. 2.
27. WO 171/592 *War Diary HQ 1st Parachute Brigade, Appendix A: Operation 'Market', Story of 1 Parachute Brigade, Consolidated Report by Brigadier Lathbury*, 31st October 1944, pp. 3–5, 8.
28. WO 171/592 *War Diary HQ 1st Parachute Brigade, Appendix A: Operation 'Market', Story of 1 Parachute Brigade, Consolidated Report by Brigadier Lathbury*, 31st October 1944, p. 4; WO 171/592 *War Diary HQ 1st Parachute Brigade, Appendix C: Diary of Events, 2nd Parachute Battalion*, September 1944, pp. 1–2.
29. WO 171/592 *War Diary HQ 1st Parachute Brigade, Appendix A: Operation 'Market', Story of 1 Parachute Brigade, Consolidated Report by Brigadier Lathbury*, 31st October 1944, pp. 3, 6–7.
30. Sims, *Arnhem Spearhead*, pp. 61–4; Urquhart, *Arnhem*, p. 199; Powell, *The Devil's Birthday*, p. 66.
31. Urquhart, *Arnhem*, p. 56; WO 171/393 *War Diary HQ 1st Airborne Division – Report on Operation 'Market', Arnhem 17–26 Sept. 1944*, 10th January 1945, p. 45.
32. WO 171/393 *War Diary HQ 1st Airborne Division, Annexure T: 1st Airborne Division Signals Report on Operation Market, 17th Sep 1944 to 26 Sep 1944*, pp. 1–2; WO 205/623 *Operational Reports Market Garden, October 1944–January 1945, Appendix A: Comments on Report on Operation Market-Garden, Lessons, Operation 'Market-Garden'*, 10th December 1944, pp. 1–3; Urquhart, *Arnhem*, p. 200; John W. Greenacre, 'Assessing the Reasons for Failure: 1st British Airborne Signal Communications during Operation 'Market Garden'', *Defence Studies* 4, No. 3 (2004), pp. 283–4, 305–6; Middlebrook, *Arnhem 1944*, pp. 37–8; Powell, *The Devil's Birthday*, pp. 111–12.
33. Urquhart, *Arnhem*, p. 36; WO 171/393 *War Diary HQ 1st Airborne Division, Annexure T: 1st Airborne Division Signals Report on Operation Market, 17th Sep 1944 to 26 Sep 1944*, p. 2.

Notes 185

34. Urquhart, *Arnhem*, p. 36.
35. Urquhart, *Arnhem*, p. 38; Harclerode, *Arnhem*, pp. 71–2; Middlebrook, *Arnhem 1944*, pp. 128–9.
36. Urquhart, *Arnhem*, pp. 39–40.
37. Urquhart, *Arnhem*, pp. 45–6; WO 171/393 *War Diary HQ 1st Airborne Division, Annexure T: 1st Airborne Division Signals Report on Operation Market, 17th Sep 1944 to 26 Sep 1944*, p. 2; Harvey, *Arnhem*, p. 73; Middlebrook, *Arnhem 1944*, p. 137.
38. Urquhart, *Arnhem*, pp. 61–6.
39. CAB 106/1078 *The South Staffordshires in the Battle of Arnhem*, pp. 4, 7–8; WO 171/393 *War Diary HQ 1st Airborne Division*, 18th September 1944; WO 171/393 *War Diary HQ 1st Airborne Division – Report on Operation 'Market', Arnhem 17–26 Sept. 1944*, 10th January 1945, pp. 9–10; WO 171/393 *War Diary HQ 1st Airborne Division – 1 Air Landing Bde – Operation Market, 17th to 26th Sept 1944, Annexure O.2*; WO 171/589 *War Diary HQ 1st Airlanding Brigade, Appendix A – Operation Market*, 18th September 1944; WO 171/1244 *War Diary 11th Battalion The Parachute Regiment, Appendix A: Account of Arnhem Battle By Lt. J.E. Blackwood*, 18th September 1944.
40. WO 171/393 *War Diary HQ 1st Airborne Division*, 18th September 1944; Harclerode, *Arnhem*, p. 89; Powell, *The Devil's Birthday*, p. 110; Ryan, *A Bridge Too Far*, pp. 309–10.
41. WO 171/393 *War Diary HQ 1st Airborne Division, Annexure C: 1st Airborne Division Op instruction No. 9 – Confirmatory Notes on GOC's Verbal Orders*, pp. 3–4; WO 171/594 *War Diary HQ 4th Parachute Brigade, Appendix C: Copy of Diary Kept by Brigadier J.W. Hackett, Commander, 4 Parachute Brigade*, 2nd October 1944, p. 2; Middlebrook, *Arnhem 1944*, pp. 248–9; Reynolds, *Sons of the Reich*, p. 32; Ryan, *A Bridge Too Far*, pp. 325–7.
42. Urquhart, *Arnhem*, pp. 78–80; WO 171/393 *War Diary HQ 1st Airborne Division – Report on Operation 'Market', Arnhem 17–26 Sept. 1944*, 10th January 1945, pp. 10–11; Tugwell, *Arnhem*, pp. 40–1; Ryan, *A Bridge Too Far*, pp. 321–2.
43. WO 171/393 *War Diary HQ 1st Airborne Division*, 19th September 1944; WO 171/589 *War Diary HQ 1st Airlanding Brigade, Appendix A – Operation Market*, 19th September 1944, p. 2.
44. WO 171/393 *War Diary HQ 1st Airborne Division*, 19th to 21st September; WO 171/393 *War Diary HQ 1st Airborne Division – Report on Operation 'Market', Arnhem 17–26 Sept. 1944*, 10th January 1945, pp. 14–16; WO 171/594 *War Diary HQ 4th Parachute Brigade, Appendix C: Copy of Diary Kept by Brigadier J.W. Hackett, Commander, 4th Parachute Brigade*, 2nd October 1944, pp. 3–8; WO 171/1247 *War Diary 156th Battalion The Parachute Regiment, Appendix C: Account of Operation Market Garden*, 18th to 20th September 1944; WO 171/1323 *War Diary 7th (Galloway) Battalion The King's Own Scottish Borderers*, 19th September 1944.
45. CAB 106/1078 *The South Staffordshires in the Battle of Arnhem, Account of 11 Para Bn*, pp. 12–13; CAB 106/1078 *The South Staffordshires in the Battle of Arnhem, Account of 1 PARA*, pp. 19–21; WO 171/393 *War Diary HQ 1st Airborne Division*, 19th September 1944; WO 171/592 *War Diary HQ 1st Parachute Brigade, Appendix B: Diary of Events, 1st Parachute Battalion*, 19th September 1944, p. 2; CAB 106/1078 *The South Staffordshires in the Battle of Arnhem, Account of 3 PARA*, pp. 20–1.
46. BA/MA RS 3-9/45 *Ia-Tagesmeldung von Kampfgruppe Spindler an SS-Division Hohenstaufen, 19.9.1944*.
47. Urquhart, *Arnhem*, pp. 103–4; Middlebrook, *Arnhem 1944*, pp. 216, 324; Powell, *The Devil's Birthday*, p. 166.
48. Urquhart, *Arnhem*, pp. 81–5; WO 171/393 *War Diary HQ 1st Airborne Division*, 19th September 1944; WO 171/393 *War Diary HQ 1st Airborne Division – 1 Air*

Landing Bde – Operation Market, 17th to 26th Sept 1944, Annexure O.2, p. 5; WO 171/589 *War Diary HQ 1st Airlanding Brigade, Appendix A – Operation Market*, 19th September 1944; Ryan, *A Bridge Too Far*, pp. 339–41.
49. Ryan, *A Bridge Too Far*, p. 211.
50. Hart, *Montgomery and 'Colossal Cracks'*, pp. 8–9.

Chapter 7
1. French, 'Doctrine and Organization in the British Army', pp. 498–9, 506.
2. British General Staff, *Field Service Regulations, Vol. II. Operations – General (1935)*, Section 5, p. 9; French, *Raising Churchill's Army*, p. 27.
3. French, *Raising Churchill's Army*, pp. 39–40; Zetterling, *Normandy 1944*, p. 22.
4. British General Staff, *Field Service Regulations, Vol. II. Operations – General (1935)*, Section 62, p. 124.
5. British General Staff, *Field Service Regulations, Vol. II. Operations – General (1935)*, Section 63, pp. 128–9; French, *Raising Churchill's Army*, pp. 89–90.
6. French, *Raising Churchill's Army*, pp. 256–8; Montgomery, *El Alamein to the River Sangro/Normandy to the Baltic*, p. 24.
7. Hart, *Montgomery and 'Colossal Cracks'*, pp. 92–3.
8. Hart, *Montgomery and 'Colossal Cracks'*, pp. 2, 8–10, 79–80.
9. French, *Raising Churchill's Army*, pp. 242–6; Hart, *Montgomery and 'Colossal Cracks'*, pp. 50–1, 57–8; Peaty, 'Operation MARKET GARDEN: The Manpower Factor', pp. 59–60; Murray, 'British Military Effectiveness in the Second World War', pp. 96–7.
10. Peaty, 'Operation MARKET GARDEN: The Manpower Factor', p. 59; Murray, 'British Military Effectiveness in the Second World War', p. 100.
11. Hart, *Montgomery and 'Colossal Cracks'*, p. 41.
12. Hart, *Montgomery and 'Colossal Cracks'*, pp. 62–5.
13. Montgomery, *El Alamein to the River Sangro/Normandy to the Baltic*, p. 10; French, *Raising Churchill's Army*, p. 259.
14. Montgomery, *El Alamein to the River Sangro/Normandy to the Baltic*, pp. 5, 145; Horrocks, *A Full Life*, p. 122; Hart, *Montgomery and 'Colossal Cracks'*, p. 119.
15. Brereton, *The Brereton Diaries*, pp. 294–5.
16. Montgomery, *El Alamein to the River Sangro/Normandy to the Baltic*, p. 64; Brereton, *The Brereton Diaries*, pp. 142–3; Dupuy, *The Evolution of Weapons and Warfare*, p. 246; French, *Raising Churchill's Army*, pp. 236–8.
17. Stephen G. Fritz, *Frontsoldaten: The German Soldier in World War II* (Lexington, KY: University Press of Kentucky, 1995), pp. 61–3; Tieke, *In the Firestorm of the Last Years of the War*, pp. 86–9, 96–7.
18. French, *Raising Churchill's Army*, pp. 92–3; Hart, *Montgomery and 'Colossal Cracks'*, pp. 67–8; Murray, 'British Military Effectiveness in the Second World War', p. 127; Fritz, *Frontsoldaten*, p. 61.
19. Middlebrook, *Arnhem 1944*, pp. 34–5; Reynolds, *Sons of the Reich*, p. 109.
20. Gordon L. Rottman, *World War II Glider Assault Tactics* (Oxford: Osprey Publishing, 2014), pp. 20–2; Myatt, *The British Infantry 1660–1945*, p. 210.
21. WO 171/393 *War Diary HQ 1st Airborne Division, 'British Guns Landed'*, September 1944; WO 171/393 *War Diary HQ 1st Airborne Division, Annexure R: Report by CRA 1 Airborne Division on Operation Market*, p. 8.
22. Ian V. Hogg, *British & American Artillery of World War Two* (London: Greenhill Books, 2002), pp. 32–3, 51–3; French, *Raising Churchill's Army*, p. 89.
23. Tugwell, *Arnhem*, p. 19.

24. WO 171/1016 *Original War Diary of 1st A/L Light Regt RA for the Month of September 44*, 17th September 1944.
25. WO 171/393 *War Diary HQ 1st Airborne Division, Annexure R: Report by CRA 1 Airborne Division on Operation Market*, p. 3; WO 171/393 *War Diary HQ 1st Airborne Division, Annexure T: 1st Airborne Division Signals Report on Operation Market, 17th Sep 1944 to 26 Sep 1944, RA Communications*, p. 1; WO 171/592 *War Diary HQ 1st Parachute Brigade, Appendix A: Operation 'Market', Story of 1 Parachute Brigade, Consolidated Report by Brigadier Lathbury*, 31st October 1944, p. 6; Harclerode, *Arnhem*, p. 168.
26. Frost, *A Drop Too Many*, p. 221; Urquhart, *Arnhem*, pp. 67, 99; WO 171/592 *War Diary HQ 1st Parachute Brigade, Operation Market: Outline of Events, 1st Parachute Brigade*, p. 4; WO 171/1016 *Original War Diary of 1st A/L Light Regt RA for the Month of September 44*, 17th, 18th, and 20th September 1944.
27. WO 171/393 *War Diary HQ 1st Airborne Division, Annexure C: 1st Airborne Division Op instruction No. 9 – Confirmatory Notes on GOC's Verbal Orders*, 6th September 1944, pp. 1–3; WO 171/393 *War Diary HQ 1st Airborne Division, 1st Parachute Brigade Operational Order No. 1, Annexure D*, 13th September 1944, p. 5; Ryan, *A Bridge Too Far*, p. 276.
28. WO 171/592 *War Diary HQ 1st Parachute Brigade, Operation Market: Outline of Events, 1st Parachute Brigade, Appendix A: Diary of Events, 1 Para Bde HQ*, Monday, 18th September 1944, p. 4.
29. WO 171/1016 *Original War Diary of 1st A/L Light Regt RA for the Month of September 44*, 19th September 1944.
30. WO 171/1016 *Original War Diary of 1st A/L Light Regt RA for the Month of September 44*, 19th September 1944; Harvey, *Arnhem*, p. 101.
31. WO 171/1016 *Original War Diary of 1st A/L Light Regt RA for the Month of September 44*, 19th September 1944; WO 171/1016 *War Diary 1st Airlanding Light Regiment RA, Report by Lt. Col. Thompson*, p. 1.
32. WO 171/393 *War Diary HQ 1st Airborne Division, Annexure R: Report by CRA 1 Airborne Division on Operation Market*, pp. 5–6. WO 171/393 *War Diary HQ 1st Airborne Division, Annexure R, Part II: Conclusions with Regards to Future Operations*, p. 2; WO 171/1016 *Original War Diary of 1st A/L Light Regt RA for the Month of September 44*, 21st to 24th September 1944; WO 171/1016 *War Diary 1st Airlanding Light Regiment RA, Report by Lt. Col. Thompson*, p. 3.
33. WO 171/1016 *Original War Diary of 1st A/L Light Regt RA for the Month of September 44*, 22nd September 1944.
34. CAB 106/1078 *The South Staffordshires in the Battle of Arnhem*, p. 33; WO 171/1016 *Original War Diary of 1st A/L Light Regt RA for the Month of September 44*, 25th September 1944.
35. CAB 106/1078 *The South Staffordshires in the Battle of Arnhem, Account of Thompson's Establishment of Contact with XXX Corps Artillery on Thursday the 21st*, p. 36; Urquhart, *Arnhem*, pp. 121–2; WO 171/393 *War Diary HQ 1st Airborne Division*, 21st September 1944; WO 171/393 *War Diary HQ 1st Airborne Division – 1 Air Landing Bde – Operation Market, 17th to 26th Sept 1944, Annexure O.2*, 21st September; CAB 106/1054 *A Short History of 30 Corps in the European Campaign 1944–1945*, p. 36.
36. WO 171/393 *War Diary HQ 1st Airborne Division, Annexure R: Report by CRA 1 Airborne Division on Operation Market*, pp. 7–8; WO 171/393 *War Diary HQ 1st Airborne Division, Annexure R: Report by CRA 1 Airborne Division on Operation Market, Appendix C to Part I:30 Corps Artillery Support*, pp. 1–2; WO 171/594 *War Diary HQ 4th Parachute Brigade, Appendix C: Copy of Diary Kept by Brigadier J.W. Hackett,*

Commander, 4 Parachute Brigade, 2nd October 1944, pp. 8–9; WO 171/589 *War Diary HQ 1st Airlanding Brigade, Appendix A – Operation Market*, 23rd and 24th September 1944; Urquhart, *Arnhem*, pp. 123, 127; WO 171/393 *War Diary HQ 1st Airborne Division – Report on Operation 'Market', Arnhem 17–26 Sept. 1944*, 10th January 1945, pp. 21, 23–4, 46.
37. Urquhart, *Arnhem*, p. 183; WO 171/393 *War Diary HQ 1st Airborne Division, Annexure P: Letter from Urquhart to CO of 64th Medium Regiment*, 27th September 1944.
38. Place, *Military Training in the British Army 1940–1944*, p. 114.
39. WO 171/1250 *War Diary 1st (Armoured) Battalion Coldstream Guards, Appendix G*, September 1944.
40. WO 171/393 *War Diary HQ 1st Airborne Division*, 21st September 1944.
41. WO 171/341 *War Diary HQ 30 Corps, Battle Logs September 1944, Sitreps Sept 21st*; WO 171/1257 *War Diary 3rd Battalion Irish Guards*, 21st September 1944; WO 171/1256 *War Diary 2nd (Armoured) Battalion Irish Guards*, 21st September 1944; Harvey, *Arnhem*, pp. 125–6.
42. WO 205/1126 *21 Army Group – Operation 'Market Garden' – 17–26 September 1944*, p. 55; LoFaro, *The Sword of St. Michael*, pp. 391–2.
43. WO 171/1256 *War Diary 2nd (Armoured) Battalion Irish Guards*, 21st September; WO 171/1257 *War Diary 3rd Battalion Irish Guards*, 21st September; Horrocks, *A Full Life*, p. 221; Ryan, *A Bridge Too Far*, pp. 412–16.
44. Horrocks, *A Full Life*, pp. 221–2; WO 171/341 *War Diary HQ 30 Corps, Battle Logs September 1944, Sitreps 21st and 22nd September 1944*; WO 171/341 *War Diary HQ 30 Corps, 30 Corps Operational Instruction No. 25*, 23rd September 1944, p. 1; WO 171/480 *War Diary HQ 43rd Division*, 18th September to 21st September 1944; WO 171/480 *War Diary HQ 43rd Division – Message from 43rd Division HQ to 130 Infantry Bde, 214th Inf Bde, and 23 Liaison HQ*, 21st September 1944; WO 171/480 *War Diary HQ 43rd Division, Warning Order from BGS 30 for Future Ops*, 1600, 23rd September 1944; Powell, *The Devil's Birthday*, pp. 180–3.
45. WO 171/1259 *War Diary 1st Battalion Welsh Guards*, 21st to 23rd September 1944.
46. WO 171/341 *War Diary HQ 30 Corps*, 25th September; WO 171/341 *War Diary HQ 30 Corps, Battle Logs September 1944, Sitreps, 22nd to 25th September 1944*.
47. French, 'Doctrine and Organization in the British Army', pp. 503–4; Samuels, *Command or Control?*, p. 103.
48. British General Staff, *Field Service Regulations, Vol. II. Operations – General (1935)*, Section 4, p. 7, Section 62, p. 124; French, *Raising Churchill's Army*, p. 27.
49. British General Staff, *Field Service Regulations, Vol. II. Operations – General (1935)*, Section 4, p. 8, Section 73, pp. 143–4.
50. British General Staff, *Field Service Regulations, Vol. II. Operations – General (1935)*, Section 4, p. 8, Section 62, p. 126.
51. Place, *Military Training in the British Army 1940–1944*, pp. 41, 79; French, *Raising Churchill's Army*, pp. 39–40.
52. Myatt, *The British Infantry 1660–1945*, pp. 195–8; French, *Raising Churchill's Army*, p. 38.
53. French, *Raising Churchill's Army*, p. 136; French, 'Doctrine and Organization in the British Army', pp. 503–4, 508–9; Murray, 'British Military Effectiveness in the Second World War', p. 127.
54. British General Staff, *Field Service Regulations, Vol. II. Operations – General (1935)*, Section 62, p. 125; French, *Raising Churchill's Army*, p. 39.
55. Bull, *World War II Infantry Tactics: Squad and Platoon*, p. 15.
56. Place, *Military Training in the British Army 1940–1944*, pp. 49–53, 58, 60; Krang, *The British Army and the People's War*, pp. 81–3; French, *Raising Churchill's Army*, pp. 203–7.

57. Place, *Military Training in the British Army*, p. 50; French, *Raising Churchill's Army*, p. 206.
58. Bull, *World War II Infantry Tactics: Squad and Platoon*, p. 19; Myatt, *The British Infantry 1660–1945*, p. 211; Place, *Military Training in the British Army 1940–1944*, pp. 53–4, 64–5.
59. French, *Raising Churchill's Army*, p. 207; Hart, *Montgomery and 'Colossal Cracks'*, pp. 7. 97; Place, *Military Training in the British Army 1940–1944*, pp. 74–5, 168–9.
60. Myatt, *The British Infantry 1660–1945*, pp. 200–1; Place, *Military Training in the British Army 1940–1944*, p. 41.
61. Bull, *World War II Infantry Tactics: Company and Battalion*, p. 17; Myatt, *The British Infantry 1660–1945*, p. 206.
62. Myatt, *The British Infantry 1660–1945*, pp. 208–9; Gordon L. Rottman, *World War II Airborne Warfare Tactics* (Oxford: Osprey Publishing, 2006), p. 49.
63. Myatt, *The British Infantry 1660–1945*, pp. 209–10; Rottman, *World War II Glider Assault Tactics*, p. 40.
64. Urquhart, *Arnhem*, p. 199; WO 171/393 *War Diary HQ 1st Airborne Division, Annexure F: 1st Airlanding Brigade Operational Order No. 1*, 13th September, pp. 1–2.
65. CAB 106/1078 *The South Staffordshires in the Battle of Arnhem*, p. 9; WO 171/393 *War Diary HQ 1st Airborne Division – 1 Air Landing Bde – Operation Market, 17th to 26th Sept 1944, Annexure O.2*, 19th September 1944, pp. 5–7.
66. Leroy Thompson, *The Sten Gun* (Oxford: Osprey Publishing, 2012), pp. 34–6, 46; Ryan, *A Bridge Too Far*, p. 332.
67. Thompson, *The Sten Gun*, pp. 38–43; Powell, *The Devil's Birthday*, p. 7; Middlebrook, *Arnhem 1944*, p. 401; WO 171/393 *War Diary HQ 1st Airborne Division – Report on Operation 'Market', Arnhem 17–26 Sept. 1944*, 10th January 1945, pp. 41–2.
68. Rottman, *World War II Airborne Warfare Tactics*, p. 57.
69. Naturally, such charges were at least as likely to see the use of grenades, snap shots by rifles, submachine guns, and pistols, and swung rifle butts as actual bayonets, but the term – emphasizing an advance into close contact with the enemy – was ubiquitous in British accounts; Urquhart, *Arnhem*, pp. 107–9; Ryan, *A Bridge Too Far*, pp. 262–3, 275.
70. WO 171/592 *War Diary HQ 1st Parachute Brigade, Appendix B: Diary of Events, 1st Parachute Battalion*, September 1944, pp. 1–2.
71. Kershaw, *'It Never Snows in September'*, p. 165; WO 171/592 *War Diary HQ 1st Parachute Brigade, Appendix A: Operation 'Market', Story of 1 Parachute Brigade, Consolidated Report by Brigadier Lathbury*, 31st October 1944, pp. 3, 8–9; WO 171/592 War Diary HQ 1st Parachute Brigade, Appendix B: Diary of Events, 1st Parachute Battalion, September 1944, p. 1.
72. WO 171/393 *War Diary HQ 1st Airborne Division*, 2315, 19th September 1944; WO 171/393 *War Diary HQ 1st Airborne Division – 1 Air Landing Bde – Operation Market, 17th to 26th Sept 1944, Annexure O.2*, 19th September 1944, pp. 7–8; CAB 106/1078 *The South Staffordshires in the Battle of Arnhem*, p. 38.
73. WO 171/393 *War Diary HQ 1st Airborne Division, 21st September 1944*; WO 171/393 *War Diary HQ 1st Airborne Division – Report on Operation 'Market', Arnhem 17–26 Sept. 1944*, 10th January 1945, p. 20; WO 171/393 *War Diary HQ 1st Airborne Division – 1 Air Landing Bde – Operation Market, 17th to 26th Sept 1944, Annexure O.2*, pp. 8, 10; WO 171/1323 *War Diary 7th (Galloway) Battalion The King's Own Scottish Borderers*, 21st September 1944.
74. Ritchie, *Arnhem – Myth and Reality*, pp. 27, 36.
75. Montgomery, *El Alamein to the River Sangro/Normandy to the Baltic*, pp. 239–40, 247–54, 263–4, 266, 275.

76. Brereton, *The Brereton Diaries*, p. 299.
77. Dupuy, *The Evolution of Weapons and Warfare*, pp. 248–9; Zetterling, *Normandy 1944*, pp. 38–40, 42, 45.
78. Brereton, *The Brereton Diaries*, pp. 319–20; Horrocks, *A Full Life*, p. 184; Jamie Slaughter, 'Allied Close Air Support during Operation Market Garden: A Lesson in Planning', in *Operation Market Garden – The Campaign for the Low Countries, Autumn 1944: Seventy Years On*, ed. John Buckley and Peter Preston-Hough (Solihull: Helion & Company, 2016), p. 99; Hart, *Montgomery and 'Colossal Cracks'*, p. 120.
79. Slaughter, 'Allied Close Air Support during Operation Market Garden', p. 99; Tugwell, *Arnhem*, p. 28.
80. Brereton, *The Brereton Diaries*, pp. 345–6; WO 205/873 *Report on Operations 'Market' and 'Garden,' September to October 1944*, p. 7; Ritchie, *Arnhem – Myth and Reality*, pp. 235–7.
81. WO 171/341 *War Diary HQ 30 Corps, 30 Corps Air Notes, No. 132*, 16th September 1944, pp. 1–2; WO 205/1126 *21 Army Group – Operation 'Market Garden' – 17–26 September 1944*, pp. 8–9.
82. WO 171/393 *War Diary HQ 1st Airborne Division, 1st Parachute Brigade Operational Order No. 1, Annexure D*, 13th September 1944, p. 6; WO 171/393 *War Diary HQ 1st Airborne Division, Annexure F: 1st Airlanding Brigade Operational Order No. 1*, 13th September 1944, p. 3.
83. Slaughter, 'Allied Close Air Support during Operation Market Garden', p. 102.
84. Cirillo, 'Market Garden and the Strategy of the Northwest Europe Campaign', pp. 48–9; Slaughter, 'Allied Close Air Support during Operation Market Garden', pp. 101–2; Middlebrook, *Arnhem 1944*, p. 68.
85. WO 171/366 *War Diary HQ 1st Airborne Corps – Operation Market Operation Instruction No. 1*, p. 4; WO 171/393 *War Diary HQ 1st Airborne Division, Annexure R: Report by CRA 1 Airborne Division on Operation Market, Part III: Air Support*, pp. 1–2; WO 171/393 *War Diary HQ 1st Airborne Division, Annexure T: 1st Airborne Division Signals Report on Operation Market, 17th Sep 1944 to 26 Sep 1944*, Air Support and Ground Communications, p. 1; WO 205/623 *Operational Reports Market Garden, October 1944–January 1945, Appendix A: Comments on Report on Operation Market-Garden, Lessons, Operation 'Market-Garden'*, 10th December 1944, p. 3; WO 205/873 *Report on Operations 'Market' and 'Garden,' September to October 1944, Appendix G, Air Support Notes on Operation Market*.
86. WO 171/393 *War Diary HQ 1st Airborne Division, Appendix K: 1st Airborne Operational Instruction No. 10 – Additional Notes on Operation Market*, 13th September 1944, p. 1; WO 171/393 *War Diary HQ 1st Airborne Division, Annexure R: Report by CRA 1 Airborne Division on Operation Market*, p. 1.
87. Ritchie, *Arnhem – Myth and Reality*, pp. 213–15.
88. Powell, *The Devil's Birthday*, p. 208.
89. WO 205/1126 *21 Army Group – Operation 'Market Garden' – 17–26 September 1944*, pp. 38–56; WO 171/341 *War Diary HQ 30 Corps, Corps Air Notes, Notes 132–39*; Slaughter, 'Allied Close Air Support during Operation Market Garden', p. 103; WO 205/873 *Report on Operations 'Market' and 'Garden,' September to October 1944, Appendix G, Air Support Notes on Operation Market*, p. 2.
90. Montgomery, *El Alamein to the River Sangro/Normandy to the Baltic*, pp. 319–21, 324; WO 205/623 *Operational Reports Market Garden, October 1944–January 1945, Appendix A: Comments on Report on Operation Market-Garden, Lessons, Operation 'Market-Garden,'* 10th December 1944, p. 1.
91. Urquhart, *Arnhem*, pp. 148, 154–5, 202; WO 171/393 *War Diary HQ 1st Airborne Division – Report on Operation 'Market', Arnhem 17–26 Sept. 1944*, 10th January 1945, p. 43.

92. WO 205/1126 *21 Army Group – Operation 'Market Garden' – 17–26 September 1944*, p. 65.
93. WO 205/1126 *21 Army Group – Operation 'Market Garden' – 17–26 September 1944*, p. 67; WO 205/873 *Report on Operations 'Market' and 'Garden'*, September to October 1944, Appendix G, Air Support Notes on Operation Market, pp. 2–3; Harclerode, *Arnhem*, pp. 168–9.
94. WO 171/366 *War Diary 1st Airborne Corps HQ, Appendix M: Message from 1 A/B Division to 30 Corps*, 0900, 24th September 1944; WO 171/406 *War Diary 1st Airborne Reconnaissance Squadron, Squadron HQ*, 25th September 1944.
95. Urquhart, *Arnhem*, p. 155; WO 171/393 *War Diary HQ 1st Airborne Division – Report on Operation 'Market', Arnhem 17–26 Sept. 1944*, 10th January 1945, p. 43.

Chapter 8

1. Eisenhower, *Crusade in Europe*, pp. 315, 340.
2. BA/MA RH 19 IV/56 *Fernschreiben von Chef Wehrm. Führ. Stab Jodl an Armeegruppe B und OKB West*, 1940, 15th September 1944; Ryan, *A Bridge Too Far*, pp. 51–2.
3. Harclerode, *Arnhem*, pp. 36–7; Reynolds, *Sons of the Reich*, pp. 91, 102.
4. Kershaw, *'It Never Snows in September'*, pp. 103–4, 311.
5. Samuel W. Mitcham, Jr, *German Order of Battle, Volume One: 1st–290th Infantry Divisions in WWII* (Mechanicsburg, PA: Stackpole Books, 2007), pp. 3–5.
6. Jeffrey Ethell and Dr Alfred Price, *Target Berlin: Mission 250, 6 March 1944* (London: Greenhill Books, 1981), pp. 153–5; Steven J. Zaloga, *Operation Pointblank 1944: Defeating the Luftwaffe* (Oxford: Osprey Publishing, 2011), pp. 86–9.
7. WO 205/693 *German Air Force Reaction to Airborne Landings in Holland – Headquarters, First Allied Airborne Army*, 2nd October 1944, p. 2.
8. WO 205/693 *German Air Force Reaction to Airborne Landings in Holland – Headquarters, First Allied Airborne Army*, 2nd October 1944, p. 3.
9. Frost, *A Drop Too Many*, p. 229; WO 171/366 *War Diary 1st Airborne Corps HQ (Main)*, 1800, 17th September 1944; WO 171/341 *War Diary HQ 30 Corps, Battle Logs September 1944, Sitrep 1405 20th September*; WO 171/393 *War Diary HQ 1st Airborne Division – Report on Operation 'Market', Arnhem 17–26 Sept. 1944*, 10th January 1945, p. 17; WO 171/406 *War Diary 1st Airborne Reconnaissance Squadron, C Troop*, 18th September; WO 171/393 *War Diary HQ 1st Airborne Division – 1 Air Landing Bde – Operation Market, 17th to 26th Sept 1944, Annexure O.2*, p. 5; WO 171/638 *War Diary HQ 32nd Guards Armoured Brigade*, 19th September 1944.
10. WO 171/376 *War Diary HQ Guards Armoured Division, Combat War Diary*, 19th September 1944; Burgett, *The Road to Arnhem*, pp. 60–2; WO 205/693 *German Air Force Reaction to Airborne Landings in Holland – Headquarters, First Allied Airborne Army*, 2nd October 1944, p. 3.
11. Condell and Zabecki (eds), *On the German Art of War: Truppenführung*, pp. 92, 329; Corum, *The Roots of Blitzkrieg*, p. 42.
12. Dupuy, *The Evolution of Weapons and Warfare*, pp. 226, 229; Samuels, *Command or Control?*, pp. 88–93, 239–40, 271.
13. Corum, *The Roots of Blitzkrieg*, pp. 42–3.
14. Condell and Zabecki (eds), *On the German Art of War: Truppenführung*, pp. 93, 95, 100–2, 107, 330, 338, 356–8, 380.
15. Bull, *World War II Infantry Tactics: Squad and Platoon*, p. 30.
16. W.J.K. Davies, *German Army Handbook 1939–1945* (New York: Arco Publishing, 1977), p. 39.
17. Davies, *German Army Handbook 1939–1945*, p. 33.

18. John Norris, *Infantry Mortars of World War II* (Oxford: Osprey Publishing, 2002), p. 33; Hogg, *German Artillery of World War Two*, p. 45.
19. Von Zangen, *Battles of the Fifteenth Army*, p. 8.
20. Quoted in Kershaw, *'It Never Snows in September'*, p. 106.
21. Kershaw, *'It Never Snows in September'*, p. 47; WO 171/393 *War Diary HQ 1st Airborne Division, Intelligence Summary No. 3*, 0900, 21st September 1944, p. 2.
22. WO 171/393 *War Diary HQ 1st Airborne Division, Intelligence Summary No. 3*, 0900, 21st September 1944, p. 2.
23. BA/MA RS 3-10/4 *Fernschreiben von 9. SS-Panzer Division 'Hohenstaufen,' Abt. Ia, an General Kommando der II. SS-Panzer Korps, Ia, 'Gliederung der Kampfgruppen'*, 28th September 1944.
24. Citino, *The Path to Blitzkrieg*, pp. 31–3.
25. Bull, *World War II Infantry Tactics: Company and Battalion*, pp. 17, 19–20; Bull, *World War II Infantry Tactics: Squad and Platoon*, pp. 26–7; French, *Raising Churchill's Army*, p. 87.
26. WO 171/592 *War Diary HQ 1st Parachute Brigade, Appendix D: Diary of Events, 3rd Parachute Battalion*, 18th September 1944, p. 3; WO 171/592 *War Diary HQ 1st Parachute Brigade, Appendix B: Diary of Events, 1st Parachute Battalion*, 18th September 1944, p. 1; Sims, *Arnhem Spearhead*, pp. 63, 65, 69.
27. Kershaw, *'It Never Snows in September'*, p. 105.
28. WO 171/592 *War Diary HQ 1st Parachute Brigade, Operation Market: Outline of Events, 1st Parachute Brigade*, p. 2; WO 171/393 *War Diary HQ 1st Airborne Division – Report on Operation 'Market', Arnhem 17–26 Sept. 1944*, 10th January 1945, p. 6; WO 171/592 *War Diary HQ 1st Parachute Brigade, Appendix A: Operation 'Market', Story of 1 Parachute Brigade, Consolidated Report by Brigadier Lathbury*, 31st October 1944, p. 3; WO 171/592 *War Diary HQ 1st Parachute Brigade, Appendix B: Diary of Events, 1st Parachute Battalion*, 17th September 1944, p. 1.
29. Sims, *Arnhem Spearhead*, pp. 63–5.
30. WO 171/592 *War Diary HQ 1st Parachute Brigade, Appendix A: Operation 'Market', Story of 1 Parachute Brigade, Consolidated Report by Brigadier Lathbury*, 31st October 1944, p. 3; WO 171/592 *War Diary HQ 1st Parachute Brigade, Appendix D: Diary of Events, 3rd Parachute Battalion*, September 1944, p. 2; Urquhart, *Arnhem*, pp. 40, 45; Ryan, *A Bridge Too Far*, p. 233.
31. WO 171/592 *War Diary HQ 1st Parachute Brigade, Appendix B: Diary of Events, 1st Parachute Battalion*, 18th September 1944, pp. 1–2.
32. WO 171/393 *War Diary HQ 1st Airborne Division, Annexure P: Copy of Pigeon Message received at Airborne Troops HQ (Rear) on September 26th – dispatched on Sept 18th*, p. 1.
33. WO 205/1124 *Battle of Arnhem, SS Panzer Grenadier Depot & Reserve Battalion 16 – German War Diary*, pp. 7, 22–3.
34. WO 205/1124 *Battle of Arnhem, SS Panzer Grenadier Depot & Reserve Battalion 16 – German War Diary*, pp. 10–11.
35. WO 171/592 *War Diary HQ 1st Parachute Brigade, Appendix A: Operation 'Market', Story of 1 Parachute Brigade, Consolidated Report by Brigadier Lathbury*, 31st October 1944, pp. 7–8.
36. Quoted in Ryan, *A Bridge Too Far*, p. 323; Tieke, *In the Firestorm of the Last Years of the War*, p. 246.
37. Ryan, *A Bridge Too Far*, p. 323.
38. WO 171/393 *War Diary HQ 1st Airborne Division, Intelligence Summary No. 4*, 22nd September 1944, p. 1; WO 171/393 *War Diary HQ 1st Airborne Division, Report on German Troops in the Arnhem Area 17–23 Sep 44, Capt PAH Hodgson, 1st AB Div IO*,

27th September 1944, p. 2; Middlebrook, *Arnhem 1944*, p. 352; Reynolds, *Sons of the Reich*, p. 160.
39. BA/MA RS 2-2/32 *Zusammengefaßter Bericht des II. SS-Pz. Korps über die Kämpfe in Raume Arnheim, mit 3 Kartenskizzen*, 10.9–15.10 1944, p. 6; Kershaw, '*It Never Snows in September*', p. 230.
40. BA/MA RS 3-9/45 *Tagesmeldung von Artillerie-Regiment 191 an 9. SS-Pz Division*, 1300, 23.9.44; BA/MA RS 3-9/45 *Tagesmeldung von Artillerie-Regiment 191 an 9. SS-Pz Division*, 24.9.44; BA/MA RS 3-9/45 *Tagesmeldung von Artillerie-Regiment 191 an 9. SS-Pz Division*, 1900, 25.9.44; BA/MA RS 3-9/45 *Tagesmeldung von Artillerie-Regiment 191 an 9. SS-Pz Division*, 1900, 26.9.44.
41. BA/MA RS 3-9/45 *Ia-Tagesmeldung von Kampfgruppe Spindler an SS-Panzerdivision Hohenstaufen, vom 23.9, 1830 bis 24.9.1900*.
42. BA/MA RS 2-2/32 *Zusammengefaßter Bericht des II. SS-Pz. Korps über die Kämpfe in Raume Arnheim, mit 3 Kartenskizzen*, 10.9–15.10 1944, p. 9.
43. Bull, *World War II Infantry Tactics: Company and Battalion*, p. 22.
44. Norris, *Infantry Mortars*, pp. 23–4, 33; Hogg, *German Artillery of World War Two*, p. 45.
45. Terry Copp, 'Counter-Mortar Operational Research in the 21 Army Group', *Canadian Military History*, 3, No. 2 (1994), p. 4; French, *Raising Churchill's Army*, p. 88.
46. WO 171/1253 *War Diary 1st (Motor) Grenadier Guards, Appendix A: 'The King's Company – July to September 1944*, p. 2.
47. WO 171/393 *War Diary HQ 1st Airborne Division*, 20th to 24th September 1944; WO 171/393 *War Diary HQ 1st Airborne Division – 1 Air Landing Bde – Operation Market, 17th to 26th Sept 1944*, Annexure O.2, pp. 11–12; WO 171/594 *War Diary HQ 4th Parachute Brigade, Appendix C: Copy of Diary Kept by Brigadier J.W. Hackett, Commander, 4 Parachute Brigade*, 2nd October 1944, p. 10; WO 171/1236 *War Diary 1st Battalion The Parachute Regiment*, 22nd September to 24th September 1944, p. 4; WO 171/1244 *War Diary 11th Battalion The Parachute Regiment, Appendix A: Account of Arnhem Battle, 11th Bn the Parachute Regiment, by Lt. JE Blackwood*, 22nd September to 25th September 1944; WO 171/589 *War Diary HQ 1st Airlanding Brigade, Appendix A – Operation Market*, 20th September 1944.
48. BA/MA RS 3-9/45 *Ia-Tagesmeldung von Kampfgruppe Krafft an 9. SS-Panzerdivision 'Hohenstaufen'*, 25.9.44.
49. WO 171/393 *War Diary HQ 1st Airborne Division – 1 Air Landing Bde – Operation Market, 17th to 26th Sept 1944*, Annexure O.2, pp. 9, 14; WO 171/406 *War Diary 1st Airborne Reconnaissance Squadron, Squadron HQ*, 20th to 25th September 1944.
50. Urquhart, *Arnhem*, pp. 146–7, 161; WO 171/393 *War Diary HQ 1st Airborne Division*, 23rd September 1944; WO 171/594 *War Diary HQ 4th Parachute Brigade, Appendix C: Copy of Diary Kept by Brigadier J.W. Hackett, Commander, 4 Parachute Brigade*, 2nd October 1944, 23rd September 1944, p. 10; Ryan, *A Bridge Too Far*, p. 435.
51. Powell, *The Devil's Birthday*, p. 189; Ryan, *A Bridge Too Far*, p. 449.
52. Urquhart, *Arnhem*, pp. 125, 153; WO 171/393 *War Diary HQ 1st Airborne Division*, 24th September; WO 171/393 *War Diary HQ 1st Airborne Division – 1 Air Landing Bde – Operation Market, 17th to 26th Sept 1944*, Annexure O.2, pp. 8, 11; WO 171/594 *War Diary HQ 4th Parachute Brigade, Appendix C: Copy of Diary Kept by Brigadier J.W. Hackett, Commander, 4 Parachute Brigade*, 2nd October 1944, 21st and 23rd September, pp. 8, 12.
53. WO 171/393 *War Diary HQ 1st Airborne Division – Report on Operation 'Market', Arnhem 17–26 Sept. 1944*, 10th January 1945, pp. 21, 41–2, 47.
54. WO 171/393 *War Diary HQ 1st Airborne Division, Annexure R: Report by CRA 1 Airborne Division on Operation Market, Part II, Conclusions with Regard to Future Operations*, p. 4.

55. Sims, *Arnhem Spearhead*, pp. 85–90, 106–7; WO 171/592 *War Diary 1st Parachute Brigade, Operation Market – Outline of Events, Appendix A: Diary of Events, 1 Para Bde HQ*, pp. 4–5, 7–8; Harvey, *Arnhem*, p. 90.
56. Harclerode, *Arnhem*, p. 35.
57. BA/MA RH 19 IX/5 *Fernschrieben von Oberkommando der Heersegruppe B an II. SS-Panzer Korps*, 1930, 18th September 1944; Harvey, *Arnhem*, p. 103; Kershaw, *'It Never Snows in September'*, p. 134; Harclerode, *Arnhem*, p. 95; Reynolds, *Sons of the Reich*, pp. 129, 137.
58. Harvey, *Arnhem*, pp. 159, 171; Harclerode, *Arnhem*, p. 129; Kershaw, *'It Never Snows in September'*, p. 274.
59. Kershaw, *'It Never Snows in September'*, pp. 170, 238–9; Harclerode, *Arnhem*, p. 91.
60. WO 171/592 *War Diary HQ 1st Parachute Brigade, Appendix A: Operation 'Market', Story of 1 Parachute Brigade, Consolidated Report by Brigadier Lathbury*, 31st October 1944, pp. 5–6; WO 171/592 *War Diary HQ 1st Parachute Brigade, Appendix B: Diary of Events, 1st Parachute Battalion*, September 1944, p. 1; WO 171/592 *War Diary HQ 1st Parachute Brigade, Appendix D: Diary of Events, 3rd Parachute Battalion*, September 1944, p. 2.
61. WO 171/594 *War Diary HQ 4th Parachute Brigade, Appendix C: Copy of Diary Kept by Brigadier J.W. Hackett, Commander, 4 Parachute Brigade*, 2nd October 1944, p. 3; WO 171/1247 *War Diary 156th Battalion The Parachute Regiment, Appendix C: Account of Operation Market Garden*, 19th September 1944, pp. 1–2; Harvey, *Arnhem*, pp. 107–8; Harclerode, *Arnhem*, pp. 91–2; Kershaw, *'It Never Snows in September'*, pp. 174–5.
62. CAB 106/1078 *The South Staffordshires in the Battle of Arnhem*, p. 22; WO 171/393 *War Diary HQ 1st Airborne Division, Report on German Troops in the Arnhem Area 17–23 Sep 44, Capt PAH Hodgson, 1st AB Div IO*, 27th September, p. 2; Harvey, *Arnhem*, pp. 103–6; Harclerode, *Arnhem*, p. 90; Kershaw, *'It Never Snows in September'*, p. 169.
63. WO 171/592 *War Diary HQ 1st Parachute Brigade, Appendix C: Diary of Events, 2nd Parachute Battalion*, September 1944, p. 2; Powell, *The Devil's Birthday*, p. 105.
64. Quoted in Ryan, *A Bridge Too Far*, p. 363.
65. WO 171/366 *War Diary 1st Airborne Corps HQ, Appendix J – Summary of Statement by Lt. D.J. Simpson, RE, 1st Parachute Battalion*, 23rd September 1944; WO 171/393 *War Diary HQ 1st Airborne Division – Report on Operation 'Market', Arnhem 17–26 Sept. 1944*, 10th January 1945, pp. 6, 12; WO 171/592 *War Diary HQ 1st Parachute Brigade, Operation Market: Outline of Events, 1st Parachute Brigade*, pp. 5, 7–8; WO 171/592 *War Diary HQ 1st Parachute Brigade, Appendix A: Operation 'Market', Story of 1 Parachute Brigade, Consolidated Report by Brigadier Lathbury*, 31st October 1944, pp. 9–10; Kershaw, *'It Never Snows in September'*, pp. 177–80; Middlebrook, *Arnhem 1944*, pp. 301–6.
66. CAB 106/1078 *The South Staffordshires in the Battle of Arnhem, Account of 1st PARA*, p. 19; CAB 106/1078 *The South Staffordshires in the Battle of Arnhem, Account of 11 Para Bn – Lt. Col. Lee*, p. 13; WO 171/393 *War Diary HQ 1st Airborne Division – Report on Operation 'Market', Arnhem 17–26 Sept. 1944*, 10th January 1945, pp. 13–14; WO 171/1244 *War Diary 11th Battalion The Parachute Regiment, Appendix A: Account of Arnhem Battle, 11th Bn the Parachute Regiment, by Lt. JE Blackwood*, 19th September 1944; Middlebrook, *Arnhem 1944*, pp. 201–5.
67. WO 171/341 *War Diary HQ 30 Corps Intelligence Summary No. 507*, 2359, 24th September; WO 171/393 *War Diary HQ 1st Airborne Division – 1 Air Landing Bde – Operation Market, 17th to 26th Sept 1944, Annexure O.2*, p. 12; WO 171/594 *War Diary HQ 4th Parachute Brigade, Appendix C: Copy of Diary Kept by Brigadier J.W. Hackett, Commander, 4 Parachute Brigade*, 2nd October 1944, pp. 9–10; WO 171/1016 *War*

Diary 1st Airlanding Light Regiment RA, Report by Lt. Col. Thompson, 20th September 1944, p. 2; WO 171/1248 *War Diary 21st Independent Parachute Company*, 22nd September 1944, p. 3; WO 171/393 *War Diary HQ 1st Airborne Division – Report on Operation 'Market', Arnhem 17–26 Sept. 1944*, 10th January 1945, p. 19.
68. WO 171/594 *War Diary HQ 4th Parachute Brigade, Appendix C: Copy of Diary Kept by Brigadier J.W. Hackett, Commander, 4 Parachute Brigade*, 2nd October 1944, 23rd September 1944, p. 10.
69. WO 171/1016 *War Diary 1st Airlanding Light Regiment RA, Report by Lt. Col. Thompson*, 20th September 1944, p. 3.
70. WO 171/393 *War Diary HQ 1st Airborne Division*, 'British Guns Landed', September 1944; WO 171/393 *War Diary HQ 1st Airborne Division, Annexure R: Report by CRA 1 Airborne Division on Operation Market*, pp. 4, 8.
71. French, *Raising Churchill's Army*, p. 95.
72. WO 171/393 *War Diary HQ 1st Airborne Division*, 'British Guns Landed', September 1944; WO 171/393 *War Diary HQ 1st Airborne Division, Annexure R: Report by CRA 1 Airborne Division on Operation Market*, p. 4.
73. Middlebrook, *Arnhem 1944*, pp. 131–3.
74. WO 171/592 *War Diary HQ 1st Parachute Brigade, Appendix E: Comments on Operation Market*, September 1944.
75. Reynolds, *Sons of the Reich*, p. 154.
76. WO 171/393 *War Diary HQ 1st Airborne Division*, 'British Guns Landed', September 1944; WO 171/393 *War Diary HQ 1st Airborne Division, Annexure R: Report by CRA 1 Airborne Division on Operation Market*, p. 8.
77. WO 171/592 *War Diary HQ 1st Parachute Brigade, Appendix A: Operation 'Market', Story of 1 Parachute Brigade, Consolidated Report by Brigadier Lathbury*, 31st October 1944, pp. 6, 9.
78. WO 171/1323 *War Diary 7th (Galloway) Battalion The King's Own Scottish Borderers*, 21st September 1944.
79. Bull, *World War II Infantry Tactics: Company and Battalion*, pp. 41–2.
80. WO 171/592 *War Diary HQ 1st Parachute Brigade, Appendix D: Diary of Events, 3rd Parachute Battalion*, September 1944, p. 6; WO 171/1244 *War Diary 11th Battalion The Parachute Regiment, Appendix A: Account of Arnhem Battle By Lt. J.E. Blackwood*, 21st September 1944; Ryan, *A Bridge Too Far*, pp. 451–2.
81. WO 171/393 *War Diary HQ 1st Airborne Division, Intelligence Summary No. 4*, 22nd September 1944, p. 2.
82. Kershaw, *'It Never Snows in September'*, pp. 274–6.

Chapter 9
1. Montgomery, *El Alamein to the River Sangro/Normandy to the Baltic*, pp. 324–6; WO 171/393 *War Diary HQ 1st Airborne Division, Annexure P: Letter from Montgomery to Urquhart, 28th Sept 1944, Letter from Dempsey to Urquhart, 29th Sept 1944, Letter from Horrocks to Urquhart, 26th Sept 1944, Letter from Browning to Urquhart, 26th Sept 1944*; WO 205/623 *Operational Reports Market Garden, October 1944–January 1945, Appendix A: Comments on Report on Operation Market-Garden, Lessons, Operation 'Market-Garden'*, 10th December 1944.
2. Montgomery, *El Alamein to the River Sangro/Normandy to the Baltic*, pp. 324–5; Eisenhower, *Crusade in Europe*, p. 349.
3. Brereton, *The Brereton Diaries*, pp. 360–1.
4. Montgomery, *El Alamein to the River Sangro/Normandy to the Baltic*, p. 323; WO 205/873 *Report on Operations 'Market' and 'Garden,' September to October 1944*,

pp. 5, 19; Burgett, *The Road to Arnhem*, pp. 101–2; CAB 106/1054 *A Short History of 30 Corps in the European Campaign 1944–1945*, p. 39.
5. Reynolds, *Sons of the Reich*, p. 174.
6. WO 205/873 *Report on Operations 'Market' and 'Garden,' September to October 1944*, p. 5; Reynolds, *Sons of the Reich*, p. 173; Middlebrook, *Arnhem 1944*, pp. 438–9, 517.
7. Middlebrook, *Arnhem 1944*, pp. 441–2; Horrocks, *A Full Life*, p. 332; Powell, *The Devil's Birthday*, p. 243.
8. Harvey, *Arnhem*, pp. 26, 29; Ritchie, *Arnhem – Myth and Reality*, p. 115.
9. Horrocks, *A Full Life*, pp. 231–2.
10. Reynolds, *Sons of the Reich*, p. 175.
11. BA/MA RH 19 IX/10 *Tagesmeldung 26.9 vom Heeresgruppe B, IA an OB West*, 26th September 1944, p. 1.
12. Kershaw, *'It Never Snows in September'*, pp. 311, 340.

Bibliography

Primary Sources

Archival Primary Sources

The National Archives (Kew)
CAB 106/1014 *A Short History of 30 Corps in the European Campaign 1944–1945*
CAB 106/1054 *The Battle of Arnhem*
CAB 106/1056 *A Graphic History of the 82nd Airborne Division – Operation 'Market' Holland 1944*
CAB 106/1078 *The South Staffordshires in the Battle of Arnhem*
WO 171/341 *30 Corps Battle Logs – September 1944*
WO 171/366 *War Diary of British Airborne Corps (Main) – September 1944*
WO 171/376 *War Diary – HQ Guards Armoured Division – January 1944 to September 1944*
WO 171/393 *War Diary – HQ 1st Airborne Division September to December 1944*
WO 171/406 *Original War Diary of 1st Airborne Recce Squadron RAC for 1st Sept '44 to 30th Sept '44*
WO 171/480 *War Diary – HQ 43rd Division – August–September 1944*
WO 171/589 *War Diary – H.Q. 1st Air Landing Brigade (Airborne Element) – January to December 1944*
WO 171/592 *War Diary – HQ 1st Parachute Brigade – January 1944 to December 1944*
WO 171/594 *War Diary – Headquarters 4th Parachute Brigade – January to September 1944*
WO 171/605 *War Diary – HQ 5th Guards Armoured Brigade – January to December 1944*
WO 171/638 *War Diary – HQ 32nd Guards Brigade – Year 1944 – January to December*
WO 171/658 *War Diary – HQ 129th Infantry Brigade, 21st Army Group 1944*
WO 171/660 *War Diary – HQ 130th Infantry Brigade 1944 – January to December 1944*
WO 171/1016 *War Diary – HQ 1st Air Landing Light Regiment, R.A., 21st Army Group 1944*
WO 171/1016 *War Diary – HQ 1st Air Landing Light Regiment, 21st Army Group – August to December 1944*
WO 171/1236 *War Diary – 1st Battalion Parachute Regiment – January to December 1944*
WO 171/1237 *War Diary – 2nd Battalion Parachute Regiment – January to December 1944*
WO 171/1238 *War Diary – 3rd Battalion Parachute Regiment – January to December 1944*
WO 171/1243 *War Diary – 10th Battalion Parachute Regiment – January to December 1944*
WO 171/1244 *War Diary – 11th Battalion Parachute Regiment – January to December 1944*
WO 171/1247 *War Diary – 156th Battalion Parachute Regiment – March to October 1944*
WO 171/1248 *War Diary – 21st Independent Parachute Company – January to December 1944*
WO 171/1250 *War Diary – 1st Armoured Battalion Coldstream Guards – January to December 1944*
WO 171/1252 *War Diary – 5th Battalion Coldstream Guards – January to December 1944*
WO 171/1253 *War Diary – 1st Battalion Grenadier Guards – January to December 1944*
WO 171/1254 *War Diary – 2nd Battalion Grenadier Guards – January to December 1944*
WO 171/1256 *War Diary – 2nd Armoured Battalion Irish Guards, 21st Army Group – January to December 1944*

WO 171/1257 *War Diary – 3rd Battalion Irish Guards – January to December 1944*
WO 171/1259 *War Diary – 1st Battalion Welsh Guards – January to December 1944*
WO 171/1260 *War Diary – 2nd (Recce) Battalion Welsh Guards – June to December 1944*
WO 171/1323 *War Diary – 7th Battalion Kings' Own Scottish Borderers – January to December 1944*
WO 171/1375 *Original War Diary – 2nd Battalion South Staffordshires – September 1944*
WO 205/623 *Operational Reports Market Garden – October 1944 to January 1945*
WO 205/693 *Operation Market Garden: Reports and Instructions – September 1944 to February 1945*
WO 205/871 *Report of Airborne Phase (17–27 Sept., 44) Operation 'Market' – XVIII Corps*
WO 205/873 *Allied Airborne Operations in Holland – September to October 1944*
WO 205/1124 *Battle of Arnhem: SS Panzer Grenadier Depot & Reserve Battalion 16 – German War Diary*
WO 205/1126 21 *Army Group – Operation 'Market Garden' 17–26 September 1944*

Bundesarchiv/Militärarchiv
RH 19 IV/56 – Heeresgruupe D/ Oberbefhelshaber West/ Oberbefehlshaber Süd/ Kriegstagebücher und Anlagen/ Bemerkung zur Serie/ Anlagen Nr. 1-2505/ Band 10: 11. Sept.–20. Sept. 1944.
RH 19 IX/5–Heeresgruppe B/Führungsabteilung/Abteilung Ia/Operationsbefehle 1944/ Bande 2: 1. Sept–30. Sept. 1944
RH 19 IX/8 – Heeresgruppe B/Abteilung Ia/Lagebeurteilungen der Heeresgruppe B, 11. Juni–11. Okt. 1944
RH 19 IX/10 – Heeresgruppe B/Abteilung Ia/Tagesmeldungen der Heeresgruppe B 1944/ Bande 2: 1. Sept.–15. Okt. 1944.
RH 24 88/123 – LXXXVIII. Armeekorps/Abteilung Ib (Quartiermeisterabteilung)/Anlagen zum Kriegstagebuch/Bande 1: 1. Juli–25. Sept. 1944.
RH 24 88/124 – LXXXVIII. Armeekorps/Abteilung Ib (Quartiermeisterabteilung)/Anlagen zum Kriegstagebuch/Bande 2: 25. Sept–2. Nov. 1944.
RH 24/203/3 – Generalkommando Feldt/Brieftagebbuch zum Kriegstagebuch 9. Aug.–14. Dez. 1944.
RS 2-2/32 – II. SS-Panzerkorps/sonstige Unterlagen/Bericht über die Kämpfe im Gebiet Arnheim, 10. Sept–15. Okt. 1944.
RS 3-9/45 – 9. SS Panzer-Division Hohenstaufen/Abteilung Ia (Führungsabteilung)/ Tagesmeldungen, Befehle (Fernschreiben und Funksprüche) 1944/Bande 2: 9. Sept.–8. Dez. 1944.
RS 3-10/4 – 10. SS-Panzer-Division Frundsberg/Abteilung Ia/Unterlagen der Abt. Ia, Ib, IC, II,Iva,V und VI –Allgemeines/Juli 1943–Sept. 1944.

Published Primary Sources
Blauensteiner, Ernst. *Employment of the II Fallschirm Korps Between the Maas and Rhine Rivers, 19 September 1944 to 10 March 1945*. MS # B-262. Allendorf: US Army Historical Division, Foreign Military Studies Collection, 1946.
Brereton, Lewis H. *The Brereton Diaries: The War in the Air in the Pacific, Middle East and Europe, 3 October 1941 8 May 1945*. New York: Da Capo Press, 1976.
British General Staff. *Field Service Regulations, Vol. II. Operations – General* (1935). London: His Majesty's Stationery Office, 1935.
———. *Field Service Regulations, Vol. III. Operations – Higher Formations (1935)*. London: His Majesty's Stationery Office, 1935.

Burgett, Donald R. *The Road to Arnhem: A Screaming Eagle in Holland*. Novato, CA: Presidio Press, 1999.
von Clausewitz, Carl. *On War*. New York: Penguin Books, 1968.
Eisenhower, Dwight D. *Crusade in Europe*. Garden City, NY: Garden City Books, 1952.
Condell, Bruce and David T. Zabecki (eds). *On the German Art of War: Truppenführung: German Army Manual for Unit Command in World War II*. Mechanicsburg, PA: Stackpole Books, 2009.
Faeckenstadt, Ernst F. *The Activities of the Western Wehrkreis/commandos (military area headquarters) VI and XII and their cooperation with the front in the defensive combat of OB West from September 1944 to March 1945*. MS # B-665. Allendorf: US Army Historical Division, Foreign Military Studies Collection, 1947.
Frost, John. *A Drop too Many*. London: Cassell & Co., 1980.
Gavin, James M. *On to Berlin: Battles of an Airborne Commander, 1943–1946*. New York: The Viking Press, 1978.
von der Heydte, Friedrich August. *6th Fallschirm Jaeger Regiment in Action against US Paratroopers in the Netherlands in September 1944*. MS # C-001. US Army Historical Division, Foreign Military Studies Collection.
Horrocks, Sir Brian. *A Full Life*. London: Collins, 1960.
Mattenklott, Franz. *Rhineland, Part 3: 15 Sept 44–21 March 45*. MS # B-044. Königstein: US Army Historical Division, Foreign Military Studies Collection, 1950.
Meindl, Eugen. *II FS Corps, Part III: Rheinland (15 Sep 44 to 21 Mar 45)*. MS # B-093. Königstein: US Army Historical Division, Foreign Military Studies Collection, 1950.
Montgomery of Alamein, Field Marshal The Viscount. *El Alamein to the River Sangro/Normandy to the Baltic*. New York: St Martin's Press, 1948.
Poppe, Walter. *2nd Commitment of the 59th Infantry Division in Holland; 18 September–25 November 44*. MS # B-149. Allendorf: US Army Historical Division, Foreign Military Studies Collection, 1946.
Reinhardt, Hellmuth. *Commitment of the 406th Division against the Allied Air Landing at Nijmegen in September 1944*. MS # C-085. Königstein: US Army Historical Division, Foreign Military Studies Collection, 1950.
Sims, James. *Arnhem Spearhead: A Private Soldier's Story*. London: Sphere Books, 1980.
Taylor, Maxwell. *Swords and Plowshares*. New York: W.W. Norton & Company, 1972.
Urquhart, R.E. *Arnhem*. London: Cassell & Co., 1958.
von Zangen, Gustav-Adolf. *Battles of the Fifteenth Army Between the Meuse-Scheldt Canal and the Lower Meuse*. MS # B-475. Allendorf: US Army Historical Division, Foreign Military Studies Collection, 1947.

Secondary Sources
Buckley, John and Peter Preston-Hough (eds). *Operation Market Garden – The Campaign for the Low Countries, Autumn 1944: Seventy Years On*. Wolverhampton Military Studies No. 20. Solihull: Helion & Company, 2016.
Bull, Stephen. *World War II Infantry Tactics: Company and Battalion*. Elite Series 122. Oxford: Osprey Publishing, 2005.
——. *World War II Infantry Tactics: Squad and Platoon*. Elite Series 105. Oxford: Osprey Publishing, 2004.
Cirillo, Roger. 'Market Garden and the Strategy of the Northwest Europe Campaign', in *Operation Market Garden – The Campaign for the Low Countries, Autumn 1944: Seventy Years On*, ed. John Buckley and Peter Preston-Hough. Solihull: Helion & Company, 2016.
Citino, Robert M. *The German Way of War: From the Thirty Years' War to the Third Reich*. Lawrence, KS: University of Kansas Press, 2005.

———. *The Path to Blitzkrieg: Doctrine and Training in the German Army, 1920–1939.* Boulder, CO: Lynne Rienner Publishers, 1999.
Copp, Terry. 'Counter-Mortar Operational Research in the 21 Army Group', *Canadian Military History*, 3, No. 2 (1994): 45–52.
Corum, James S. *The Roots of Blitzkrieg: Hans von Seeckt and German Military Reform.* Lawrence, KS: University Press of Kansas, 1992.
Crang, Jeremy A. *The British Army and the People's War 1939–1945.* Manchester: Manchester University Press, 2000.
Davies, W.J.K. *German Army Handbook 1939–1945.* New York: Arco Publishing, 1977.
Dupuy, Trevor N. *The Evolution of Weapons and Warfare.* New York: Bobbs-Merrill, 1980.
———. *Understanding War: History and Theory of Combat.* New York: Paragon House, 1987.
Echevarria, Antulio J. 'Auftragstaktik in its Proper Perspective', *Military Review* 66, No. 10 (1986): 50–6.
Ethell, Jeffrey and Dr Alfred Price. *Target Berlin: Mission 250, 6 March 1944.* London: Greenhill Books, 1981.
Förster, Jürgen. 'The Dynamics of Volksgemeinschaft: The Effectiveness of the German Military Establishment in the Second World War', in *Military Effectiveness, Volume 3: The Second World War.* ed. Allan R. Millett and Williamson Murray. New edition. New York: Cambridge University Press, 2010.
French, David. 'Doctrine and Organization in the British Army, 1919–1932', *The Historical Journal* 44, No. 2 (2001): 497–515.
———. *Raising Churchill's Army: The British Army and the War Against Germany 1919–1945.* Oxford: Oxford University Press, 2000.
Fritz, Stephen G. *Frontsoldaten: The German Soldier in World War II.* Lexington, KY: University Press of Kentucky, 1995.
Greenacre, John W. 'Assessing the Reasons for Failure: 1st British Airborne Division Signal Communications during Operation 'Market Garden', *Defence Studies* 4, No. 3 (2004): 283–308.
Harclerode, Peter. *Arnhem: A Tragedy of Errors.* London: Arms & Armour Press, 1994.
———. *Wings of War: Airborne Warfare 1918–1945.* London: Cassell & Co., 2005.
Hart, Russell A. 'Mission Impossible? The Mobilization of the German Replacement Army and its Role in the Thwarting of Operation Market Garden', in *Operation Market Garden – The Campaign for the Low Countries, Autumn 1944: Seventy Years On*, ed. John Buckley and Peter Preston-Hough. Solihull: Helion & Company, 2016.
Hart, Stephen Ashley. *Montgomery and 'Colossal Cracks': The 21st Army Group in Northwest Europe, 1944–45.* Westport, CT: Praeger Publishers, 2000.
Harvey, A.D. *Arnhem.* London: Cassell & Co., 2001.
Haythornthwaite, Philip. *Frederick the Great's Army (2) Infantry.* Men at Arms Series 205. Oxford: Osprey Publishing, 1991.
Hogg, Ian V. *British & American Artillery of World War Two.* London: Greenhill Books, 2002.
———. *German Artillery of World War Two.* London: Greenhill Books, 2002.
Kershaw, Robert J. *'It Never Snows in September' The German View of MARKET-GARDEN and The Battle of Arnhem, September 1944.* Hersham: Ian Allan Publishing Ltd, 2004.
Kjoerstad, Ola. 'German Officer Education in the Interwar Years: Frei im Geist, fest im Charakter', MA Thesis, University of Glasgow, Scotland, 2010.
Krang, Jeremy A. *The British Army and the People's War 1939–1945.* Manchester: Manchester University Press, 2000.
LoFaro, Guy. *The Sword of St. Michael: The 82nd Airborne Division in World War II.* Philadelphia, PA: De Capo Press, 2011.

Middlebrook, Martin. *Arnhem 1944: The Airborne Battle, 17–26 September*. Barnsley: Pen & Sword Military, 1994.
Millar, Simon. *Zorndorf 1758: Frederick faces Holy Mother Russia*. Campaign Series 125. Oxford: Osprey Publishing, 2003.
Mitcham, Samuel W., Jr. *German Order of Battle Volume One: 1st–290th Infantry Divisions in WWII*. Mechanicsburg, PA: Stackpole Books, 2007.
Murray, Williamson. 'British Military Effectiveness in the Second World War', in *Military Effectiveness, Volume 3: The Second World War*. ed. Allan R. Millett and Williamson Murray. New edition. New York: Cambridge University, 2010.
———. *German Military Effectiveness*. Baltimore, MD: The Nautical & Aviation Publishing Company of America, 1992.
Myatt, Frederick. *The British Infantry 1660–1945: The Evolution of a Fighting Force*. Poole: Blandford Press, 1983.
Norris, John. *Infantry Mortars of World War II*. New Vanguard Series 54. Oxford: Osprey Publishing, 2002.
Peaty, John. 'Operation MARKET GARDEN: The Manpower Factor', in *Operation Market Garden – The Campaign for the Low Countries, Autumn 1944: Seventy Years On*, ed. John Buckley and Peter Preston-Hough. Solihull: Helion & Company, 2016.
Place, Timothy Harrison. *Military Training in the British Army 1940–1944: From Dunkirk to D-Day*. London: Frank Cass, 2000.
Powell, Geoffrey. *The Devil's Birthday: The Bridges to Arnhem, 1944*. London: Buchan & Enright, 1984.
Preston-Hough, Peter. 'The Viktor Graebner Assault, 0900 hrs Monday 18th September 1944', in *Operation Market Garden – The Campaign for the Low Countries, Autumn 1944: Seventy Years On*, ed. John Buckley and Peter Preston-Hough. Solihull: Helion & Company, 2016.
Reynolds, Michael. *Sons of the Reich: II SS Panzer Corps – Normandy, Arnhem, the Ardennes and on the Eastern Front*. Barnsley: Pen & Sword Military, 2009.
Ritchie, Sebastian. *Arnhem – Myth and Reality: Airborne Warfare, Air Power and the Failure of Operation Market Garden*. London: Robert Hale Limited, 2011.
Rottman, Gordon L. *World War II Airborne Warfare Tactics*. Elite Series 136. Oxford: Osprey Publishing, 2006.
———. *World War II Glider Assault Tactics*. Elite Series 200. Oxford: Osprey Publishing, 2014.
Ryan, Cornelius. *A Bridge Too Far*. New York: Pocket Books, 1974.
Samuels, Martin. *Command or Control? Command, Training and Tactics in the British and German Armies, 1888–1918*. London: Frank Cass, 1995.
Slaughter, Jamie. 'Allied Close Air Support during Operation Market Garden: A Lesson in Planning', in *Operation Market Garden – The Campaign for the Low Countries, Autumn 1944: Seventy Years On*, ed. John Buckley and Peter Preston-Hough. Solihull: Helion & Company, 2016.
Strohn, Matthias. *The German Army and the Defence of the Reich: Miltary Doctrine and the Conduct of the Defensive Battle 1918–1939*. Cambridge: Cambridge University Press, 2011.
Thompson, Leroy. *The Sten Gun*. Weapon Series 22. Oxford: Osprey Publishing, 2012.
Tieke, Wilhelm (trans. Frederick Steinhardt). *In the Firestorm of the Last Years of the War: II. SS-Panzerkorps with the 9. and 10. SS-Divisions 'Hohenstaufen' and 'Frundsberg'*. Winnipeg, MN: J.J. Fedorowicz, 1999.
Tugwell, Maurice. *Arnhem: A Case Study*. London: Thornton Cox, 1975.
Zaloga, Steven J. *Operation Pointblank 1944: Defeating the Luftwaffe*. Campaign 236. Oxford: Osprey Publishing, 2011.
Zetterling, Niklas. *Normandy 1944: German Military Organization, Combat Power and Organizational Effectiveness*. Winnipeg, MN: J.J. Fedorowicz, 2000.

Index

A Bridge Too Far
  book 10–13, 16
  film 10, 55, 102
Adair, Allan 88–9
aircraft
  Hawker Typhoon fighter-bomber 88, 109, 122, 132, 134, 136
  transport gliders 1, 45, 64, 104, 114–15, 132, 156–7
    Airspeed Horsa glider 115, 156–7
    General Aircraft Hamilcar glider 157
air forces *see* Luftwaffe, Royal Air Force, United States Army Air Force
air power
  air supply of ground forces 58, Plate 16
  air support of ground forces 16, 20, 72, 82, 85, 90, 112, 122, 127, 131–7, 148, 153
  air transport of ground forces 1, 7, 114, 169, 162–3
    in Market Garden planning 6, 7, 14–15, 16–17, 58, 60, 71, 97–8, 132
  Close Air Support (CAS) 16, 113, 122, 131–7
  Forward Air Controllers (FACs) 88, 113, 122, 133–4
  ground-to-air communications 113, 122, 133–5, Plate 16
  limitations of 131–5
  role in Normandy campaign 3, 72, 85, 109, 113–14, 131–2, 135–6, 139–40
Alarmeinheiten (alarm units) *see* German military units
Allied military units
  1st Allied Airborne Army 1, 5, 7, 16, 40, 108, 131, 161

Supreme Headquarters Allied Expeditionary Force (SHAEF) 73
Allied strategy
  'broad front' vs 'narrow front' 3–5
  'Colossal Cracks' 23, 111, 127, 168
Antwerp (Dutch city) 5, 164
armoured fighting vehicles
  British tanks
    M4 Sherman medium tank
      in Market Garden 65, 66, 67, 69–70, 88–9, 90, 91, 120–2, Plate 12, Plate 18
      in First World War 31, 110
  German
    armoured cars and half-tracks 40, 55, 139, 153, 154, 159, Plate 4
    Panther (Panzer V) medium tank 67, 153
    Panzer III medium tank 153–4, Plate 20
    Panzer IV medium tank 153–4
    self-propelled guns (SPGs) 64, 90, 122, 138, 155, 157, 159–60, Plate 5, Plate 7
    Sturmgeschütze (Assault Guns) 153–6, 159, Plate 5
    Tiger II (Panzer VIB) heavy tank 154
Arnhem (Dutch town) 1, 5, 6, 13–14, 39–40, 41–2, 45–50, 54, 55, 57, 63, 64, 65, 69, 74, 86–7, 90–2, 93, 97–120, 123, 127–31, 134–6, 145, 147–9, 152–3, 156–60, 161, 163–6, 168–9
  Arnhem road bridge 5, 40, 42, 45, 46, 47, 55–8, 64, 97, 100–1, 104, 106–7, 116, 117, 129, 146, 147, 152, 153–5, 158
artillery
  British
    organization 110, 114–15, 121, 128

Index   203

doctrine and tactics 22, 31, 72,
  76–8, 79, 84–5, 109–14, 120–1,
  124, 126–7, 152, 166
equipment 115, Plate 14
role in Market Garden 69, 87, 90,
  109, 114–20, 120–3, 134
German
  organization 139, 149
  doctrine 141
  mortars as 'supplementary artillery'
    142–3, 146, 149–52
  role in Market Garden 49, 52,
    138–9, 149, 155, Plate 8
Auftragstaktik (mission tactics) *see*
  doctrine, German

Barlow, Hilary 106
battle drills *see* doctrine, British
bayonet charges 129–30
Bemmel (Dutch village) 123
Betuwe (Island) 65, 69, 91, 122–3, 149,
  Plate 20
Bewegungskrieg (war of movement) *see*
  doctrine, German
Bittrich, Wilhelm 11, 40–3, 45, 48, 50–1,
  64, 149, Plate 1
Bradley, Omar 73
Brereton, Lewis 131, 161
British military units
  2nd Tactical Air Force 88, 109, 112,
    122, 131, 133, 134, 136
  83 Group, RAF 88, 109, 133, 134,
    136
  Desert Air Force (DAF) 83, 112, 113
  Home Forces 85, 96, 111, 126
  Royal Army Service Corps (RASC)
    54, 152
  army groups
    21st Army Group 1, 4, 5, 8, 23, 80,
      85, 86, 109, 111, 112, 133, 164
  armies
    2nd Army 1, 7, 39, 66, 71, 85, 108,
      110, 122, 133, 134, 161, 163, 164
    8th Army 83, 84, 112, 113
  corps
    XXX Corps 1, 5, 14, 47, 60, 66, 69,
      70, 74, 85–7, 89–92, 118, 120,
      123, 132, 135, 140, 152, 162, 166

divisions
  1st Airborne Division 5, 6, 11–14,
    42–3, 45, 47, 49–55, 57–60,
    65–70, 74, 81, 88, 90, 93–8,
    102–7, 114–20, 122–3, 127, 129,
    131, 133–6, 142, 147, 150–3,
    155–62, 164–7, Plate 9,
    Plate 10
  6th Airborne Division 96
  43rd Infantry Division 52, 69,
    122–3
  Guards Armoured Division 14, 22,
    62, 64–5, 69, 87–92, 94, 120–3
brigades
  1st Airlanding Brigade 49, 51, 59,
    97, 104–6, 117, 120, 128
  1st Parachute Brigade 45–7, 49–50,
    55–6, 95, 97–106, 116–17, 128,
    147, 154, 157–8
  1st Polish Independent Parachute
    Brigade 52, 97–8, 104, 162
  4th Parachute Brigade 49–50, 94,
    97, 104–7, 115–17, 154, 158,
    Plate 9
  5th Guards Armoured Brigade 87
  32nd Guards Brigade 69
  231st Independent Infantry Brigade
    95
battalions/regiments
  1st Airborne Reconnaissance
    Squadron 45, 47, 103, 105, 147,
    Plate 17
  1st Airlanding Light Artillery
    Regiment 115–17, 128, Plate 14
  1st Battalion, the Border Regiment
    51–2, Plate 15
  1st Parachute Battalion 39, 45, 58–9,
    93, 98–102, 105, 129–30, 155
  2nd (Armoured) Battalion, Irish
    Guards 88–91, 122, Plate 12
  2nd Battalion, The South
    Staffordshire Regiment 52, 104,
    128, 130, 148, Plate 13
  2nd Parachute Battalion 46–7, 53,
    56, 81, 93, 99–100, 116, 146–7,
    155
  3rd Battalion, Irish Guards 88–9,
    91, 122

3rd Parachute Battalion 47, 98–101, 103, 107, 116, 130, 146, 148, 155, 157
4th Battalion, The Dorsetshire Regiment 52
7th Battalion, Somerset Light Infantry 123
7th Battalion, The King's Own Scottish Borderers 51–2, 59, 95, 104–5, 130–1, 158–9
10th Parachute Battalion 105, 154
11th Parachute Battalion 104–5, 130, 148
44th Royal Tank Regiment 69
64th Medium Artillery Regiment 87, 118, 134, 152
156th Parachute Battalion 94, 105, 154
combat groups
    Coldstream Guards Group 65, 69
    Grenadier Guards Group 69, 150
    Irish Guards Group 91, 122
    Welsh Guards Group 123
Broadhurst, Harry 133
Browning, Frederick 12, 61, 94, 161

Clausewitz, Carl von 24, 26–7
Close Air Support (CAS) *see* air power
'Colossal Cracks' (British battle doctrine) 23, 111, 127, 168
communications
    and command 43–4, 58, 70, 73, 75–6, 80, 102–3, 106, 116, 134, 152
    ground-to-air 113, 122, 133–5
    radio failures at Arnhem 58, 102–6, 122, 133, 152
Coningham, Arthur 112, 133

Dempsey, Miles 71, 85, 161
doctrine
    British
        battle drill 126–7
        'bite and hold' tactics 77–8
        historical origins 21–5 74–81
        on command 8, 20–5, 36–7, 72–3, 74–84, 89–92, 94–5, 97–9, 101–6, 108, 130–1, 166

German
    Auftragstaktik (mission tactics) 8, 24, 27–37, 41, 43–4, 47, 48, 101, 165, 168
    Bewegungskrieg (war of movement) 33, 168
    on command 8, 18–20, 24–5, 40–4, 47–8, 52, 59–60, 63, 70–1, 165
    origins 26–38
Dombrowski, Wolfgang 48

Eindhoven (Dutch city) 1, 39, 42, 43, 60, 66, 70, 88, 90, 140
Eisenhower, Dwight D. 3–5, 138, 161, 164
El Alamein, 2nd Battle of 23, 84, 108, 109, 111, 112
Elst (Dutch village) 122–3
Exercise 'Golden Miller' 94

Falaise (French town) 3, 138
Feldt, Karl 62–3
Field Service Regulations (1935) 79–80, 124–5
First World War 18, 21, 26, 30–4, 58, 75–80, 82, 110, 124–6, 140–1, 150, 168–9
Fitch, John 103, 146–7
France 1, 3–4, 38, 40, 43, 49, 62, 67, 78, 86, 91, 109, 126, 134–5, 138–40, 143
'friction' in combat 26–8, 75, 165
Friedrich II '*der Große*' of Prussia (Frederick the Great) 27–30, 35, 71
Friedrich Wilhelm of Brandenburg, *Der Großer Kürfurst* (The Great Elector) 27–8, 71
Frost, John 46–7, 55–6, 58, 64, 101, 152, 158
Führung und Gefecht der verbundenen Waffen (*Combat and Command of the Combined Arms*) (German Army doctrinal manual) 33, 35, 37

Gavin, James 11, 61, 63
General Staff, German 18, 28, 30, 32, 138
German military units
    Alarmeinheiten (alarm units) 41, 48

Index   205

Ersatzheer (Replacement Army) 62
Feldheer (Field Army) 62
Heer (German Land Army) 141, Plate 2
Kriegsmarine (German Navy) 49, 51
Luftwaffe (German Air Force) 51, 52, 63, 139–40, 144, Plate 2
Oberkommando der Wehrmacht (Armed Forces High Command) 138
Reichswehr (interwar German Army/Armed Forces) 18–19, 32–6
Waffen-SS (military wing of the SS) 11, 12, 18, 39–42, 44, 47–51, 53, 55, 62–3, 66, 71, 87, 98, 138–9, 142–4, 148, 153–6, Plate 1, Plate 2, Plate 11
Wehrmacht (Armed Forces) 7, 12, 26, 32–3, 35–7, 53, 114, 138, 141, 144
Wehrmachtbefehlshaber Niederlande (Armed Forces Command Netherlands) 42, 51
Westheer (Western Army) 1, 4, 62, 86
army groups
  Heeresgruppe B (Army Group B) 7, 8, 12, 26, 39, 40, 42, 43, 138–40, 149, 153, 166, 168
armies
  5. *Panzerarmee* (Armoured or Mechanized Army) 3, 138
  7. *Armee*, 138
  15. *Armee* 43, 67
  1. *Fallschirmarmee* (Parachute Army) 42, 66, 69, 70, 87
  Wehrkreis Kommando (Military District Command) VI 42, 62–5
brigades
  107. *Panzer Brigade* 67, 69, 153
  280. *Sturmgeschütze Brigade* 153–5, Plate 5
battalions
  9. *SS-Panzer-Aufklärungs-Abteilung* (SS Armoured Reconnaissance Battalion) 18, 53, 55–7, 59, 154, 158
  Jungwirth Parachute Regiment 69
  SS-Panzergrenadier Ausbildungs und Ersatz Battalion 16 (motorized infantry training and replacement battalion) 44–8, 57, 98–100, 103, 144, 147
  Worrowski Battalion 52
battle groups *(Kampfgruppen)*
  Artillerie Kommando (Arko) 191 149–50, Plate 8
  Gruppe von Tettau 48, 51–2, 149
  Kampfgruppe von Allworden 49, 143, 145
  Kampfgruppe Brinkmann 153, 155
  Kampfgruppe Chill 69
  Kampfgruppe Frundsberg *see* 10. SS-Panzerdivision 'Frundsberg'
  Kampfgruppe Gropp 49
  Kampfgruppe Harder 49
  Kampfgruppe Huber 69
  Kampfgruppe Knaust 154–5, Plate 20
  Kampfgruppre Krafft 144
  Kampfgruppe Möller 48–50, 143
  Kampfgruppe Spindler 46–52, 56, 57, 98, 100, 103, 105–7, 139, 147–9, 154–6
  Kampfgruppe Walther 69
corps
  II. *Fallschirmkorps* (Parachute Corps) 65
  II. *SS-Panzer Korps* 11, 39–42, 47–51, 62, 66, 71, 87, 138–9, 142–4, 148–50, 153–6
  Korps Feldt 62–5
divisions
  9. *SS-Panzerdivision 'Hohenstaufen'* 40–2, 47–50, 53, 138–9, 143, 148, 153–6
  10. *SS-Panzerdivision 'Frundsberg'* 40–2, 48–9, 63–4, 91, 138–9, 153
  59. *Infanterie-Division* 69
  406. *Landesschützen Division* 17, 60, 62–5
'German way of war, the' 19, 29
Gorman, John 89
Gräbner, Viktor 18, 55–7, 59, 158
Great Britain
  manpower shortages faced in 1944 17, 23, 111–12, 163
Groesbeek Heights 60–3

Hackett, John 12, 104–5, 151, 156
Harmel, Heinz 11, 41, 91, Plate 1
Harzer, Walther 11, 41, 148
Heeresdienstvorschrift 300: Truppenführung (Army Service Regulation 300: Troop Leading or *Unit Command)* (German Army doctrinal manual) 33–5, 37, 140–1
'Hell's Highway' 66–71
Heveadorp (Dutch village) 52
Hicks, Philip 104–5
Horrocks, Brian 69, 74, 84–5, 89, 92, 122–3, 161, 164

Jomini, Henri 74

Koevering (Dutch village) 70
Krafft, Josef 44–8, 57, 98, 103, 105, 144, 147

Lathbury, Gerald 46, 98–101, 103–4, 146–7
Lindquist, Roy 61
logistics
   aerial resupply 58
   Allied logistical crisis in late 1944 3–5, 134, 163
   ammunition supplies 53–8
Lower Rhine River (*Nederrhin*) 1, 5–6, 45, 52, 65, 66, 70, 74, 91, 106, 120, 122, 147, 148, 150, 154, 162
Luftwaffe (German Air Force) *see* German military units

Maas (Meuse) River 5, 61
Maas–Waal Canal 60
Market Garden *see* operations
Meuse–Escaut Canal 87, 97
Model, Walther 12, 39–44, 48, 62, 66–7, 154, 168, Plate 1
Moltke, Helmut von, The Elder 27–30, 98
Montgomery, Bernard Law 1–6, 8, 11, 16–17, 23, 71–4, 81, 83–6, 92, 108, 111–12, 132, 135, 161–4, 167–8
mortars *see* weapons

Neerpelt bridgehead 1, 39, 66, 87
Nijmegen (Dutch town) 1, 39, 40, 42, 60–6, 71, 90, 91, 118, 122, 161–2, 165

Nijmegen bridges 5, 40, 42, 60, 61, 63–5, 71, 90–1, 122, 161–2, 165, Plate 18
Normandy, Battle of 3, 8, 11, 23, 39–40, 57, 72, 85–7, 89, 96, 108–9, 113–16, 127, 131–2, 136, 139, 150, 153, 164, 167–8

Oosterbeek (Dutch village) 13, 45, 48, 50, 57–8, 69, 106, 114, 116–19, 122–3, 130, 135, 148–9, 152, 156, 158–60, 168, Plate 10, Plate 16
operations
   The Ardennes Offensive (Operation *Wacht am Rhein*) 6, 11, 163
   '*Kaiserschlacht*' (Emperor's Battle) (First World War) 32, 78
   Market Garden
      operational plan 1–3, 5, 8, 11, 15–17, 43, 58, 61, 71, 73–4, 86–8, 92, 97–8, 103–4, 116–17, 120–1, 132–5
      outcomes 5, 161–4
      casualties
         Allied 6, 162–3
         German 6, 168
   Overlord *see* Normandy, Battle of

Pannerden (Dutch village) 64
Patton, George 4–5
Prussia 19, 27–30

radios *see* communications
Regimental System, the (British Army) 21
Reichswald forest 60–5, 68 (map)
Rhine River 1–5, 64, 71, 108, 134, 162–4, 166
Ritchie, Sebastian 6–7, 16–17
Royal Air Force (RAF) 1, 82, 88, 109, 112–13, 122, 132–6, 139, 163
Ruhr (German industrial region) 2, 5, 163
Rundstedt, Gerd von 39, 73
Ryan, Cornelius 10–14, 102, 107

St Oedenrode (Dutch village) 67
Scheldt Estuary 67, 164

Schlieffen, Alfred von 30–1, 169
Seeckt, Hans von 18, 32–3, 35, 71, 79, 141
Seydlitz, Friedrich Wilhelm, Freiherr von 29–30
Sims, James 53, 56, 81, 146, 152
Somme, Battle of, 1916 125
Son (Dutch town) 60, 66, 67, 90, 161
Spindler, Ludwig 49–50, 57, 103, 105, 107
stormtroops (First World War)
  tactics 18, 31–2, 141
  armament 141

tactics
  British 20–2, 24, 31, 53–7, 58–9, 75–8, 83–4, 87–90, 94–5, 99–101, 104–6, 110–14, 116–17, 121–3, 124–7, 129–31, 135–6, 142, 151, 156–9
  German 18, 27–30, 31–4, 45, 48, 50, 52, 55, 56, 64–5, 71, 77, 140–3, 144–53, 154–6
tanks *see* armoured fighting vehicles
Taylor, Maxwell 67
terrain
  Dutch terrain and influence on the campaign 45, 57, 101, 121–3, 136, 145–6, 157, 158, Plate 12, Plate 13
XXX Corps (British Army) 1, 5, 14, 47, 60, 66, 69–70, 74, 85–92, 118, 120, 123, 132, 135, 140, 152, 162, 166
von Tettau, Hans 149
Thomas, Ivor 123
Thompson, William 118, 151, 156
training
  British Army 8, 20–5, 54, 73, 76, 79, 81–3, 85, 88, 90, 93–6, 97, 100–1, 107–8, 121, 166
  German Army 18–20, 32, 35–7, 40–1, 43–4, 49, 52–3, 63–4, 149, 168
Trapp, Rudolf 48
Truppenführung see Heeresdienstvorschrift 300: Truppenführung
21st Army Group (British Army) *see* British military units

United States Army Air Force (USAAF) 1, 113, 139, 163

United States military units
  8th Air Force 113
  9th Tactical Air Force 131
  divisions
    82nd Airborne Division 5, 11, 42, 60–1, 63–6, 90, 162, 165
    101st Airborne Division 5, 42, 60, 66–70, 88, 90, 153, 162, 165
  regiments
    327th Glider Infantry Regiment 70
    501st Parachute Infantry Regiment 70
    502nd Parachute Infantry Regiment 70
    504th Parachute Infantry Regiment 90–1
    506th Parachute Infantry Regiment 69–70
    508th Parachute Infantry Regiment 61, 63
Urquhart, Roy 12, 47–8, 58, 59, 73, 92, 95, 97, 101–4, 106–7, 118, 128, 135–6, 146, 161

V-1 flying bomb 4
Valkenswaard 88, 132
Vandaleur, J.O.E. 122
Veghel (Dutch village) 66–9
Versailles, Treaty of 32, 35

Waal River 5, 51, 60–1, 65, 90–2, 122
weapons
  artillery
    25-pounder gun/howitzer, ordnance, QF 115
    75mm pack howitzer, M1 115–18
  anti-tank guns
    British 156–9, Plate 9
    German 45, 61, 88, 90, 120–2, 143, 144
  bayonets 125, 129–30
  machine guns
    British
      Bren light machine gun 53–4, 56, 127, 144, Plate 17
      Lewis light machine gun 125
      Sten submachine gun 53–4, 56, 128–9, Plate 10, Plate 15

Vickers medium machine gun 127–8, 144
German
  MG34/42 general purpose machine guns 143–4, Plate 3, Plate 4
man-portable-anti-tank weapons
  Panzerfaust 88
  Projector, Infantry, Anti-Tank (PIAT) 159, Plate 17
mortars
  British 124–5, 127–8
  German 31, 45, 53, 61, 117, 136, 141–4, 145–6, 148–52, 160, 166
Tables of Organization and Equipment (TO&Es)
  British
    divisional artillery 114–16
    divisional machine-gun battalion 127
    infantry battalions 127–8
  German
    divisional artillery 139
    infantry battalions 142–4
weather, effects upon the campaign 133, 135, 161
Weisenführung (leadership by directive) 28, 30
Westerbouwing Heights 52
Westheer (Western Army) *see* German military units
Westwall 2, 40, 62
Wigram, Lionel 126

Ziegler, Alfred 143, 145–6, Plate 6